Washington Davis

Camp-Fire Chats of the Civil War

Embracing the Tragedy, Romance, Comedy, Humor and Pathos in the Varied

Experience

Washington Davis

Camp-Fire Chats of the Civil War
Embracing the Tragedy, Romance, Comedy, Humor and Pathos in the Varied Experience

ISBN/EAN: 9783744794602

Printed in Europe, USA, Canada, Australia, Japan

Cover: Foto ©Thomas Meinert / pixelio.de

More available books at **www.hansebooks.com**

CAMP-FIRE CHATS

OF THE

CIVIL WAR;

BEING THE INCIDENT, ADVENTURE AND WAYSIDE EXPLOIT OF THE

BIVOUAC AND BATTLE FIELD,

AS RELATED BY MEMBERS OF THE

GRAND ARMY OF THE REPUBLIC.

EMBRACING THE TRAGEDY, ROMANCE, COMEDY, HUMOR AND PATHOS IN THE VARIED EXPERIENCE OF ARMY LIFE.

By WASHINGTON DAVIS.

CONTAINING AN AUTHENTIC HISTORY OF THE G. A. R. AND OTHER VALUABLE INFORMATION.

CHICAGO:
A. B. GEHMAN & CO.
1886.

TO THE

GRAND ARMY OF THE REPUBLIC,

THE VETERANS AND THE VOLUNTEERS

OF THE

CIVIL WAR,

UPON WHOSE LOYALTY AROSE THE STANDARD OF PERPETUAL UNION;
AND TO THEIR WIVES, SISTERS AND MOTHERS,

THIS VOLUME

Is Respectfully Dedicated,

IN THE HOPE THAT IT MAY REMAIN
A TESTAMENT TO THEIR HEROIC ENDURANCE, AND A TRIBUTE TO THEIR
HALLOWED MEMORY.

IT is hoped that no "crying need" or "long-felt want" has been satisfied by the publication of CAMP-FIRE CHATS. Nor has the manuscript been prepared for the private perusal of a few of the author's friends; but this volume has been published for the same purpose as are other books in these latter days (save the reports issued by good old honest Uncle Sam), with the additional intent of preserving a few points of history, and some features of army life not before delineated. To this end the subject matter has been selected, with sufficient humorous incident, it is thought, to relieve the work of dryness.

Only one claim is made: the stories are fresh and heretofore unpublished; and in gathering the material from the field the publishers and the author have spared neither labor nor expense. It was realized that much wholesome romance, together with many details in the history of the Civil War, remained treasured only in the memories of the veterans, or at least had not found their way into print, and must necessarily perish with the soldiers, unless the many interesting stories told at the various camp-fires of the Grand Army of the Republic, were preserved. The preservation of these also achieves a very praiseworthy result: It furnishes to youthful minds a far better class of reading than the mass of exciting and pernicious literature thrust upon them from all sides.

Each speaker has been given due credit, and is therefore responsible for the tale he has told. No character sketches have been attempted, for, since the characters are all living, it has been deemed unsafe for the author's physical well-being; and then such sketches, either pen portrait or caricature, have been odious to the writer ever since his school-boy days, when he was cartooned on the old school-yard fence by a youthful genius with a stolen piece of chalk.

Thanks to the many who have furnished the anecdotes herein contained, and for their kind assistance so freely tendered the author while collecting the data; and especially to Symmes M. Jelley, A. M. If the book is welcomed by the public as heartily as the author has been received by the members of the Grand Army, no anxiety will be felt by

W. D.

CHICAGO, January, 1884.

CAMP-FIRE I.

The S. P. U. H.—The First Camp-Fire—The Camp of Instruction—The Farmer and the Watermelons—"How Tedious and Tasteless the Hours"—The Closing Scene.

CAMP-FIRE II.

How a Balky Horse did not Surrender—The Execution of Deserters—A Pension for a Pin-Scratch.

CAMP-FIRE III.

The Maddest Man in the Army—A Regimental Foot Race—Effects of Excitement—"Bress de Lor'."

CAMP-FIRE IV.

Buttermilk Without Money, but not Without Price—Freaks under Fire—"Johnnies" and "Yanks" stop Shooting to Shake hands—Soldiers at the Fort Different from "Home Guards"—Origin of "Hold the Fort."

CAMP-FIRE V.

A Surprise for the Johnnies—With Banks up the Red River—Prison Life in Texas—Soldiers yet on Parole—Trouble Between the 13th and 19th Army Corps.

CAMP-FIRE VI.

"Slap-Jacks"—A Trip up the Tennessee—The Horrors of Valley Forge Repeated—Bullets and Etiquette—"Copper-Heads."

CAMP-FIRE VII.

A Banquet to the S. P. U. H.—"S. B."—A Classical Exposition of the Term, and some Reminiscences for Illustration.

CAMP-FIRE VIII.

Libby Prison—The "Horned Yankee"—Andersonville, whose Surname is Death—A Modern Miracle—The Altar of Kleptomania Receives a Sacrifice of Seven.

CAMP-FIRE IX.

The Florence Prison—Homeward Bound—Pathetic Incidents.

CAMP-FIRE X.

War on the Water—Daring Deeds—How Many Regiments each Man Captured—Remarkable Escapes—The Biggest Liar in the War.

CAMP-FIRE XI.

Sutlers—Quartermasters—Mules—How Rich a Soldier must be to Buy Anything from a Sutler—The Profits in the Government Appointment of Quartermaster on a Regular Salary—Eulogy on the Sutler and the Army Mule.

CAMP-FIRE XII.

Bushwhacking—What Circumstances do with Cases—A Jest on Gen. A. J. Smith—Foraging.

CAMP-FIRE XIII.

Battles Unsung by the Muse of History—Origin of the Stars and Stripes—Genealogy of George Washington.

CAMP-FIRE XIV.

A Rollicking Recruit—Love and War—The S. P. U. H. Sutler— "When Gabriel Blows his Trumpet in de Morning."

CAMP-FIRE XV.

The Race for Columbia—"To Amputate or not to Amputate?"

CAMP-FIRE XVI.

"Brazen Effrontery"—Corduroy Roads—Long John, the Darkey.

CAMP-FIRE XVII.

Lazy Jim's Stratagem to Avoid Walking Back to Camp—"They got our Flag"—Anecdote of General Sherman.

CAMP-FIRE XVIII.

Many were Called, but One was Chosen—A Sad Occurrence—" Let the Dead and the Beautiful Rest."

CAMP-FIRE XIX.

A Reminiscence of General Nelson—A Sham Battle Demolishes a Sutler's Store.

CAMP-FIRE XX.

"When this Cruel War is over"—A Continuation of Camp-Fire XVIII.—A " Muley" Yoke of " Muley " Oxen.

CAMP-FIRE XXI.

The Grand Army of the Republic not a Political Organization—Its Principles: Fraternity, Charity, Loyalty—A Complete, Brief Record of its Organization and Growth to the Present Time.

CAMP-FIRE XXII.

A Romance of the War—A Story Strange but True—What an Insane Fisherman Caught.

CAMP-FIRE XXIII.

The Wrong Ox by the Horns—The Tables Turned on an Officer's Strict Discipline—A Decision by Mansfield, General—Rivalry in Religion.

CAMP-FIRE XXIV.

Wrong Kind of a Cat—" More About the Broken Window," or Crawford Again.

CAMP-FIRE XXV.

A Raw Recruit's Anxiety—Another Story about Another Mule—On the St. Francis River—A General Incog. Refused a Cup of Coffee.—A Confederate's Idea of what the Gospel is.

CAMP-FIRE XXVI.

The Sequel to the Farmer and the Watermelons—The Un-wisdom of a Raw Recruit—A Joke on the General—The Temperance Major—The Captain who didn't Water his Whiskey.

CAMP-FIRE XXVII.

Home on a Furlough—A Premonition of Death—Hours of Peril.

CAMP-FIRE XXVIII.

Dinnis M'Ginley as the "Secretary of War"—Mart McCoy and the General—How the 15th Corps came by its Badge—The Romance that a Spent Ball Brought About—How Wheeler's Cavalry got some Corn Meal—Sensations upon Seeing a Comrade Killed by a Bullet.

CAMP-FIRE XXIX.

The Truth about the Capture of the Guerilla Chieftain, John Morgan —Audacious Audacity—The Last Plank of the Ship of State.

CAMP-FIRE XXX.

A Mule Driver's Peculiarities—Foragers—Major Collins' Negro Boy, Fraction—The Sad Story of an Unknown Michigan Soldier.

CAMP-FIRE XXXI.

"Desecrated" Vegetables—What they were and how they Cooked 'Em—Shaming the "Biggest Liar."

CAMP-FIRE XXXII.

Two of Mosby's Men Personate Union Officers—A Successful Military Manœuver—Character Maintained Notwithstanding the Demoralizing Influences of Army Life.

CAMP-FIRE XXXIII.

Reminiscences of the Battle of Corinth—A Brave Boy in Gray—The Old Canteen.

CAMP-FIRE XXXIV.

The Last Camp-Fire—The End of the Season—The S. P. U. H. Valedictory—A Hymn of Peace.

ILLUSTRATIONS.

A Camp-fire Chat.................................Frontispiece
Knapsack... 24
Cartridge Box.. 31
The Old Mill... 35
"Bress de Lor'".. 41
Shell-gun.. 43
Skirmish Line.. 49
Camp Ford, Texas... 65
Haversack.. 72
"Fall in for Grub"... 85
Bombs.. 91
Libby Prison... 97
Andersonville... 107
Pontoon Bridge.. 137
Shot out of a Cannon...................................... 145
Redoubt... 149
Foraging.. 167
Shrapnel Shell.. 169
Charge of Cavalry... 314
A Halt on the March....................................... 187
Corduroy Road... 199
The Latest News... 280
Lull in the Battle.. 269
The Morning Reveille...................................... 223
A Midnight March.. 329
G. A. R. Badge.. 245

CAMP-FIRE CHATS.

INTRODUCTION.

NEVER was there war or military conflict more prolific of incident than the Civil War of America. The explosion of a shell was frequently followed by the crack of a joke, and a bullet or a bayonet produced more fun than fear; yet neither were ever so close that they left no time for a prayer. The raging battle was never so intense that a dying comrade could not be given a drink of water; and no march was ever so long, nor fatigue so great, that a biscuit could not be divided with a messmate. Such was the sympathy which held the army with its common cord.

But this is easily understood; for behind the war of musketry was a war of mind. Each bullet and each bayonet was guided by a thought and an inspiration, whose constancy placed upon each fort and parapet an emblem of fraternity and liberty which put to shame the ancient banners of spoliation and conquest.

Spartan bravery could not have coped with American courage in such a struggle; nor the ominious crescent of the Saracens have been more awe-inspiring, nor the cross of the Crusaders more worshipful, than the flag which quieted the trembling sovereignty of the western world.

The history of this war has been written, the causes and results have been discussed, and the record made; but the narration of personal adventure and observation can never fail to be of interest, and the tales, by those who survive, of the true bravery of America's noblest sons, with their daring deeds and marvelous exploits, will ever remain in the hearts of the people, like the traditions of old, and become the fireside history of a modern conflict between the brothers of a nation, in which both believed themselves in the right.

And, indeed, it is here that we must look for the real history and the exposition of the true character of a people in time of war. The movements, campaigns and statistics of armies may be chronicled, and in their cumbersome dryness be placed away among the archives of the nation; but the veritable disposition of those who harbor the passion, the coolness, the love, the hate, the sympathy, the cruelty, the right, the wrong,—must ever be sought from individual sources.

It is not possible to give every soldier's experience through the entire war, but the incidents in this volume are taken from actual experiences. If the aim has been accomplished, a variety of information has been disclosed which will give to the general reader a picture of war and army life such as has never been presented to the people.

Many books give a drawn-out list of battles as the history of our Civil War. The war was not in all a military conflict; it was a complete revolution, in which the many customs and whole life of *one* people were changed, and as a result of which new energy thrilled another people. The war was not all battles nor all marches; but a stern struggle of combined intellectual and physical forces. Intelligence and reason pervaded rank and file; and while the sword was in its scabbard, between acts, discussion held sway. It was in this way that the revolutionary features were slowly wrought out, and this will be clear only when we have paused by many a camp-fire to witness the manifestations of a change in our national character, as disclosed by the actors themselve .

CAMP-FIRE I.

THE S. P. U. H.—THE FIRST CAMP-FIRE—THE CAMP OF INSTRUCTION—THE FARMER AND THE WATERMELONS—"HOW TEDIOUS AND TASTELESS THE HOURS"—THE CLOSING SCENE.

THE Society for the Preservation of Unpublished History, having been duly authorized and organized, with each of its members a living embodiment of all the accomplishments desirable in a minor historian, and each a commissioned and lawful emissary of the great Muse, went forth determined to prove the beneficence of its existence, by first gathering in and giving shelter to such facts and observations in the history of the Civil War in America as had not felt the protecting hand of the "art preservative of all arts." What the society lacked in numbers it made up in spirit, and if its physical shortcoming was marked, its Muse-ical development was proportionally great.

One feature, however, was especially noticeable, and this was the unusually large ears of the members, which was only another evidence of their fitness for the work in hand. Aided by this abnormal development they would collect the dying accents of many an unwept hero; and, moreover, in the modern school of ethics, an attentive ear is more to be admired than an oily tongue; yea, than a tongue doubly oiled. Likewise, they were well equipped in every appointment. But it must not be inferred from this that the members of the S. P. U. H. belong to the long-eared race of zoology, or that all historians have long ears, or that the long-eared race are all historians, for such an inference would be historically incorrect, and far from the purpose of the fraternity.

Enthusiastic over their worthy intention, the S. P. U. H. arrived at a post of the Grand Army of the Republic, immediately sought out the commander, and notified him that their great ears itched for stories of the war, and memoirs of army life. That eminent was astonished. Whether to consider the society a fraud or a humbug he did not know. Certainly it was not real, and yet the age of myths and miracles was past.

"War!" said he; "I surrender. Your assault has found me unarmed. The attack is a complete surprise."

Twenty years of active business life had dispelled all military thoughts. In his efforts to recall his early life the gray-haired veteran was almost tranced. But the balm of assurance was administered, his soldierly instincts returned, and the commander invited the S. P. U. H. to be at the rendezvous when the sun's rays should be succeeded by those from the camp-fire.

They consented, and at the appointed time met the assembled veterans, who had been summoned into camp by the commander. After the fire burned well and threw its comfort into the faces of those present, the historical hard-tack and coffee were served in the style *a la* 1861-'65. When this was done the chief bade the soldiers be quiet, and thus exhorted them:

"COMRADES—I have called you into camp this evening for special duty. We have present a representative of the Society for the Preservation of Unpublished History. The ears of this society itch for stories of our old camp-fires, marches, battles and crude experiences, and memories of our ancient valor. Let him among you who has the easiest tongue and best memory now speak. Whoever may give any curious information about the many features of soldier life, or describe the manners and customs of the rank and file, the saddle, the battery or the gunboat, or give a strange adventure, or some point of history heretofore unrecorded, shall have his name and regiment written in the great book of the Muse, which the Society for the Preservation of Unpublished History has now in charge. If any of you have such incidents and observations of unwritten history, let it now be divulged, or forever be cast into oblivion."

Thereupon the pipe of peace was passed around the campfire of plenty. When the "boys" were all settled, Rev. A. R. Thain, a private of the 96th Illinois Infantry, remembered an anecdote, and said:

"I think of one incident that occurred in our camp of instruction at Rockford, Ill., but, for the benefit of our visitors I will give what comes to my mind of our first experience in war, before I relate it.

"Our country knew very little about war when the Civil War broke out, and the task of forming an army from raw recruits, many of whom had never seen a soldier, was great indeed. Our only consolation in those days was that our antagonists were in somewhat the same condition of ignorance. And yet we did possess one advantage over them; we *knew* that we were ignorant of the art of war, while many of them thought themselves thoroughly proficient. Each Southerner was ready to meet as many 'Yankees' as he had fingers and toes, doubtless imagining himself the eldest son of Mars. I remember reading the statement of one writer concerning the Confederate Army in its first organization; that 'every man brought a colored servant with him to stand guard, or relieve his master of fatigue duty;' that 'every amateur officer had his own pet system of tactics, and the effect of the incongruous teachings, when brought out on battalion drill, closely resembled that of the music of Bob Sawyer's party, where each guest sang the chorus to the tune he knew best.'

" But in the Union camps of instruction, all the boys who were there will remember how strictly the discipline was enforced. The raw recruit was tied up so tightly with red tape that he could hardly stir without an order from headquarters. Every day he was ground between the upper and nether millstones of company and battalion drill, and between times was, perhaps, sifted and bolted by squad drill. His slow, careless gait had to be transformed into a prompt marching step. His habit of executing all movements in easy curves must be corrected, his muscles must have a certain jumping-jack jerkiness, his frame a ramrod uprightness, chest thrown back, eyes to the front, little fingers at the seams of the pants; must learn which was his left foot, and for some this was very difficult, for I know one man who was sent home from the camp of instruction because he could not master the mysteries of 'hay-foot, straw-foot.'

" But, perhaps, one of the most difficult things for the new soldier to appreciate and do, was the performance of guard duty—camp-guard in the home camp. It might do well enough in the daytime, to keep citizens out and soldiers in, and impress visitors with the pomp and pageantry of war; but at night, when the soldiers were sleeping on the soft side of a pine board and dreaming of the beds they had left behind them, what necessity was there, military or otherwise, for posting men all around the camp at intervals of ten or fifteen rods?

" The camp of instruction at Rockford was bounded on one side by the Rock River, but I suppose if the camp had been on an island it would have been surrounded by guards, if for nothing else than to keep the river from creeping out of its bed, or the frogs from jumping across the guard line. At first, the men who stood camp guard adopted a somewhat novel, but certainly very noisy way of relieving the tedium of the night watches. If Mr. Darwin had been present he might have said that it was a recurrence of ancient practices in the line of man's descent, for each guard adopted the cry of some beast or bird, and made the night hideous with imitations. From Post No. 10 would come the crow of a cock; Post No. 12 would answer with the headlong, heels-over-head gobble of a turkey; Post No. 15 seemed to be held by a dog, and from Post No. 20 would come the stridulous hee-haw of a donkey. And this was practiced in many camps throughout the war. Close imitations were greeted with great applause. The most famous man in our line of barracks was a private in Company D, 96th Illinois, who could imitate the cry of a turkey so closely that the listener involuntarily thought of Thanksgiving. The sequel showed, however, that he could gobble better than he could fight.

"In the camp of instruction we also learned to forage. It was wrong, of course, to practice on friends, but the soldier's stomach sometimes got the better of his conscience. One ludicrous incident occurred. A farmer came into camp with a load of watermelons, and a crowd of soldiers gathered around his wagon, as if eager to purchase his wet goods. One soldier selected a melon and began to bargain very earnestly for it, gradually drawing the farmer a few steps further away from the wagon. He told the farmer that he and his comrades had left their ancestral melon-patches to go and fight the battles for the Union; that Uncle Sam did not pay them very liberal wages; that as yet they had received no pay, but that they were fond of melons, and he wanted to know what was the lowest price which he would take for the particular melon which he held in his hands. He argued very pathetically for a low price. Being patriotic, the farmer sold it for a few cents, and after some delay in making change, turned toward the wagon to supply the other customers. But sad to tell, his wagon was empty, and not a melon was in sight. Bringing eatables into the locality was like pouring water on a sand heap. With a disgusted look, the farmer tried to get a last glimpse of one of his melons, at least, but it was in vain, and he mounted his wagon, remarking: 'Guess I'd better git my wagon out o' here pretty soon, or you'll eat that.' He left the camp soon after with an empty wagon, a flat pocket-book, and a rather low opinion of camp morals."

When Mr. Thain had finished, Mr. Wm. Tasker, Chaplain of an Illinois Infantry Regiment, began:

"That reminds me of one that occurred in Northern Missouri, in a swamp called Mud Creek. It was the first guard for many of the boys after leaving the camp of instruction, and it was hard for some of them to accustom themselves to the loneliness of sentinel duty. It was especially hard for one young fellow, I remember, who had never been from home very much, and already began to be homesick. His post was in a thicket of undergrowth from which the large trees had been cut, and it was his first night on guard. It had been raining all the afternoon, and by eight o'clock in the evening the usual camp-life was hushed, and all was quiet. The night was very dark, and the rain still poured down—one of those dreary, drizzly, dismal times so unwelcome to a homesick soldier—in fact, the place and time could only be duplicated by the dreariness of a Missouri thicket on a rainy night.

"The lad paced his weary beat to and fro, to and fro, all the evening. Nine o'clock came, and the stillness became oppressive. Ten o'clock came; still nothing could be heard except the monotonous patter of the rain. Eleven o'clock; twelve o'clock; all was quiet. The sentinel walked up and down again. Then he sat down. Nothing would break the silence. He thought of home. Then a tear trickled down his cheek. To clear it away he began to sing:

"'How tedious and tasteless the hours
When Jesus no longer I see;
Sweet prospects, sweet birds, and sweet flowers
Have all lost their sweetness to me.'

"Just then the officer of the guard, a gruff, irreverent specimen, came around, heard the music, and thought to have a little sport. Creeping quietly up, he suddenly raised to his feet within a few steps of the startled soldier. The music ceased.

"'Halt!' the sentinel commanded. 'Who goes there?'

"Placing his hands up to his mouth for a trumpet, the officer loudly whispered, '*Jesus Christ!*'

"'Oh! I thought it was the Second Relief,' said the soldier."

Then Mr. Svanson John Petersen, of De Grace's Twenty-Pound Paragon Battery, Company H, First Ill. Light Artillery of the United States of America Volunteers, arose. He began with his favorite tribute to Gen. W. T. Sherman, and was not alone in his admiration of the great chieftain; but the boys had heard his story before, and knew its length. The fire burned low, many of the soldiers had been doing fatigue duty during the day, some of them had mixed their coffee with a stronger beverage during the evening, and the majority longed for the bunk. Mr. Petersen continued:

"It vas de march vrom Savannah to Raleigh. De camp vas lade at night, und dere vas early rizing all de time. De vedder vas bad, und de boys discourage. Ven de boys vas discourage dey vould cuss de offisairs. Ve vas cussin' Sherman und de offisairs, ven ve vas riding along von day, because de war vas too long. Ve vas vith de third gun, und I vas de lead driver. De second driver he say to me, 'Keep still,' all at once.

"Preddy zoon Sherman und his shtaff files along up de rear. Sherman says, 'Vat's de matter?'

"'Ve are tired oud,' 've zay.

"Den Sherman vas very polite. De soldiers are von by his expression. He say: 'Boys, it's preddy zoon over. I know it's hard, but a little longer ve'll be home—ve are on our vay home!' If he had been a captain he vould svear at us. It vas very sad."

"Is that the end?" asked the Society for the Preservation of Unpublished History.

"Vell, I haf anudder von," said Mr. Petersen.

"We will hear that another time," said the society. On looking around it was discovered that there were a great many dry eyes in the audience after this sad story. In fact, all eyes were dry, and there emanated from the various breathing apparatuses sounds indicative of weariness. The god Morpheus had weighed their eyelids down; upon beholding which the society beckoned Mr. Petersen to be seated. In course of half an hour the soldiers began to leave camp, one at a time, each quietly departing after he shook off his drowsiness, and feeling too much victimized to arouse his fellow-slumberers.

CAMP-FIRE II.

HOW A BALKY HORSE DID NOT SURRENDER—THE EXECUTION OF DESERTERS—A PENSION FOR A PIN-SCRATCH.

WHEN the veterans convened on the following evening, some one soberly alluded to the discourtesy of the previous meeting in withdrawing from the camp-fire so unceremoniously. With great humiliation the guilty each made a low bow, and assured the others that nothing but the best intention—which has excused far greater crimes—had possessed them; that they had quietly withdrawn that they might leave their weary comrades to the full enjoyment of unbroken slumber. This explanation being accepted, Mr. Joseph Dewey, of the 7th Iowa Cavalry, Company C, said:

"Let me relate the glorious tradition of how a balky horse saved the life of Captain Bartlett. It was just before the capture of Memphis, and our boys were returning from a three-days' raid. We had come in sight of what we thought were two regiments of Federal infantry, and wheeled about to join them. But when we were within a few rods of the supposed Federals, we suddenly discovered that they were about two thousand 'Johnnies' in blue coats.

"Captain Bartlett had a very remarkable horse. He was a dark bay, bob-tail, straight neck, and short ears. This horse always held his head about twenty-nine degrees higher than the heads of his fellows, probably from his sense of pride. But with all his imperfections he was not blind. I have never known of a blind horse that was balky. Jehu—that was his name—had two good I's, one for intelligence, the other for indolence. However, he rarely used both at the same time. He would glance backward with the eye of intelligence to see what was going on in the rear, and then, all of a sudden, he could see nothing more except through the indolence eye. Yet withal, this noble animal was trustworthy—you could always trust him to eat a peck of oats and call for more; and he was equally reliable for standing still when there was too much weight on his back.

"Upon discovering the true character of the blue-coated infantry, the cavalry wheeled again, and were off. Jehu stopped. He had become tired of horse society. He desired solitude. The captain whipped and spurred, all to no purpose. Then the Confederates opened fire, and it began to be uncomfortable for Jehu, though no damage was done. Then another volley came, and Jehu at once concluded to join the enemy. To carry out this determination, he turned his head to the left, stiffened his neck, and darted off in a 2:40 gait, side-wise, to the right. This brought him into the midst of the enemy, who yelled to the captain: 'Surrender! surrender! You Yankee s— o— b—!'"

[This military term may need some explanation. It originated with the Confederates early in the war, and was an appellation given to all soldiers of the Union Army, from whatever point they hailed. In civil life it became shortened to "Yankee *sob*," but here it is used in its strictest hostile sense.]

"But no surrender for Jehu. The enemy's ranks parted and let him through, but the firing continued, and still was heard:

"'Surrender! surrender! you Yankee s— o— b—!'

"'How in thunder *can* I surrender,' answered the captain, still borne through the ranks on the back of the horse. 'I will if you'll stop my horse.' Several shots were fired, but strange to say, Jehu made good his escape without a scratch to himself or the captain, amidst great applause."

Mr. H. P. Thompson, Orderly Sergeant of Company H, 49th New York, and later in charge of the provost guard, then asked if the S. P. U. H. would like to hear concerning the execution of two deserters.

"Yes," said their representative; "give us a description of how deserters were executed."

"Well, I remember what I am going to tell as well as if it happened only yesterday. The prominent part I bore in the sad affair fixed it indelibly on my mind.

"It was near Brandy Station, Va., on the 3d of December, 1863. Desertions were becoming too frequent, and something had to be done to stop the disloyalty. Seventeen deserters had been tried and sentenced at this time; but fifteen were pardoned by the general proclamation of President Lincoln, pardoning all deserters who would return and take their places in the ranks. The two who were not pardoned were George Blowers, of Company A, 2d Vermont, and John Tague, Company A, 5th Vermont. There were a great many trials for desertion during the war, but deserters were seldom executed; they usually received a lighter sentence. The most general sentence was that the deserter should return to the army and serve out all of his original time of enlistment which had not been served, without pay or allowance. For instance, if a soldier who had enlisted for four years had deserted at the end of six months, he would be brought back when caught, and be compelled to serve three years and six months more. This was the penalty, except in flagrant cases.

"Some were sent to Dry Tortugas, which was almost equivalent to banishment. Dry Tortugas is a group of islands belonging to the United States, at the entrance of the Gulf of Mexico, 120 miles west southwest of Cape Sable, the southern extremity of Florida. The islands are very low and swampy, partly covered with mangrove bushes, which is a species of tropical fruit resembling the paw paw and banana. It was a dismal place, and deserters were compelled to serve out a term of years with ball and chain, the same as other prisoners.

"Occasionally there was a man hung; but Tague and Blowers were to be shot. The provost marshal of the county or locality where they were caught had returned them, as was the custom, to their regiment, and drawn his bounty, which was a reward of $50 apiece (I believe), offered by the State in which they were found.

"The court-martial then tried and sentenced them, and they were placed in tents by themselves in charge of the provost guard, which was chosen pro rata from the different regiments of a division. The guard in this instance was a detail of twenty men chosen from the regular provost guard. When a deserter was put under guard, two or three of these men would stand with loaded muskets around the tent of the deserter, being relieved every two hours. No soldier was ever made to stand guard over a deserter from his own company or regiment, for, of course, it was always painful for one comrade to be compelled to enforce a severe law upon a fellow comrade, and possibly a schoolmate, or even a brother, and then there was danger of a plot to escape if an intimacy of this kind were allowed. So these two boys from Vermont were handed over to our regiment, the 49th New York.

"It was a beautiful morning. The sky was clear, the sun shone brightly, the air was soft and still, and two ambulances, containing rough wooden coffins, were brought up to the tents where the prisoners were under guard. Each soldier was then placed in an ambulance, on his coffin, and the retinue proceeded to the place of execution, about a mile from the headquarters of the guard. The ambulances were drawn this distance by the soldiers who were to do the shooting. When they arrived at the chosen place, the division, composed of about ten thousand soldiers, was formed into a hollow square to witness the sad affair. A hollow square is a double line of soldiers on three sides of a square, fronting the fourth side, which is left open, as the objective point of operations. It was used on this occasion for an imposing display, and to intimidate and prevent other soldiers present from committing a like crime.

"It was a scene full of awe, never to be forgotten by those who took part. All who witnessed it seemed to feel the solemn presence of death. When the coffins were placed in the open part of the square, John Tague attempted to be jovial by rapping in the bottom of his coffin and asking some of the boys if they could not put shavings or something in it, as it would be a pretty hard nest; but no applause greeted his remark, and it reacted upon him with solemn force. The adjutant general then stepped out into a position a little forward from the center of the square, and in a clear, but tremulous voice, read the finding of the court-martial to the troops. The guns used by the provost guard on occasions like this were always loaded by a person appointed for the purpose. It would not do to let soldiers load their own guns, as they would probably put in blank cartridges. The feeling of responsibility for a death was too intense in such cases. However, one blank cartridge was always put into one of the guns, so that each of the men who did the shooting might suppose that he had the blank, and that his shot did not kill the prisoner.

"When the adjutant finished reading, the guard was ordered forward, divided into two platoons of ten each, and the guns were handed to them. As I have said, I shall never forget this particular moment. I had charge of one of the platoons, and the orders were that the man having such charge should step up with a loaded musket and blow out the brains of the victim in case the volley discharged at him by the platoon failed to kill! I held my musket ready in my hand, and was to shoot John Tague. The other platoon was in charge of Sergeant Otis B. Hayes. He was a man of strong nerve and moral courage, but at this time he was as pale as death and as weak as a child; in fact, he could hardly stand. He was to end the life of George Blowers, if the ten shots from his platoon failed.

"While the finding of the court-martial was being read by the adjutant, the doomed men stood up. But they were now ordered to kneel on their coffins. A quarter-sheet of ordinary note paper—called by the boys a 'paper heart'— was then pinned on the coat of each victim, over his heart. When this was done, there was an awful silence. The doomed boys had not been blindfolded, and each countenance, though brave to the last, betrayed the solemn consciousness that within a minute more they would be within the pale of death. All was suspense. Clapping his hands to his heart, John Tague said, 'Boys, shoot me here—make no mistake!' Then came the final order from the provost marshal:

"'Ready! Aim! Fire!'

"Tague fell forward on his face and never breathed again; but Blowers was horribly mangled, and fell forward on his hands and knees, exclaiming:

"'Oh! my God—my God!'

"Sergeant Hayes trembled like an aspen. He was to end the poor fellow's existence! He advanced toward the spot, while ten thousand soldiers held their hushed breath. But, to the relief of all, Blowers died before the Sergeant reached him; and the troops formed company front, and marched in review past the coffins to view the bodies of their dead comrades."

"That is true to the letter, and well given," said Andrew W. Brazee, late major of the 49th New York. "I was the provost marshal who gave the order, and remember it well."

A general from Ohio, who had charge of a brigade, then gave this incident to illustrate the eagerness with which a certain element in our army sought redress from the government for injuries sustained, even before the pain of a hurt had subsided; in fact, an injury was hardly received before they began to weigh, in their minds, the amount of annuity to which they would be entitled.

"A Dutchman had been detailed as an orderly on duty at the general's headquarters, and in an engagement was unfortunate enough to have the index and second finger of his right hand shot off. He was running to and fro across the battle field when he met the general, and, with tears rolling down his cheeks, he exclaimed, 'Oh, Sheneral, Sheneral, shoost look at my hand.' The general, after expressing sorrow and sympathy, was about to move on, when the man again turned his tearful face toward him, and, holding up his bleeding hand, in pitiful tones cried out:

"'Oh, Sheneral! Sheneral! how much pension I gets for him? Don't you tink I would get two pensions, one for each finger what I lose?'"

This story was considered a good one to close with, and the second camp-fire was dismissed.

CAMP-FIRE III.

THE MADDEST MAN IN THE ARMY—A REGIMENTAL FOOT RACE—EFFECTS OF EXCITEMENT—" BRESS DE LOR'."

BOYS, do you recollect the race between our regiment and the 2d Iowa?' said Mose Huntley, of the 52d Illinois.

" Yes," said Mr. Kessler, a First Lieutenant of one of the companies, " it was just before the battle of Corinth, and I remember about that time of seeing the maddest man I ever saw in my life. He belonged to our company, and was a fine soldier, patriotic and courageous, but impetuous. His name was Peterson, I believe, a strong, burly Swede.

" The rebel Forrest had just made an audacious raid near us. Peterson could stand it to fight an honest soldier in the front, but when he thought of being hoodwinked by a treacherous guerilla, he almost tore his hair. We were ordered out immediately after Forrest, and pursued him all night. Just before daybreak we were passing through a low wooded land, and thought we heard the noise of the enemy in our advance. Peterson broke into a run, thinking he would get a shot at ' dem kersud gareelahs.' But alas! just as he started to run a vine tripped him, and he fell forward against a sapling of two or three years' growth. His rage was uncontrollable. Swearing a chain of oaths, and clenching his musket with a death-grip, he slashed away at the sapling with the butt end, breaking the stock and ruining the barrel. But this was not enough. He grappled with the enemy, gnawed, kicked and twisted until he tore the tree up by the roots and flung it away."

"Ehic! 'nuther vict'ry fur United States arms," said Boozy Dick, who was intoxicated to a stupefying degree.

"Well, Mr. Huntley, will you not give us the race now?" said the Society for the Preservation of Unpublished History; when Boozy Dick again essayed to exhort:

"Yes, let 'em go, Mose! I'll bet on the—on the—hic!—"

"The Sergeant-at-arms will please assist the sick veteran to retire," ordered the commander, and accordingly Dick was taken to the guard-house.

Mose Huntley then proceeded:

"Well, as I said at starting out, it was between our regiment (the 52d Illinois) and the 2d Iowa, but Kessler stopped me—"

"I beg your pardon, Comrade Huntley," said Mr. Kessler.

"My pardon is beggable," replied Mose, and continued:

"It was about two weeks before the battle of Corinth. We were out on a forage, and came to an old out-of-the-way house, about which weeds and bushes had grown. We heard a noise in the house and found six Rebs with one Yankee prisoner, whom they were trying to convert.

"'Humph!' said the Yankee, 'I'll never join your crowd as long as the United States has a flag and an army. You darned nigger-keepin' traitors ought to be ashamed to fight against such a flag as mine. If I was loose, I'd hang the whole lot of you!' The prisoner had looked through a crack and seen our boys coming, and it made him sort o' brave. 'If I wanted to I could call twelve legions to my help.'

"'Ha! ha! ha!' laughed the rebs. 'Why don't you do it? *Do* it—call 'em.'

"'Well, I will call a *few* of 'em—come on, boys,' said the Yank, and just then our boys broke through the door and took the whole six prisoners.

"We tore everything up, and finally found a barrel of whiskey and one of black-strap."

["Black-strap" is a kind of syrup unskilfully made from frost-bitten sugar-cane. It resembles a mixture of coal-tar, glucose and stale soda water. Sometimes it was mixed with whiskey, and swallowed with much relish by soldiers whose stomachs must have been lined with something like cast-iron. This chemical analysis has been obtained at great expense by the S. P. U. H., and is known to be correct.]

"Near by was an old mill," continued Mr. Huntley, "and strange to say, several bushels of wheat in a bin. We took some o' the wheat and put it in the hopper, and some of the boys would grind while the others watched. We ground about a bushel before the wheels got hot, and then they began to screech. We had nothing but cotton-seed oil, and that gummed so that it was no use to put it on. We ground about six bushels, when the old rattle-trap stopped short, never to go again! Squee-squawk, squee-squawk—you could hear it for twenty-five miles!"

"Aw! come down a peg," said one of the boys.

"Well, you could hear it for five miles—I'll swear it," said Mose.

"Then we took the bran, whiskey, and black-strap, and started for camp. We did not open either of the barrels, as we thought we would save it all and have a good time with the whole regiment that night. But alas! General Oglesby confiscated our entire stock. He told the teamster to drive the ambulance up to his tent and sleep on those barrels that night. The general was all right in this, because he had just chased the Rebel general, Rowdy, off fifty miles that day, and expected him back that night. He ordered the brigade to lie on their arms in line, for an emergency.

"We wrapped ourselves in our blankets and lay down— but not to sleep. The news of the whiskey had been circulated among the boys, and made 'em restless. They rolled up in their blankets and began to 'spoon!'"

THE OLD MILL.

"What is 'spooning'?" asked the Society for the Preservation of Unpublished History.

"'Spoonin',' my dear children," explained a veteran in the art, "is when soldiers wrap up in their blankets and roll back'ards and for'ards over one 'nother for fun. It is done when they have too much 'budge' aboard. But this time they were only anticipatin', and sort o' goin' through the motions like. They hadn't had anythin' to drink, an' so it was purty dry spoonin'.

"It was 10 o'clock and the Rebel general, Rowdy, hadn't come yet. The boys didn't like the idea o' being cheated out of their 'regular,' and so they 'pointed a commission to look after them barrels of General Oglesby's. The commission crawled up quietly to the wagon, and enough of the boys formed a line on their knees to pass the canteens back from the wagon to the bivouac, so that no noise would be made. It was not long before the commission got an auger an' commenced to bore through the bottom of the wagon up into the barrels. The first barrel they bored into was the black-strap, but they plugged that up, and it did not take long to get the whiskey out of the other one. The canteens were passed back, and the boys had a good old 'spoon,' never waking the driver, who slept on the barrels.

"In the morning the officers thought they would sample the whiskey, and sent to the wagon for some. But of course the boys had emptied the barrel, and when it was reported to General Oglesby, he came out, called the boys together, and asked:

"'Who in (Hades) stole that whiskey?'

"'The 2d and 7th Iowa!' said our boys.

"'No, sir! the 52d Illinois,' said the Iowa boys.

"Just then General Sweeney (then our Colonel) came out, and he looked awfully dry and disappointed. 'Who stole that whiskey?' he inquired.

"'The 2d and 7th Iowa!' we answered, and the Iowa boys again said we did it.

"'By the powers! I'll arrest every one of you,' said Sweeney.

"But he didn't. When it comes to arrestin' two or three regiments o' soldiers, it's not easily done. Then we were suddenly ordered to Corinth on double-quick, to resist an attack by the Johnnies. The sun was hot, and the air sultry. The march was heavy, and we double-quicked it every step. As we proceeded, some of the boys became so worn-out that they dropped out, and lay down on the roadside. Some were sunstruck, and many were disabled for life, who are drawing pensions now for that very march. Before we got to Corinth, it was told among the boys that General Weaver (then Colonel of the 2d Iowa) had bet General Sweeney $500 that the 2d Iowa could beat the 52d Illinois to Corinth. This nerved the boys up, and the ranks kept thinning out. I think there were some deaths reported from fatigue. When we got to Corinth in the evening there were only sixteen of our company to report—the rest had dropped on the way. Our company was the first to get in, but I never wanted any more races in mine.

"There were no rebels there, nor any signs of any. The boys said the race was on account of the bet, but I thought it was to punish us for stealing the whiskey."

"All that might have been avoided," said Capt. J. M. Shields, of Company F, 77th Illinois, "but let me remind you of something that could not have been avoided—a curious result which was the experience of almost every soldier in the war, and shows how various are the effects of excitement under fire, upon different temperaments.

"We were ordered to the extreme right in the battle of Chickasaw Bluffs, which placed us on the bank of the Mississippi. It was necessary to skirmish our way along, and before we arrived there, serious trouble occurred. We had never been in an engagement, and none of us knew whether we could stand fire or not. Troops could never be depended upon the first time, though they generally came through all right.

"Our way was through a wooded country, and as usual in skirmishing, the orders were for every fellow to look out for himself. We pushed on in our irregular line for several hundred yards, the boys becoming more and more scattered. They realized now, for the first time in their lives that they were to be shot at. Some were eager and almost rash in their recklessness to push forward and get a shot at the rebs. At times they would be so far in advance that they would have to be ordered back. Others advanced in mortal fear, though they were patriotic and sincere enough, and made good soldiers afterward. But the terror and excitement that seized numbers of them, made them almost powerless to act, for they would lose all control of their nerves, and it is a singular but well-established fact, that under such circumstances the bowels are the first portion of the human system to feel this prostration of the nerves."

Hundreds of soldiers in our civil war became deathly sick under their first fire, though through no cowardice of their own.

"As we went on, the woods became thicker, and the firing sharper. The excitement grew greater, and then the trouble began. Fully five hundred of our regiment were seized with the complaint, and affairs grew serious indeed. Among them was one poor fellow whom I shall never forget. He had kept well to the rear all along, but I cheered him up, pushed him ahead, and managed to keep him in the company.

"Presently we came out in a turnip patch, and when we were well in view, the rebs poured a volley into us. This was the climax. The bullets rattled and stirred the dust about our feet, yet no one was hurt. But the panic was upon us, and it was not possible to hold the weakest. One or two of the boys rushed forward and gained the shelter of a fence beyond, but the rest rapidly retreated.

"I went back with the company, and in the rear found the young man I had aided. He was lying on the ground, deathly pale, writhing in supposed pain, and was so weak that he could not stand. I ordered him to get up and advance immediately, knowing that with one strong effort he would regain his courage. But he was in a sad state, and with his arms tightly pressed about his stomach, he pleaded: 'Oh! my God, my God! captain, do, *do* let me stop here. Oh! I am *so* sick—oh!—oh!'

"I could only pity the poor boy, and so I let him remain until he recovered. Yet he was only one of many who passed through the same experience, and afterward became the most courageous soldiers."

The 7th Iowa was then glorified in this manner by Mr. William F. Montgomery:

"When Sherman reached Columbia, S. C., 300 Union officers were imprisoned there. These were liberated and the city was fired. But before this the prisoners were slurred with all kinds of foul insults. Nothing seemed too base for the home-guards and women to utter. They were worse than the women of New Orleans before Butler's 'Woman Order.'

"But there was one consolation, even though it came in the form of ebonized humanity. Every insult thrown at the Union prisoners only increased the enthusiasm of the negroes. Multitudes of negro women and children always hung about the army, and hailed the Union soldiers as their deliverers. They meant well enough, but their sympathy was generally carried to excess, and they became almost a general nuisance, especially the ignorant and superstitious field hands. It was a strain on moral courage to endure the majority of the negroes who worked about the houses, but these were infinitely more decent than the field hands.

"In our company was a little wiry, sawed-off man, who hated a negro worse than a snake. When the boys wanted a little sport they would call on Tom to 'cuss the niggers,' and he invariably responded. He repeatedly declared that, 'if the niggers is emancipated I'll leave the army.' But he didn't leave. He staid right along until the climax was reached at Columbia. As we marched up, the negroes swarmed out on all sides to meet us. Among them was an old field hand, a big, stout wench, who would weigh over 400 pounds avoirdupois. Her cheeks hung down, and so did her lower lip, which was something near an inch in thickness, and her hair seemed like the tail of a horse that had been feeding in a cockle-burr field, except that it had the hereditary kink not found in horse-hair.

"The excitement among the negroes grew greater and more intense, and their eyes protruded far beyond their usual limit, as the army came near. They sang, and danced, and shouted. The big woman was especially wild. She raised her arms, snorted like an elephant, and started straight for me. I had been in twenty-two hard-fought battles; had heard the bullets sing past my ears, and shells over my head; many a time had faced death in a thousand forms, and was in the present emergency well armed; but for once in my life I beat a hasty retreat. The old negress gained on me, and I was almost within her reach, the ranks ringing with applause, when I stepped behind the wiry little nigger-hater, and the negress wrapped her great arms around him, lifting him off his feet, and shouting:

"'Bress de Lor'! Bress de Lor'! Yooz de ones we's bin prayin' faw dese fo yeahs! Lor' bress ye, honey! I lub

"BRESS DE LOR'."

ye—I lub ye! Hm—hm—,' and she squeezed the little wiry man the tighter, while the boys cheered louder than ever."

Some of the veterans present remembered the incident, and together with the Society for the Preservation of Unpublished History, they re-echoed the applause of twenty years ago.

When the auditors were quiet again, the commander said that a drum corps from the Freedmen's Exodus Society would like to favor the camp-fire with an attack. The campfire submitted, and the drum corps filed in. Unfortunately, however, the man who tuned the drums had died soon after the war, and the position which he vacated had been unfilled up to date, so that the instruments were somewhat out of repair, and somewhat more out of tune. Then the stifled ether was stirred with rut-tut-tut, bum-bum! rut-tut-tut, bum-bum! and it was thought, from the most scientific musical analysis, that the drum corps had started out on the appropriate tune of

"Ain't I glad I'm out of the Wilderness,"

—an old edition, perhaps, revised and enlarged, with variations and side-notes complete, rearranged especially for the drum corps of the Freedmen's Exodus Society. The drummers warmed up to their performance, and the melody became more intense. After they had played a short time there began to be a remarkable prevalence of headache, and then the audience began to ache all over. The commander was petitioned for mercy. The tenor became louder and shriller, the bass deeper and heavier. The commander then deliberately but loudly ordered the music to face about and halt. But no command could be heard amidst "the clash of arms." Each burly son of Ham had now closed his eyes and nerved himself for the first grand crescendo. The result was inevitable. If the soldiers waited for the climax they would all be placed on the pension-list for broken ear-drums. There was only one way out of the difficulty—that was past the guard. That individual, they found, had already fled, and the whole camp soon stampeded after him. When the drummers opened their eyes, after they had finished their selection, they looked about them, found nothing but darkness, and probably adjourned.

CAMP-FIRE IV.

BUTTERMILK WITHOUT MONEY, BUT NOT WITHOUT PRICE—
FREAKS UNDER FIRE—"JOHNNIES" AND "YANKS"
STOP SHOOTING TO SHAKE HANDS—SOLDIERS AT THE
FRONT DIFFERENT FROM "HOME-GUARDS"—SOUTHERN
NEWSPAPERS—ORIGIN OF "HOLD THE FORT."

ALL the veterans answered at roll-call this evening, as did all the visiting brethren—including the S. P. U. H.—except the drum corps of the Freedmen's Exodus Society. No one asked any question, not caring even to call to mind the experience of the previous evening.

Mr. John G. Morrison began to speak:

"In the fall of 1863, our Regiment (the 101st Ill.) was transferred from West Tennessee to Bridgeport, Ala., and attached to the 11th Army Corps. Supplies for the army at Chattanooga were at that time carried on mules from Bridgeport by a circuitous route along the north bank of the Tennessee River. To open up a shorter and better route, the 11th and 12th Army Corps, not then reorganized into the 20th, were ordered to march across to Chattanooga.

"On the second day's march a discussion arose in Company D, as to which army then occupied Lookout Mountain. One man stoutly maintained that Rosecrans did not lose at Chickamauga, and to settle the matter, one of D's men broke ranks and ran up to a house, and politely asked a lady who was standing in the door, and trying to feel that she wasn't subdued and never would be, whether there were any Confederates on Lookout Mountain. She replied very tartly that when he came back he might tell her.

"The midnight fight in the valley, the battles of Mission

Ridge and Lookout Mountain were soon fought, and after the terrible mid-winter march to the relief of Knoxville, and a rest at Kelley's Ferry, our regiment marched back over the same road through the valley, to Bridgeport. We had all of us forgotten the woman and her evasive answer, except the soldier who questioned her. As we passed the house, he again left the ranks and went up to the house, taking another comrade and half a dozen canteens with him.

"'Madam,' he said, making his best bow, 'I am going back now, and stopped to tell you that there is not a single Confederate on the mountain.'

"'Clar out!' said the woman.

"'Well, madam, I saw some very nice buttermilk when I was here before, and I thought I would bring my canteen along and have it filled.'

"'Naw sir!' growled the woman. 'I don't never give no Yankee no buttermilk o' mine.'

"'You seem to be decidedly in the negative, madam, but I'll *pay* you for the milk—you'll never have to *give a Union soldier* any buttermilk.'

"With this assurance, the woman filled the canteens, in high hope that she would get some United States money, for Confederate scrip was already depreciating, notwithstanding the stringent laws in force against a discrimination in favor of United States money.

"'How much are these worth?' asked the soldier, putting the several canteens into his several pockets.

"'Two dollars apiece!' said the woman.

"'Ain't that pretty high?' asked the soldier, fumbling in every pocket he had to find some money.

"'Thought yer said I wouldn't have to give no Union soldier no buttermilk,' said the woman, surmising the true state of affairs.

"'You will not,' said the soldier—'I'll get the money of

my comrade just out in the yard,' and he started out; with his hands he beckoned the comrade to go back toward the passing columns, while with his voice he called him toward the house. Of course the comrade was in a hurry to get back to the ranks, and the soldier with the canteens moved on after him with apparent reluctance, leaving the woman standing in her doorway watching her buttermilk disappear over the hill, her great expectation slowly changing into disappointment, and then disgust."

When Mr. Morrison finished speaking Mr. Thain asked if the society would like to be initiated into skirmishing, and the active business life of the line of battle.

"Yes," was the reply, "it may be read with ravenous interest by the two-thousand-one-hundred-and-third generation hence."

"Well, let us take Sherman's Atlanta campaign as the main basis of illustration; for the war was not conducted scientifically, and with absolute certainty of success, until after General Grant was placed in command of all the Union forces, and had arranged a concert of action between the East and the West. There is a completeness about the campaigns of 1864, which renders that year of the conflict an interesting study as illustrating the art of war.

"Sherman's army when he began the Atlanta campaign, was 100,000 strong; Johnston's 60,000 strong, but he had the advantage of a friendly country in his rear, and the additional advantage of a succession of carefully fortified lines in the line of his possible retreat. A large force of negroes was at work all the while in his rear; and when he abandoned one line of works he had another to take shelter in. Sherman's advantage consisted in the fact that he could spare at least 40,000 men to lap around the right or left of Johnston's position, and by threatening his communications compel him to fall back. Every direct attack made ¹y Sherman failed, but the flank movement was always successful, though it had a demoralizing effect on the Confederates, who thereby had to confess their weakness by falling back each time, and finally were shut up in Atlanta.

"Having given this general outline of the way in which the campaign was conducted, let us now suppose that Sherman is beginning to feel one of Johnston's strong positions, for instance, the line including Kenesaw, Pine and Lost Mountains. But this is ticklish work, approaching a strong line in a country which is rough and hilly, and much of it heavily timbered. The enemy may sally out on us while we are forming our line, or before our front is protected by earthworks. Yet the Union soldiers are mighty diggers, and if the Johnnies as much as stop to tie their shoe strings before starting, they will find a line of works barring their advance, raised as if by magic. On the Atlanta campaign, the spade was mightier than the sword. Our men did not need to be *urged* to fortify; the enemy's shell urged them in language which needed no interpretation. As soon as a line was formed, and arms stacked, they began to dig, almost as instinctively as a mole begins to burrow when placed on the ground. In every new deal that Sherman and Johnston made, spades were trumps, and as our boys knew how to play the game, we usually won.

"It was amazing to see how quickly a line could be thrown up in that timbered country. Logs, rails, stumps, stones—anything which could form a slight protection, was piled along the regimental front, and inside of this a trench was dug, the earth being thrown outside to form a breastwork. In a few minutes it is strong enough to resist a musketry fire, and a sudden charge could be successfully repelled by the aid of this frail work. When there was no danger of immediate attack, or when this first breastwork became a part of the regular line of investure, a strong parapet was built, faced with logs, poles, or rails, perpendicular on the inside, and four or five feet high. The trench on the inside was then widened to from four to six feet, and deepened to two feet, the earth being thrown over in front again, and making a wall on the outside, four to six feet thick. The parapet was generally crowned with a head-log, a space being left between its under side and the parapet to fire through. The head-log rested on skids, which sloped off across the trench to keep the log from injuring the men, if displaced by a cannon-shot. These works were sometimes further strengthened by an *abatis* of tree tops, placed a number of rods in front, with their sharpened branches turned toward the enemy. Through this an attacking column would find great difficulty in making their way under fire. Such works could be held against almost any direct attack, as Sherman found to his cost in his unsuccessful charge on the Kenesaw line on the 27th of June.

"The skirmish pit was much like the main line in construction, except that it was lighter and only twelve or fifteen feet long. The skirmish pits were placed as far in advance of the main line as the location of the enemy's pits would permit, the opposing skirmish lines often being uncomfortably near each other.

"The establishment of a skirmish pit in an exposed position, in the face of a watchful Confederate line, was a task requiring the wisdom of a serpent, the courage of a lion, and the building powers of a beaver. I distinctly remember one particular skirmish line in front of Johnston's Allatoona line of defense; and though the situation now presents itself to me in a somewhat ludicrous light, it was serious enough on Saturday, the 28th of May, 1864. We went on the skirmish line before daylight, as it was in an open field in plain sight of the enemy's main line, and not more than 300 yards from their skirmish line. The particular post where I found myself was sheltered by two lengths of rail-fence in the shape of a letter

THE SKIRMISH LINE.

V, strengthened somewhat by additional rails. At first we confined our attention to the enemy's skirmish pits, and many sharp shots were exchanged. But along in the forenoon we became ambitious, and began to try the effect of long-range shots on the main line. Directly in front of us was one of the enemy's batteries, and as we could now and then see a man not sheltered by the parapet, or an officer riding along on horseback, it amused us to see how our long-range shots would quicken their pace. Some of the shots must have taken effect, or, at any rate, they could bear our fire no longer, for about the middle of the forenoon that battery opened a terrible fire on our particular pile of rails.

"We had thought that our insignificance was our best protection, but now the tables were sadly turned. We knew that the loose rails would aid in our destruction if a shot should strike them, but we clung to our fence corner, dreading the skirmish fire if we should leave it.

"Serious as the situation was, a ludicrous feeling flashed through my mind for a moment as I looked around for a place to lie down. My comrades, including the lieutenant of the guard, were piled together in the corner of the V, each trying to make himself as flat as—" [some of the sermons preached by the chaplains—the S. P. U. H. thought he said—as their great ears for once failed to catch the comparison; but it might have been as flat as they lay when robbing henroosts while the property man was near. However, the society concluded, without any reflection upon the speaker, that posterity must necessarily suffer the loss of some eloquent points of history; otherwise the historian of three thousand years hence would have no ancient manuscripts to ponder over.]

"The boys were so mixed together," continued the narrator, "that I could not distinguish one from the other. I lay down behind the pile, and wished myself behind the main line. Shell after shell shrieked over us so close that we could almost feel the wind of them, and one or two burst just behind the post, but nothing struck our pile of rails.

"The fire from the enemy's batteries became so sharp that our batteries began to answer it, and this turned their attention from such small game to pay their respects to our main line. Other batteries began to join in, and as gun after gun awoke from both sides it seemed as if old Nick had let loose all his dragons. When the firing ceased we became badgers, one and all, and began to dig for dear life. Bayonets, tin plates, pieces of rails—anything that could turn up earth, was used.

"By-and-by, when the Confederate skirmishers were not alert, one of our number crept along, Indian-fashion, past a light growth of bushes to the next post to the right. He soon returned with a spade, and if that spade had been solid gold, handle and all, presented to our post for our sauciness in stirring up such a hub-bub, it could not have been received with greater delight. At first it was used with great difficulty, for to rise to one's feet, even in a stooping posture, was almost sure death from a rebel musket-ball. By slow degrees a shaft was sunk in the fence-corner, deep enough for a man to stand upright, and by making frequent changes, that spade was so diligently used, that by the middle of the afternoon we had transformed our frail defense into a shot-proof redan.

"Then we opened on that battery again, loading and firing as fast as we could, and they opened on us more furiously than before, but we answered them shot for shot. We had one advantage, for, by watching the puffs of smoke from their cannon we could seek safety in the subterranean region of our little fort before the shot reached us. We could dodge their shots, but they could not dodge our musket-shots, which were imperceptible. They tried us with solid shot, then shell, then grape-shot; but all in vain. We "silenced" that battery, that is, they ceased firing because their shots were of no effect; then we rested on our laurels. Those of my hearers who have never been in a battle may get some idea of the skirmish line of a great battle by multiplying many times the experience just related.

"The Atlanta campaign might be called a skirmish one hundred and twenty days long, rising now and then into a battle; for, from the time that we took the enemy's works at Tunnel Hill on May 7, until we parted company with Hood's army at Jonesboro, below Atlanta, the skirmish fire hardly ever ceased.

" The two armies became familiar with each other on the skirmish line; and familiarity bred *respect*. On the Kenesaw line the skirmishers began to parley with each other, and friendly meetings between the lines became frequent.

" I happened to be on the skirmish line when the practice first began. One afternoon there was a pretty lively fire for awhile, and then a lull. It seemed as if both sides had become tired; and then the Johnnies hailed us thus:

"' Hello, Yanks! Let up awhile. Stop firing, and send out two unarmed men half way, to talk with two of ours.'

" ' Do you want to surrender? ' we asked.

"' No! Give us a rest, and we'll have a chat with you.'

"' All right, Johnny; you do the same.'

"A man from company A and myself started through the woods toward the rebel line, and before we had gone very far, we saw coming toward us two butternut-clad men, who were almost duplicates of Hercules. The rebs had not yet learned to trust our word, and so they had sent two men famous for their fighting powers in a rough-and-tumble encounter. I do not say that we had been selected for the same reason, though, in fact, my companion was a noted fistfighter—the terror of the whole camp when he was intoxicated.

" These two tall men were brothers from Texas, but our meeting was so friendly that suspicion was disarmed at once, and we sat down for a talk. The first question of the Johnnies' was:

"'Ain't you 'uns most tired o' this thing?'

"It was evident that they were; but we told them that we had come to Dixie to see the thing through, and that when they were ready to say quit, and call us brothers under the Stars and Stripes, we would gladly go home.

"'But why have you 'uns come down here to take away our niggers?'

"We assured them that such was not our object, and tried to enlighten them as to the cause of the war. They were very ignorant, and hardly knew what they were fighting for; but were wise enough to know that they were being beaten. They were anxious for some 'Lincoln coffee,' as they called it, and we gave them some from our haversacks. At this time the Johnnies were living on rye coffee, corn bread and bacon.

"'You Yanks drink Rio,' they said, 'but we drink *Ry-e!*'

"After exchanging Northern papers for some of the wretchedly-printed sheets then published in the South, we parted company with our two tall Texan friends, and soon both parties were safe within their own lines.

"Here is a sample of the newspapers published in the South in the latter part of the war," and the speaker held up a copy of the "Vicksburg Citizen," of July 2, 1863.

It was an interesting relic. Stationery was somewhat scarce in Confederate society, and even in business circles, when this edition of the " Citizen" was printed. Everything available in the line of paper had been used in making government "scrip," so that there was little supply for the baser needs of civilization. However, the editor of the "Citizen" was enterprising, and would not suspend his publication as long as anything like paper could be found with one white side to it. By the merest chance he obtained a quantity of fifth-grade wall-paper at a fabulous price, and at once proceeded to issue the "Citizen," only two days before the surrender of the city. It was a daily paper—daily whenever the proprietor could find anything to print it on—and the copy exhibited was sixteen inches long by eleven inches wide, with four minion columns of war news quite clearly printed on the uncolored side. The coloring of the other side was a rough, gloomy green for the solid color, having a brown vine-like figure with a red flower for the ornamentation. It was a novel publication—a monument to the endeavor of the proprietor, who could in reality present his readers with a chromo this time—and only commemorates the extremities developed by war.

The relic was passed around for the curious to examine, while the speaker continued:

"As soon as we were safe in our own lines there would come a hail, 'Look out, Yanks! we're going to shoot!'

"'All right, Johnny, pop away!' And for some time the skirmish fire would be kept up with unusual briskness, like children who break into an uproar after a period of enforced silence.

"There was nothing malicious about it; indeed, there was very little personal malice at this time between the men of the two armies. We had learned to respect each other on many a well-fought field, and when our men fell into their hands the regular soldiers treated them kindly. It was the wretched State militia, home-guards, and soldiers who had never seen a battle, who treated our prisoners so cruelly at Andersonville and other Southern prisons.

"In concluding, I will offer a little incident which inspired the song, 'Hold the Fort.' The original was not very religious, but in battle, under great excitement, men do and say things which would not be excusable in civil life. It was at the bloody battle of Allatoona Pass; and Sherman, fearing that General Corse, who held an important position, might weaken, dispatched him to 'hold the fort' at all hazards. To this General Corse replied: 'I am short a cheek-bone and an ear, but can whip all h—l yet.'"

"Your reference to the skirmish lines," said Gen. Ira J. Bloomfield, of the 26th Illinois, "reminds me of some of the freaks the boys committed at the siege of Atlanta. When the siege was in full blast, we moved our entrenchments to within fifteen or twenty paces of the enemy in many places, and the men resorted to all kinds of tricks and devices to get a good shot. One was to get a piece of looking-glass, and then turn a loaded gun-barrel down, pointed over the top of our works; and by lying down below it, and using the looking-glass, a soldier could sight his gun without exposing himself at all. But a very ingenious contrivance was to hollow a conical minie-ball and fill it with powder, and then fit a percussion cap to the point of the ball, with an opening down to the powder. One man would load his rifle with this ball, and several of his comrades would stand with their weapons cocked, ready to fire. The man with the conical ball in his rifle would fire at a stump, fence-rail, or any solid substance that could be seen near the enemy's rifle pits. When this bullet struck, it would explode and sound as if some one just outside their works had fired a gun. This naturally would make them raise their heads to see what it meant. Then came the opportunity for the men in waiting to surprise their antagonists with the most effective shots, much to the gratification of our men, and the chagrin of the boys in gray."

CAMP-FIRE V.

A SURPRISE FOR THE JOHNNIES—WITH BANKS UP THE RED RIVER—PRISON LIFE IN TEXAS—SOLDIERS YET ON PAROLE—TROUBLE BETWEEN THE 13TH AND 19TH ARMY CORPS.

THE incidents related at the close of the last camp-fire, revived many another experience, and the roll-call was scarcely finished before a comrade belonging to the 100th Indiana besought that the following might be chronicled:

"While at New Hope Church, Ga., we advanced our lines each night, until our brigade—the second of the first division of the 15th Army Corps—had advanced and entrenched, by actual count, to within 114 steps of the rebel works. The only guard duty we did was to make a detail of three men to each company to do camp guard at night, with instructions to watch very carefully, lest the enemy should surprise us while it was dark.

"We could plainly see the Confederate works during the day, and no man dare raise his head above the fortifications, lest he be a target for the watchful sharpshooters.

"So on the 4th of June, 1864, Colonel Heath, of the 100th Indiana, concluded to give the Johnnies a little surprise. He called on the Colonel of the 46th Ohio, and giving him the cue, they soon had everything in readiness. The 46th Ohio being armed with the Spencer rifle (seven shooters), they were ordered to load, and every man be ready to fire at the sound of the bugle. The 100th Indiana had orders to give the 'Yankee yell' at the first blast of the bugle. Soon all was in order, and the boys were eager for the work in hand. The bugle sounded the 'forward,' and the cheers of the 100th Indiana followed.

"The rebs, hearing the bugle and the shouting of the boys, concluded we were charging their lines, and sprang to their feet to meet us, thus exposing themselves. Then the 46th Ohio opened fire upon them with their Spencers, and it began to tell. The Johnnies quickly turned and sought cover, enraged beyond expression, each cursing and swearing to the full extent of his blasphemous vocabulary. They heaped all sorts of abuse on us, and one fellow was particularly exasperated. As he was going back, full of disgust, he faced about and yelled, at the top of his voice, 'Shoot away—*you can't hit anything. You think you're mighty smart, but it's only another one of your darned Yankee nutmeg tricks.' A round of Yankee applause was followed by a volley, but the fellow got behind the works just in time to escape."

Major J. M. McCulloch, of the 77th Illinois, then asked if prison life in the South had been discussed at any previous camp-fire. Unfortunately he had not been present at any of the meetings, but would miss none of them hereafter.

"Since you have mentioned the matter, we will hear from you first," said the commander.

"Well, I am hardly prepared to speak impromptu," said the Major.

"Major McCulloch!" "Prison life!" "Major McCulloch!" "Speech!" "Speech!" and other exclamations were heard from the auditors.

"Well, if there is no escape, I will tell you of my experience, not in Andersonville, for I was not there; but there were other prison pens, and I served more than a year in one in Texas, which may not be altogether uninteresting to talk about.

"About the 1st of March, 1864, it was my lot to join the

expedition up Red River in Louisiana, under the command of General Banks. The previous winter months had been occupied in preparation for the expedition, and on the 8th of March the best equipped and best clad army that I was with during my term of service, commenced a forward movement from Brashear City, Louisiana, and marched directly through to Alexandria without delay. This was also one of the best conducted marches. Many of the boys had desired to go with Sherman, but as they did not get their wishes, the trip up Red River was made more pleasant than usual. The column was in motion early in the morning, and went into camp early in the evening. No promiscuous foraging was indulged, but everything necessary was amply provided by detailed foraging parties, so that there was no necessity for the weary soldier to spend part of the night in getting something fresh to eat.

"We reached Alexandria on the 26th of March, and joined the main column of the expedition conducted by General Franklin. One week later we reached Natchitoches (pronounced Nakitosh by the natives), where General Banks took command in person. On the morning of the 6th of April the column was again in motion toward Shreveport, the advance meeting with considerable opposition from the enemy. Our regiment was ordered to the front as skirmishers on the 8th, and about 3 o'clock P. M., after repeated skirmishes with the enemy (in one of which our Lieut.-Colonel L. R. Webb was killed), we found them strongly posted to resist our further progress. A line of battle was formed by the advance troops, consisting of the 2d division of the 13th Army Corps and a few regiments of cavalry.

"General Ransom, who commanded this section of the 13th Army Corps, seeing the dangerous situation of the advance, asked permission to withdraw some distance to get a better position, but was ordered to hold his ground. The other division of our corps was three miles in the rear, and the 19th Corps, consisting of about ten thousand, was about eight miles, and a force of ten thousand under Gen. A. J. Smith, fully a day's march in the rear of that. Why we were thus scattered I never heard explained. The rebels, under Gen. Dick Taylor, to the number of fifteen or twenty thousand, seeing we would advance no further, and knowing our scattered condition, commenced an attack upon us, and brought on a terrific engagement, afterward called the battle of Sabine Cross Roads, by our army, but Mansfield by the Confederates.

" The center of our line held their ground manfully and did terrible execution in the ranks of the advancing foe, repelling three separate attacks; but the rebel line, being so much longer than ours, pressed the wings of our line back, and, before the center was aware of it, a line of rebels was formed in their rear. Being nearly out of ammunition, they submitted to the inevitable, and surrendered. This surrender included the 48th Ohio, the 19th Kentucky, and two companies from the right of our regiment, the 77th Illinois.

" The retreating wings met the 3d division a short distance in the rear, and with them formed another line, but the same fate befel it. The 19th Corps being six or seven miles still further in the rear, the rebels met no further opposition until they encountered this corps well-formed in line of battle, behind which our retreating fragments found shelter. Flushed with victory the rebels rushed upon this new line of battle, but were repulsed with great slaughter, and retired. Darkness closed the scene.

" Having escaped from the first line of battle, I formed with the second, and was there made a prisoner of war. I had often before felt, when entering a battle, that I might be killed or wounded, but I had never once thought of being captured. You can therefore imagine my consternation.

"The utter route of our army and the general demoralization which surrounded me, made me feel for the moment as if the whole United States had collapsed. I soon met Captain White, of the Chicago Mercantile Battery, who had been acting as chief of artillery on the division commander's staff, and said to him in a low tone:

"'Captain, doesn't this beat anything you ever saw?'

"'Oh, no!' he replied, 'it's nothing to Shiloh!'

"He had been a lieutenant in Taylor's battery at that battle.

"I then took courage and congratulated myself on the thought that it was probably not so bad after all, and that while many of my comrades had 'bitten the dust,' I still had my life. But as I had never thought of being taken a prisoner, nor of a prisoner's condition, a new, and what proved to be a fearful experience, now began to open up to me. I was taken with others to Mansfield, three miles distant, where we arrived after dark, and were confined in the court house all night. Those who had been captured earlier in the day were guarded in an open field about a mile from town.

"During the night we saw sad evidence of the havoc we had created in the battle. It was told us that a Louisiana regiment of about 1,200, made up from that vicinity, had been cut to pieces; and the ambulances seemed to confirm the report, as a continual stream of dead and wounded came in during the whole of the night. Great lamentation was manifested. It was impossible for us to sleep, as there was scarcely more than standing room in the building. In the morning we were marched out of the town toward Shreveport, and when a mile out our comrades, who had spent the night in the field, joined us and made a delegation of eleven hundred. We marched three abreast, with a row of mounted guards on each side, and a squad in front and rear.

"After marching about sixteen miles we camped for the

night; and for the first time since our capture rations were issued to us—consisting of corn meal and salt beef. Having no cooking utensils of any description, it was more than Yankee ingenuity could do to prepare much for eating; but we managed after this fashion: The meal was mixed on a rubber blanket, with water and a little salt from the beef barrel, and then spread on a piece of board and held to the fire to bake. The salt beef was cut in pieces and stuck on the end of a sharpened stick, then held in the blaze, and thus, during the night, we managed to partially stop the gnawings of hunger. After the second night, the guard arranged to do their cooking by detail during the day, giving us their utensils at night; and by cooking in turns all night, we managed to get our new fare into better shape.

"Adverse news from the front during the first night caused our course to be changed the next morning toward Marshall, Texas, and on the fifth day after leaving Mansfield we passed through that town, which is a place of considerable size near the Louisiana line; thence directly west from Shreveport. The inhabitants of the town and vicinity had been informed that Gen. Banks' entire army had been captured and was coming. So the streets were lined with men, women, and children of the various shades of color from black to white, to see the Yankees. We were ordered to march two abreast, in order to make a longer column and a more impressive appearance. When about the center of the town we struck up our national war-song, ' The Union Forever,' and sung:

"'We are coming from the East and we're coming from the West,
Shouting the battle cry of Freedom!
And we'll hurl the rebel crew from the land we love the best,
Shouting the battle cry of Freedom!

"'The Union forever! Hurrah, boys, hurrah!
Down with the traitors and up with the stars,
While we'll rally round the flag, boys, rally once again,
Shouting the battle cry of Freedom.'

" While we were singing, some of the women tried to persuade the commander of the guard to stop us, but he seemed to think it was our privilege, and paid no attention to their solicitations. In fact, the guard, who already had heard much of our singing, seemed to enjoy it, much to the chagrin of the spectators. We tried to make the best of our circumstances, and often sang by the way. On several occasions we passed by camps of negroes whose masters were taking them to the interior of Texas, in order to keep them out of reach of our army. On such occasions our boys would sing:

> "'Ole massa run, ha! ha!
> De darkies stay, ho! ho!
> It must be now dat de kingdom's comin'
> And de year of Jubilo.'

" We arrived in the vicinity of the prisoners' camp on the 15th of April, having marched about 125 miles in seven days. The camp was situated about three miles east of Tyler, in Smith county, Texas, and called Camp Ford. It was inclosed by a stockade made of heavy timbers split in halves and firmly set in the ground on end. Originally it contained only three acres, but had been enlarged recently to about seven, in order to accommodate the new arrival. We remained where we camped for the night, until the afternoon of the next day, when we were moved inside the stockade. We had not expected a paradise, but we felt that after such accommodations as we had on the march—no shelter or blankets, except such as we bought or traded for—it would be a relief to get some place in which to lie down in shelter at night. Imagine our surprise when we came in sight of the camp. Inside the pen there were a few log-cabins and dugouts, crowded together promiscuously in one corner. On the tops of these, and on the highest points, were gathered a motley crew of about six hundred, in very ragged clothing, to get a glimpse of the new-comers, about whom big tales had been told them. The remainder of the inclosure was a newly cleared piece of woodland, with nothing on it but stumps, a few brush heaps, and some old logs. Our hearts almost sank within us. But into the stockade we went, and on the unoccupied part were drawn up in parallel lines about twenty feet apart. Here we were counted and delivered to the commandant of the prison, one Colonel Allen, who addressed us in a few words, telling what he expected us to do, and closing with: 'Now, gentlemen, these are your quarters— make yourselves as comfortable as possible.' With nothing but the blue heavens for a covering and the naked earth for a bed, and nothing within reach but a few brush heaps, to be told to make ourselves comfortable, we thought was *decidedly cool.*

"The old prisoners gathered around us, anxious to hear the news from the outside world, and the remainder of the evening was spent in chatting and partaking of what the older inhabitants could spare from their scanty fare. The officers of our party were taken into the cabins of the officers already there, who shared with us their limited quarters; but the privates could only set fire to some of the brush heaps and logs, and huddle around them as best they could for the night. Many following nights were passed in the same way before shelter of any kind could be had. The officers were first permitted to go out to the woods under guard, and cut and carry in timbers to build themselves quarters, which was accomplished in a few days. Then the men were allowed to go out in small parties, but the process was so slow that the best that could be done was to get poles and brush with leaves to make arbors for shelter from the sun by day and the dews by night. Some of the more energetic and persistent ones succeeded in getting a clapboard roof, but a great many spent most of the summer with nothing but brush roofs. Some made dug-outs, and covered with earth a place just large enough for two or three to sleep in. As winter approached we were allowed to go out in greater numbers, under a strong guard, and carry timbers for more than half a mile. By Christmas most of the inmates had pretty fair quarters, and the camp assumed a better appearance.

"Our rations were delivered in bulk to persons designated by ourselves to receive and distribute them, and consisted of corn meal, fresh beef and salt. A pint of corn meal and a pound of beef was our daily allowance per man, with sufficient salt to season them. Occasionally during the earlier part of our stay, rye was issued for coffee. Twice the corn meal failed for several days at a time, and whole corn shelled was issued instead. Some amusement was created during its delivery. When the wagon would make its appearance, the boys would start from different parts of the camp toward the delivery place, calling "Whoo-e-e! Whoo-e-e!" as though calling hogs to their feed. The corn, however, answered a good purpose, as it was a change, the boys making it into hominy. Our beef during the summer was *passable*, but late in the fall it got so poor that it scarcely tasted like beef. A detail of our men butchered the beeves and quartered them, then the rebel guard picked out the best of the hind quarters, and the remainder was brought into the stockade. When the beef got so poor the guard complained to their officer, but no attention was paid to them. Finally, one day after drawing their portion, they carried it in procession to the woods, dug a hole, put it in, fired three rounds of musketry over it, then buried it. After that they got bacon, and in two weeks afterward bacon was issued to us regularly, a quarter of a pound being the allowance per man for a day, and we were rejoiced at the change.

"No clothing was issued to us by the Confederate authorities during our imprisonment, except a few very coarse hats

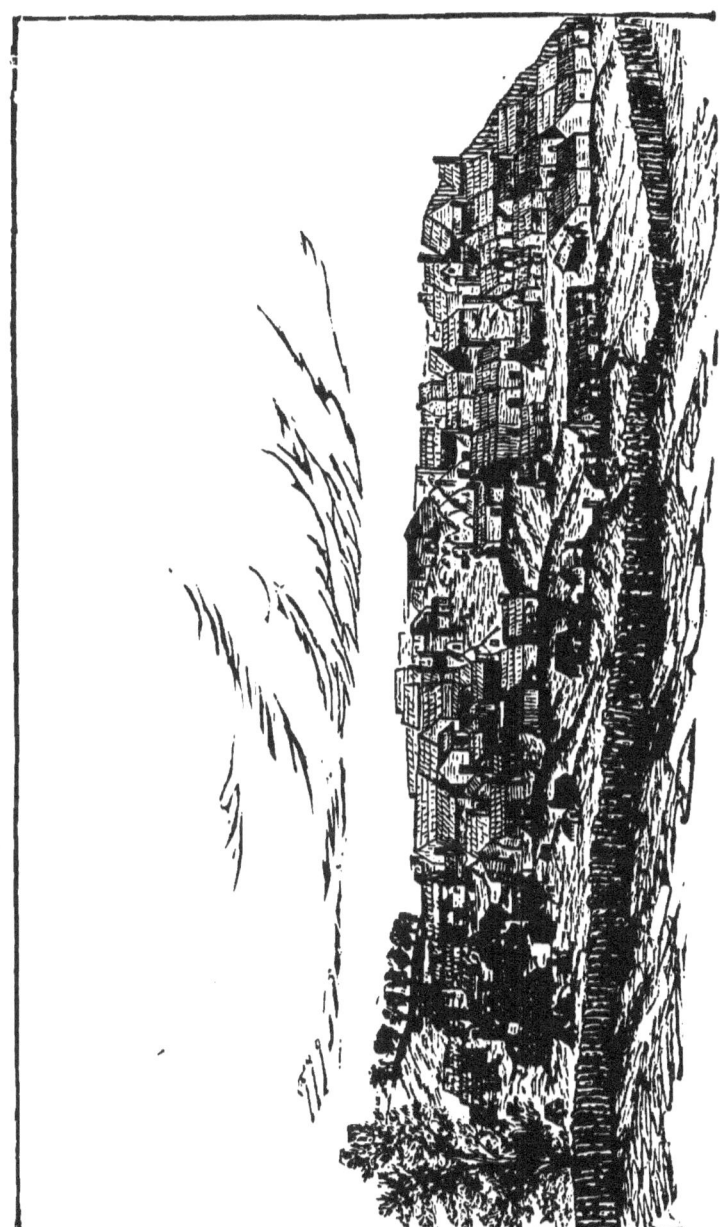

CAMP FORD, TEXAS.

and shoes. I saw men go for months without a shirt to their back, and no covering but a pair of ragged pants or drawers. Lieut.-Colonel Leake, of Iowa, with about four hundred men, had spent the previous winter in the stockade, and were forwarded for exchange in July. When they arrived at Shreveport the authorities became ashamed of their naked appearance, and offered to issue them clothing, but the brave Colonel promptly refused the offer, saying:

"'We will go into our lines in the same condition that we have been prisoners.'

"When they arrived at New Orleans, those hardy and brave Iowa soldiers marched down Canal street, and up St. Charles, past the headquarters of General Canby, in almost a nude condition. This exhibition of rebel barbarity, together with the statements of the officers exchanged, stirred up our authorities, and started negotiations with the rebel authorities, which resulted in our receiving on the 2d day of October, from our authorities at New Orleans, 1,500 complete suits of United States clothing and 1,500 blankets. At the time the clothing was received there were about 3,300 prisoners, and an inventory of the camp, ordered by myself to ascertain the destitution before the issue of the new clothing, showed but 1,500 blankets or parts of blankets in the stockade. The issue of this clothing, and especially the blankets, was truly a godsend to the camp, and gave it a very different appearance. On the 25th of January another batch of clothing of about 1,200 suits arrived from the same source, and this supplied our wants fairly during the remainder of our imprisonment. From the first of our imprisonment, rumors of exchange were kept afloat, and hopes of getting free never seemed more than a month or six weeks ahead. While this was probably done by the rebels to keep us from escaping, it answered a good purpose in keeping us hopeful. Many, however, grew restless, and made the attempt to exchange themselves. Plans of escape were numerous. The digging out process was resorted to, but did not succeed, although one hole was made for more than 150 feet, and had reached the outside before discovery. Bribing the guard was done in many instances, forged passes in others, and quite a number were taken out in the dirt cart that removed the rubbish from the camp. When this was found out, the boy who drove the cart was suddenly relieved of his position, and each load thereafter was probed with swords or bayonets.

"The greatest difficulty in escaping was after we were outside. With three hundred miles between us and the nearest point in our lines, every white man between eighteen and sixty years a soldier, and packs of bloodhounds kept for the purpose which could take a trail twenty-four hours old, it was almost impossible to get through. Yet quite a number succeeded. But the majority were recaptured, brought back, and at first severely punished. Captain Reid, of a Missouri regiment, was ordered to stand on the head of a barrel bareheaded and barefooted in the hot sun eight hours a day for two weeks. Some were tied up by the thumbs; others stood on a stump cut with a right and left scarf for two hours at a time, with a guard standing by who had orders to shoot if a foot was lifted. Those who tried it said it was exceedingly severe.

"One of the hardest cases of failure I remember was that of Major Bering and Lieutenant Srofe, of the 48th Ohio. They had been out twenty-one days, and were within three days' travel of our lines when recaptured. On their way back they met the rest of their regiment going forward for exchange, but were not permitted to go with it, and thus endured six months more imprisonment for their effort to free themselves.

"The devices to while away time while prisoners, were many and varied. Chess was the principal game, and the demand for chessmen created quite a business for a former prisoner who had erected a turning lathe. The games of checkers, cribbage and cards, were also prominent. Then we had the gambler with his chuck-a-luck board and keno bank, which relieved many a poor fellow of what little cash he had brought with him. The banker was there to exchange greenbacks for Confederate money or specie. At our entrance Confederate money was ten to one in greenbacks, and gradually increased to twenty, thirty, forty and sixty, and for some months before our imprisonment closed, it was entirely defunct. Specie took its place in trade with the outside. Our specie cost us on an average from eight to ten dollars in greenbacks to one in gold or silver. I bought flour at the rate of six dollars per hundred pounds in specie, when each specie dollar cost us ten dollars in greenbacks. We also had the baker who sold biscuits at twenty-five cents apiece, and sweet potato pies for one dollar. The barber, the tailor, and the shoemaker plied their avocations, and many of the prisoners manufactured combs, pipes, rings, and trinkets in abundance from the horns of the slaughtered cattle. Violins and banjos were made, the strings being taken from the sinews of the beeves, so that, notwithstanding the solitude of the place, we had music and dancing during the long winter evenings. The religious element was also strongly manifested. A Bible class was held every morning in good weather, and a prayer meeting every evening. Public services were held on the Sabbath, at first by captured chaplains, and after they were released, by laymen. On two occasions the chaplain of the guard preached to us, and was listened to attentively by an audience of at least one thousand. He exhibited surprise at the result, but I told him we were at least partially civilized.

"Yet thieves and the lower classes of humanity were there also, and human nature was exhibited in lower phases than I ever saw it before. A few thieves, who were at one time caught in the act, were punished by being dipped in the sinks by the exasperated crowd.

"We had four different commandants while I was there. First, Colonel Allen, a Kentuckian, who wore the uniform of a United States officer of the line, when he wanted to appear well. He said he could sometimes wish we would all find Southern graves. The next was Colonel Sweet, who was at one time a resident of Chicago. In conversation he told me he did not want a Republican government—that it was nothing but a *mob*, and the will of the majority was the worst tyrant on earth. The next was Colonel Brown, commander of a regiment of what appeared to be F. F.'s, of Texas. He had been in the Texan war, and a prisoner in Mexico; and although he was one of the roughest men I ever met, he had a heart in him, and did many things for our comfort, when suggested to him. The last was Lieut.-Colonel Jamison, who had been wounded in the army of Virginia, and was now given command of a regiment of home guards. This man, while one of the most bitter of rebels, was gentlemanly, and used more leniency than any of his predecessors.

"When the spring opened the boys inaugurated a scheme to get some fresh vegetables for summer use. Captain Watt of the 130th Illinois, an old man, was granted the privilege of taking out a few men on parole of honor to make a garden in a field near by, and after fencing a lot was promised a mule and plow. He failed to get the mule, but took out ten Yankees and hitched them to the plow, and did good execution. Before we left, he and others had the pleasure of eating some vegetables of his own raising. And thus Colonel Jamison, while he could do but little for us with the means under his control, was disposed to let us do for ourselves many things which benefited us.

"Our knowledge of the outside world came mainly through the Houston 'Daily Telegraph,' which was sent to

Captain Crocker, a gunboat-man, by a friend; and also from new prisoners. We received no mail from our line for about five months, and after that probably once a month. The Christian Commission sent us a box of books from New Orleans at one time, which was greatly prized.

"Our prison was watered by a spring which rose in one corner of the stockade, and was sufficient, most of the time, for drinking and cleansing purposes, but in their dejected condition many made poor use of it. The atmosphere of the stockade during the late summer months became almost unbearable, from a bad arrangement of our sinks; but a new person being put in command of the inside about the 1st of October, made suggestions which the commandant allowed him to carry out, and relieved us ever afterward. He gave us a fine ball ground which was well occupied and proved a blessing.

"We were guarded by a cordon of guards outside the stockade, who had orders to shoot any prisoner who came nearer than ten feet to the stockade. In a number of cases men were shot who neither violated the rule, nor showed any intention of doing so. The guards generally were not hostile to us, and in very many cases friendly; but there were sons of Belial among them who took advantage of their position to immortalize themselves by killing a Yankee; yet the officers gave us no relief.

"The mortality of prison life was varied, some regiments and squads losing one-fourth, some one-third, and in one instance one-half their number, while in others scarcely any died. So that while the treatment was inhuman and will always be a foul blot on the Confederate record, yet my observation was that the disposition, character, and habits of the men had a great deal to do with the mortality of prison life. The greatest number in the prison at one time was about 4,700, and that was reduced by various exchanges to 1,700 when the camp was broken up. We left 282 dead on a hill opposite the stockade, which was neatly fenced with post and rail by a squad of our own men before we left.

"Thirteen months had passed since we entered the stockade, and now the end approaches. News had been received of the surrender of Lee and Johnston, and we knew the time for our departure must be near. The paroling officer, whom we were always glad to see, came with the news that we were all to be sent home. I shall never forget my feelings and emotions, as I reveled in them the whole of the following night without any sleep. The next day we were paroled for exchange, as a mere form on their part. We had the notoriety of being the last prisoners held by the defunct Confederacy, *and 1,700 of us are yet on parole for exchange.* The next night the militia who had been guarding us for several months packed up their traps and left for their homes, leaving us but a few regular soldiers, who did not pretend to guard us further. On the 17th of May, 1865, we started on the march for Shreveport, 120 miles distant, where we arrived through considerable trial and suffering on the 22d. Thence we took boats down Red River to its mouth, and on the 27th glided safely into the father of waters, once more under the protection of the old flag."

"The reason the troops were scattered so at Sabine Cross Roads," said Mr. Arnold, of the 23d Wisconsin, "was this fact: In the final arrangement after the endless reorganizing that followed the Vicksburg campaign, the 13th and 19th Army Corps were set off together. The boys of the 19th had not seen quite such hard times as the 13th boys, and had better clothes. Some of the soldiers from Illinois regiments at this time were wretchedly clad, which condition, of course, they themselves could not remedy. Thinking to show off a little, a few of the 19th boys began to call their Illinois comrades rag-a-muffins, threadbare guerillas, etc. This wounded the pride of the Sucker State soldiers, who felt that such epithets were unmerited, and they replied that if they had had no clothes at all, they could out-fight the 19th Corps on the stormiest day of the war. The remarks were soon current, and the feeling spread among the respective corps, until the whole was leavened. For a time it was thought that there would be business right there and then; but the commanders kept the corps camped separately until the ill-starred breeze blew over, and thus saved a possible disgrace to both corps. But this, I believe, was the reason that the 13th and 19th Corps could not be kept within six or eight miles of each other for awhile."

The above explanation was heard with considerable interest, and then the camp-fire adjourned.

CAMP-FIRE VI.

"SLAP-JACKS"—A TRIP UP THE TENNESSEE—THE HORRORS
OF VALLEY FORGE REPEATED—BULLETS AND ETI-
QUETTE—"COPPER-HEADS."

MILLIONS of readers of the records made by the Society for the Preservation of Unpublished History will fully understand at the first glance the exact and practical significance of the compound word which introduces this camp-fire; but that it may be intelligible to the million-and-first student of history, and that it may be one more fact put on record for the benefit of unlearned posterity, the Society hereby gives to the world the subjoined etymological and historical conclusion, obtained at great outlay of money and sacrifice of health in the research, and great delay in the proceedings of the chats.

As has been communicated in the rhapsody just got rid of, "slap-jacks" is a compound word. It is compound not only in form, but in meaning; for the material which entered into the preparation of "slap-jacks" consisted of almost any powdered substance from brick-dust up to crushed saw-logs, the series including wheat, oats, corn, horse-feed, "wood, hay, stubble," and so forth. The word is also hybrid, being wrenched from the literature of two separate and distinct races of humanity; and a mongrel of the ages, as it is an offspring of two classical developments which were parted by a period of two thousand years. This is believed to be the history of the word, and the following is the etymology: "Slap-jacks" is derived from the Greek Βάλλω, *hurl, hit;*

or, the Anglo-Saxon *strike* (see Webster's Unabridged Dictionary, p. 1308, col. 1), hence, Anglo-American *slap;* and from the German *John*, hence the Anglo-American *jack*, which was in its primitive use, a proper noun, and traces of that use still linger in the dialect of the marine corps of the day; but from its symphony and the ease of its application it came to have a variety of meanings. From this it will be observed readily that "jacks" was just the word to combine with "slap" in order to make "slap-jacks."

"Slap-jacks" was always used in the plural, owing to a difficulty which arose in their manufacture. The pulverized material, usually corn meal or flour, which was the principal ingredient, was placed on a rubber blanket, or in any convenient small cavity—sometimes the end of a hollow log—and then the other ingredient, water, was poured into it, and a mush made. Salt was sometimes added, when the soldiers had it, but it was not necessary. A handful of this mush was then suddenly put against the side of a board, and placed near the camp-fire to brown, or at least to dry out. The mush was called "jack" and the operation of placing it on the board was called "slap;" but just as the consummation was being devoutly carried out, some of the "jack" would slip through the fingers of the slapper, fall to the ground, and make more than one "slap-jack." Again, after the mixture was on the board near the fire, part of it would slip down the tilted edge of the board, and become plural once more. So that it was not possible to manufacture "slap-jacks" in the singular, and the use of the word in that number became obsolete.

It is hoped that, after the foregoing elaborate treatise on the language of the army, the Society for the Preservation of Unpublished History will not have to explain that "slap-jacks" is the military word for pan-cakes. The following incident, related by F. O. White, Company A, Cavalry, 36th

Illinois, may give the student some idea of this article of army diet:

"It was near Keatsville, Mo., just before the battle of Pea Ridge. Many of our boys were expert bookkeepers, and when they passed a country store, they usually took an inventory of the stock on hand, though they were never very careful whether they left anything in the store.

"We finally came to a store which had drugs on one side and groceries on the other; so we made a good haul. We got plenty of flour and other material for 'slap-jacks,' including some saleratus, as we thought; but to make sure of it, we passed it to one of the boys who knew something about chemistry, for him to analyze. He assured us that we were right; so we felt a glow of satisfaction that we were to have 'slap-jacks' that evening with saleratus in them.

"We went into camp and made up a large quantity of them, but as they did not get very light, we thought that the cook had put too much saleratus in; yet we would not allow that to make any difference, as we had had no saleratus in our 'slap-jacks' for a long time, and could tolerate a goodly dose. They were served up in good style, and the boys ate plentifully of them. Soon, however, the boys began to leave camp, one at a time; then they went by twos and threes, and finally the camp was nearly deserted, almost the entire number having been attacked with sudden illness. Alas! all who had partaken of the delicious but traitorous 'slap-jacks' were now compelled to play the part of artesian wells—the cakes had begun to *rise!* In the morning the suspicious saleratus was taken to a reliable chemist, who found that it was *tartar emetic.*"

This incident was followed by one from a soldier of Company C, 20th Illinois:

"While on the march near Rolla, Mo., our rations ran short, and Lieutenant Moore, of our company, picked up about

100 pounds of new buckwheat flour. He carried it more than two miles, and meeting Lieutenant Hall, gave him an invitation to call at headquarters for supper that evening, and they would feast on buckwheat cakes. The army had gone into camp, and Lieutenant Moore delivered the flour to the cook, with instructions to make up a good supply of cakes, as he expected Lieutenant Hall to sup with him.

"The cook proceeded to mix the cakes, applying the necessary seasoning (all he had), and the supper was soon ready. Lieutenant Hall arrived, and the cakes were brought before the host and his guest. The guest was the first to partake of the delicacy, and after he had waited until the host had tasted it, said:

"'Is this the buckwheat you carried two miles?'

"'Yes,' said Lieutenant Moore; 'tastes rather queer, doesn't it?'

"'I am quite of your opinion,' replied Lieutenant Hall, 'as it is nothing in the world but plaster-of-Paris.'

"Lieutenant Moore declared that it was no joke, and this assurance was made doubly sure by the cook, who just then made his appearance and said:

"'Mars' Cap'n, thought dat risin' didn't take effec' in dat buckwheat jes right, ha! ha! ha!' Exit cook, right; Lieutenants Hall and Moore, left."

This disclosure put the camp-fire attendants into a merry mood, and the regular order of business was proceeded with, Gen. Ira J. Bloomfield, of the 26th Illinois, speaking:

"After the battle of Chickamauga we came up the river from Vicksburg to Memphis, and marched across the country to Chattanooga just in time to take part in the battle of Mission Ridge, on the 25th day of November, 1863. The next morning we pursued the Johnnies to Ringgold Gap, and then turned up the Tennessee River to the relief of Burnside, who was penned up in Knoxville by Longstreet.

"We had left all our baggage-wagons and supplies behind, and as we went up the Tennessee Valley we lived off the country, having foraging parties out ahead of us to collect provisions from the houses, and to grind the wheat and corn in the numerous mills. Details of soldiers kept the mills running all night.

"I never saw greater manifestations of loyalty in my life than were shown by the people of East Tennessee. All the able-bodied men were in the army, but the women and children would stand at the roadside and say to us:

"'Go to the house and take all we have. We have friends where we can get more.' One woman, when she saw the Union troops, shouted:

"'Glory to God! I knew you would come! I have two brothers in the Union army, and I wish I had forty more.'

"We lived well going up toward Knoxville, but when we came back, a few weeks later, it was hard foraging. One night at the Hiawassie we had nothing to give the men but wheat bran that we had left in the mill there when we went up. Next morning, as we sat upon our horses and the men filed out into the road to resume the march, Private Lemmon, of Company D, a comical genius, who was always playing some kind of a joke, cried out: 'Colonel! colonel! are you going to issue us oats in the sheaf to-night?'

"Most of the time during our trip up the Tennessee River that fall the weather was fine, and except when out of food, we got along splendidly, but being so long without a change of clothing, officers as well as men became infested with vermin, so that when a halt was made every one must needs seize the opportunity to relieve himself of such forbidding intruders.

"Many of the men suffered greatly for tobacco. One night, near Marysville, I heard of a tobacco factory about six miles off from our line of march. I sent a lieutenant and a squad of men to bring in a supply, and the next day about

10 o'clock they overtook us with a wagon-load of 'Silver Heels' tobacco, which we distributed to the men. Many a poor soldier was made happy that day, and the effects of the tobacco could be seen in the livelier step on the march and in the renewed joking and laughter.

"The weather remained fine until within two days' march of Chattanooga, when it suddenly turned cold. The ground froze, and ice formed on the streams and along the road. The long march from Memphis to Chattanooga, and from there up to Knoxville without supplies, had worn out the shoes of the men so that when the cold set in many of them were barefooted, and had to make the last day's march in that condition over the ice and frozen ground. Their feet were so lacerated that we sent them from Chattanooga to Bridgeport, down the Tennessee River, in an open scow. That was the day before Christmas, and the suffering of those poor fellows with their sore feet and the exposure to the cold winds in their open boat, was sad indeed. Their feet became so inflamed and sore that when they got back to Springfield, Ill., Jan. 22, 1864, on veteran furlough, many of them were unable to wear shoes, having their feet bundled up in old rags. I never expected to see the horrors of Valley Forge or anything akin to it, but what I have related is only a faint picture of what those poor soldiers suffered.

"While speaking about feet, I have been reminded of a state of affairs that came about at the close of the war. In the spring of 1865, at the grand review at Washington, a number of my men were without shoes, but then the weather was warm, and it caused no suffering. The long march from Savannah, Ga., up through the Carolinas, and thence, via Richmond, to Washington, had worn out their shoes, and when we stopped at Alexandria, Va., to refit, I could not find with any of the quartermasters shoes large enough to fit eight or ten of my men. They had not calculated on supplying our big Western boys, and had neither Nos. 11 nor 12. I told the men that they need not take part in the grand review. But they wanted to be there, and did actually march down Pennsylvania Avenue barefooted, but with steady step, keeping time to the music of the Union.

"To show you how tough and hard these men were after their long marches, sieges, and battles, I must give you a little incident that occurred near Mount Vernon. We had turned aside there to visit the tomb of Washington. While marching along one day near a small town called Dumfries, where a bright little stream ran across the road to empty itself into the Chesapeake Bay, we came to a narrow foot-bridge which spanned it. Our usual marching order was in a column of four front, but the bridge was so narrow that we had to undouble, which caused some little delay in the march. While sitting on my horse waiting for the crossing, I heard some angry words, and turned just in time to see one man strike another a terrible blow across the face with his musket, tumbling the latter off the foot-bridge into the water below. I rode back to see about caring for the injured man, but before I could reach him he picked up his knapsack and gun, and took his place again in the ranks as if nothing had happened. The next morning when I went out to look after him, the only signs left of the blow was a slight black spot under each eye. Such a blow across the face of a civilian would have laid him up for a month; but these men were tough and hard, for they had been brought down to solid fighting weight by long service in the open field."

General Bloomfield, who now depends on his legal skill for his rations, then informed the hearers that he could not be with them hereafter, as he was about to take command of a relief expedition in a divorce suit; but, whether it was apropos or not, he would relate one more incident to show that bullets in war often become ungraceful and over-step the rules of etiquette.

"A volley of musketry has very little respect," he said, "for titles or rank in army society; and it is generally true that there are soldiers in both opposing armies who aim at sashes and badges.

"On the morning of the battle of Mission Ridge, Col. Timothy O'Meary, of the 90th Illinois, came into line of battle wearing a blue flannel suit and a bright red sash around his waist. Col. John Mason Loomis, the brigade commander, warned him of the danger, saying:

"'Colonel, we have to go down over that open field, and the hill on the other side is full of sharpshooters. Your sash will furnish a good mark for them!' But the gallant colonel only smiled and held up a picture of the Virgin Mary that he always wore suspended by a cord around his neck, replying:

"'They cannot hurt me while I have this.' A few minutes later he lay weltering in his blood, mortally wounded by a rifle ball through his left side, just below the heart."

Doubtless this incident will remind the veterans of 1861-'65 of whole bookfuls of similar happenings. It reminded Maj. M. B. Parmeter, of the 77th Illinois, of one, which must be prefaced with an explanation:

There was a type of combatant in the North during the war known as "copper-head," the more virulent class of which were members of the "Knights of the Golden Circle;" the milder developments were less haughty, and were sometimes known as "plain copper-heads." But it is to the good feeling of all who stood by their country in the hour of her need, the S. P. U. H. included, that this entire type of citizens was limited, though the epithet was applied to many without desert.

It must not be understood by the term "combatant" that the main pillars of the K. of the G. C., with their adherents, were soldiers; for they kept as far to the rear as possible. They were combatants in everything except business at the front, and lacked the first principles of soldiership—patriotism and moral courage. They combated the policy of war from innate cowardice, more than from their love of peace; they decried emancipation because their opponents upheld it; opposed the government because it was not under their own direction. When the last call for troops was made, they were in sore lament. Already there were nearly a million soldiers in the field (and this was a thrust at *all* soldiers)—every man who became a soldier, and was detailed to forage, was no better than a thief, they said. Think of it—a million thieves turned loose upon the unprotected citizens of the country! *O tempora! O mores!* How homely to these "unprotected citizens" was the beautiful picture of the great concourse of a nation's children scattering to their peaceful homes across broad prairies, over mountains and through glens, to plow, preach, and pound anvils!

But there came a day when the clatter of their loose tongues was hushed. No more did they stand behind a tree and demand peace. For then it was that their great relative, Uncle Sam, made a suggestion in the form of a draft that all his able-bodied male relations over twenty-one years of age and under forty-five, should come to his assistance at once. But now was "the winter of their discontent." They disclaimed all kinship. They sought "British protection." Their able bodies began to pedestrianize, and did not cease that operation until they had found a home in Canada. Like other fractions of humanity, when a relative is in affluence he is very dear to them; but place him in durance vile, and they seem like residents of Neptune. When the tills of the nation are overflowing with the golden coin, each of the former "unprotected citizens" is a noble foster of the "best government God ever gave to man;" but let the Executive call for needed service, and they deny their allegiance—vile treason sits on manhood's throne!

With the foregoing revery rehearsed, Major Parmeter's remarks may be better appreciated:

"It was just before the capture of Vicksburg, and the draft had just come into full blast. The majority of the Peace Faction at the North had either become quiet or gone on an expedition to Labrador, or in that direction. At any rate, they were not very boisterous around their former neighborhoods. Some of them went South, but not for the purpose of joining the army.

'Among the latter was a physician from my old home who was apparently well read, but nevertheless was a mild copper-head. It made him nervous to see so many of the boys going off to the war, and he took it upon himself to act as a sort of missionary for their return. He seemed especially interested in a young fellow by the name of Buckingham, and came to Vicksburg to persuade the young man with others to return home.

"But no persuasion for Buckingham; he was too enthusiastic. The doctor remained several days, and as he became bolder and found more old acquaintances, he began to get nearer to the front. One day he came out on skirmish line, where several of the home boys were, and began his missionary work, talking about the old times at home. Pretty soon the Johnnies opened fire on us, and the skirmishers began to seek shelter. Having had considerable experience in the business, the boys were expert in getting behind the works, but the doctor was left out. A spent ball just then grazed his clothes, and, with a look of fright and surprise, he ran for the works, exclaiming:

"'Why, I didn't suppose they would shoot a *citizen!*'

"'Yes, sir,' said one of the boys, 'shoot you as soon as any other copper-head—bullets are no respecters of persons.'"

With the last two incidents to show that the etiquette of bullets is yet unwritten, the camp-fire adjourned.

CAMP-FIRE VII.

A BANQUET TO THE S. P. U. H.—"S. B."—A CLASSICAL EXPOSITION OF THE TERM, AND SOME REMINISCENCES FOR ILLUSTRATION.

"ORDER!" said the commander, as the tattoo sounded, and the bugle came to its relief; but the bugle was hoarse, and the noise which it made was akin to that of a masculine cat in distress, in the little hours. The boys all laughed, but the commander rapped on a log with his musket, and the rattle of the bayonet commanded peace.

Then he said, " Comrades, I have been for sometime anticipating a feast on the rare old dish of S. B., and hard-tack. Let's build up the fire, satisfy our hunger, and give the S. P. U. H. a banquet."

Accordingly, more sticks and tree-boughs were placed on the fire, and the preparations proceeded. While the work was going on, the Society for the Preservation of Unpublished History ascertained that "S. B." meant that particular part of swine anatomy which, with the exception of the feet, is nearest the earth. The civil name for it was "salt bacon;" later changed to "breakfast-bacon," while the designation on the social menu is "fat of pork." This abbreviation, however, was applied to more than one army delicacy. It sometimes signified "soaked beans," sometimes "salt beef;" but more frequently was given to a very choice dish, made from hard-tack which had been carried on a long march through the rain, then soaked in river water during the night, with several changes of the water, and fried for breakfast.

"Hard tack," the S. P. U. H. learned, was a kind of bread, light in color, which could not be affected by age. In size, shape and durability, it was similar to the sections of a slate roof.

Meantime the Society for the Preservation of Unpublished History sat by with great dignity, full of high satisfaction that its members were soon to be banqueted and toasted. When the coffee and eatables were ready, the veterans began without ceremony, in the fashion *a la* if-I-don't-get-my-share pretty-soon-somebody-else-will; and before the S. P. U. H. could come to a clear understanding of the situation, and secure the attention of the veterans, there was not enough left for one meal for a ghost. When the food had all disappeared, the boys perceived that the S. P. U. H. had been forgotten. Many apologies were offered, but no hard-tack nor S. B. *Sic vita militaris est.*

Then the national air was sung:

(Tune—AMERICA.)
   My rations are S. B.,
   Taken from porkers three
    Thousand years old;
   And hard-tack cut and dried
   Long before Noah died,—
   From what wars left aside
    Ne'er can be told.
   *   *   *   *   *

There were originally three stanzas to this hymn, but after it was sung, while being handed across the fire to the S. P. U. H., two stanzas fell into the blaze and were consumed. The society now has the ashes of the sacred paper in its museum.

Mr. George Justice, of Company H, First Battery 18th U. S. Infantry, then remembered an experience which simultaneously illustrates three things: The craving of the boys for fresh meat, the sincerity of Gen. Geo. H. Thomas, and the able discipline he imposed.

"FALL IN FOR GRUB."

"I participated in one little experience which I have never related, and have never heard told. When the 14th Army Corps laid at Stephenson, Ala., in 1863, General Thomas issued orders to the effect that he did not want any foraging; but despite such orders from as good a man as ever commanded a soldier, there were some who disobeyed them. We had been without fresh pork for some time, and my partner, James D. Killdow, and myself, concluded we would have some. So one afternoon we started out; but we did not have to go very far before we spied a porker that would weigh about 200 pounds, and we were not long in taking him. We withed his legs together, run a pole through them, and started for camp. By keeping the woods, we could slip in at the foot of the company; but we had a road to cross, and there was where the trouble commenced. As we came out into the open space, who should gallop around the bend but General Thomas and staff,—just as we were thinking about what a nice mess we were going to have. He ordered us to halt, and riding up to us, asked:

"'Where do you men belong?'

"'To the 18th U. S. Infantry,' I said.

"'Don't you know the order against foraging?'

"There was no use denying it, so I replied that we did.

"'What did you kill that hog for?'

"'We wanted some fresh pork,' I said.

"'Well, you will have to be disciplined for disobedience,' and the general turned to one of his aids, and added: 'Bring these men and that hog up to headquarters.'

"The aid ordered us to pick up the hog, which we did, and wagged along with our load. To our surprise, we found a ring made and a guard waiting for us, with orders to make us carry the hog around that ring until further notice. Being nothing but a boy at that time, the hog got very heavy for me in a short time. I told the guard that I was too small for that kind of work, but he told me not to lay that hog down. I told him I must rest or die right there.

"'All right, be brave and die at your post,' he replied, with a laugh.

"When we had carried the hog around about an hour an officer approached, and told us that General Thomas had said we might have the hog, as he thought we had earned it, and that we would not be guilty of such a trick again. Our punishment was complete, but didn't we drop that hog in a hurry? I tell you, rest never was so sweet.

"When we had rested sufficiently, we took up our burden, and started for camp. We were heroes now, and instead of slipping in the back way, we walked right down the front, across the parade ground, between the line officers' tents and the heads of the companies, past the head of our own company to our tent. The orderly sergeant appeared on the scene at once, and ordered us to take the hog to the cook's tent, and have it issued out. We had already killed it, but I said 'No!' Then the orderly ordered two soldiers to pick it up and take it to the cook's tent. I told Killdow to watch the hog until I could go up and see the captain. In a few minutes I was at the captain's tent, and soon related the story about General Thomas giving us the hog. The captain appreciated the joke, laughed heartily, and said:

"'Well, I guess the hog belongs to you.'

"I went back and told the orderly that the hog belonged to Killdow and myself. He went up to see the captain, but did not return; so we skinned the hog and issued it out to the boys ourselves. But that was the last hog that poor Killdow ever helped to kill, for he was taken prisoner at the battle of Chickamauga, Sept. 20, 1863, and died in Andersonville prison on the 1st of September, 1864."

"That is not very much unlike one I recall, which occurred just before we were going into Huntsville, Ala.," said Mr. J. J. Marquett, of Company B, 37th Indiana.

"It was reported that there were four Johnnies secreted on a large plantation about two miles from the line of march, and our lieutenant, eleven other men, and myself were detailed to look after their welfare.

"We arrived about dark, deployed out, and came up on all sides of the house, so that none of them could escape. There were two or three at some of the doors, but I had a door to myself. When we were ready we began to force our way in. My door opened readily, and I stepped in. All was dark. I began to feel almost like a burglar. About the second step I took I ran against something, and putting my hand out to explore, I ran it squarely into a rich dish of corn meal pudding [known as 'samp' in the South] which was steaming hot! Near it was a plate of hot biscuit, and you may imagine that it didn't take me long to get those biscuit into my knapsack. The family had been just ready to eat, but had taken the light from the dining-room, so that the soldiers would not discover the supper. I helped myself to a few other things, and then, after exploring the room, left the house.

"The other boys had been in the various rooms, but found no Johnnies, except a lady and her daughter—the men had all escaped to a small piece of woods. However, they left two guns and a pistol, all loaded, but the ladies did not try to use them. Near by was a nice spring-house, and when the boys came together we went in and filled our canteens with milk. Then we ate the biscuit and what other food I got, and started back for the main line. One of the boys had captured a ham, but we did not stop to cook that.

"It was some time before we overtook the marching column. About midnight we came to a small village with one store, which had been partly sacked, and there were yet a few soldiers hanging around the place. As we came up to the store we discovered the cause of this, for just then one of the boys came out of the cellar, reeling with drunkenness. One or two of our boys began to investigate, and found whiskey ankle deep all over the cellar floor. It seemed as if every one who had gone into the cellar had pulled the cork from a new barrel, drawn a canteen full, and let the liquor run. From the odor that came from the cellar, and from the effect the fluid had on the boys, it seemed to me that it must have been forty-rod whiskey."

[The S. P. U. H. chemist, who had been retained on the liberal privilege that he might have all the knowledge he could gain from the several analyses, if he would defray his own expenses, ascertained that " forty-rod whiskey " took its name from the effect it produced upon those who smacked their lips over it. After quaffing the zephyr-like ambrosia it has the angelic faculty of making a fellow feel as if he were forty rods from the place of his real existence. In short, he is distant from his equilibrium, and usually makes a desperate effort to restore himself.]

"When the boys caught up with the troops in the morning, all who had any forage went in the back way (for they had not been detailed to forage) except the fellow who had captured the ham. I say 'captured,' because when the day broke it was discovered that the ham possessed unmistakable signs of life. Observing this the soldier concluded that he had not carried that ham all night for nothing, and would yet have some sport from it, if not food. So he took another draught of 'forty-rod' from his canteen, run his bayonet through the ham and started into camp past General Turchin's headquarters, apparently more intoxicated than he really was.

"'Here!' demanded the general, 'where have you been?'

"'E—hic!—down the road a ways.'

"'Who gave you permission to go foragin'?'

"'Didn't—hic!—have any; didn't think we—hic!—think we needed any, just to steal one ham.'

"'Come up here, you drunken vagrant.'

"'Allrigh', general; you can have the ham—s'pose that's what you want; take it right along—compliments of your dearly be—hic!—loved.'

"The general looked at the ham, and at once saw its true condition, whereupon he laughed:

"'Sold again;—have a cigar. You can have the ham—take it away, but look out that it don't bite!'"

"Three cheers for S. B.," said the commander of the camp-fire, and the vicinity echoed three hearty hurrahs.

"That is like one I know, wherein the S. B. came off victorious," said Mr. Henry A. Keve, of the 7th Illinois:

"In the spring of 1862, our division (Dodge's) was sent out from Corinth, Miss., on an expedition into the Tuscumbia Valley in Alabama. On the 28th of April we were deployed as skirmishers at Town Creek, to watch for the approach of rebel cavalry under Roddy. The cavalry not making its appearance, the boys began to look about for means to pass the time away. A few stretched themselves upon the grass in the warm sunlight, and were soon fast asleep. Among the sleepers was Private Theodore, of Company K.

"Theodore was one of those wise fellows, whose experience in the regular army and in Mexico had furnished him with a wonderful stock of wearying tales and pointless jokes. He was personally acquainted with Generals Scott, Taylor, Wool, Twiggs, Jeff. Davis, and Robert E. Lee; was always ready with a solution of all difficult questions in military strategy, politics, philosophy or religion—in short, was a walking emporium of wisdom, and contrived to make himself generally unpopular.

"Not far from the sleeping Solomon was an old hog with a young family. The hog was very lean, which accounts for her being able to perform her part in the following comedy.

"But Private Brown was not asleep; on the contrary he was wide awake and looking about for some harmless amusement. He saw the old hog, and he saw the slumbering Theodore. Brown was an Illinois farmer and knew all about hogs and their habits; and his fertile brain soon developed the following scheme to bring Theodore back to consciousness:

"He stole softly toward the bed of swine, grabbed a pig and started for the unconscious Theodore, the pig squealing and the old hog following on a run. Dropping the pig by the side of Theodore he stepped aside to view the result. On came the savage and terrified beast, and with a booh-hooh-hooh! she pounced upon the unguarded sleeper. The scene that followed was exhilarating in the extreme—the old hog boohing-hoohing and shaking, and poor Theodore, thinking in his half-awake condition that the enemy was upon him, struggling and shouting:

"'I surrender! I surrender!' He finally made his escape by leaving part of his clothing in the hog's possession; but with all his ability as a solver of knotty problems, Theodore could never imagine what made that old hog so mad at him."

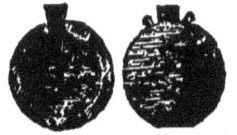

CAMP-FIRE VIII.

LIBBY PRISON—THE "HORNED YANKEE"—ANDERSONVILLE, WHOSE SURNAME IS DEATH—A MODERN MIRACLE—THE ALTAR OF KLEPTOMANIA RECEIVES A SACRIFICE OF SEVEN.

AT the close of the last camp-fire, Mr. W. Frank Bailey, of the 6th Pennsylvania Reserves, who was known to have been wounded when he entered Andersonville, and to have had a rough experience, was requested to give what reminiscences he could of prison life, at the next camp-fire. When the usual preliminaries were gone through with, Mr. Bailey said he had thought some of Andersonville since his fourteenth months' visit there, and did not believe that any one who had spent any length of time in that village would ever forget Southern hospitality.

He then continued:

"Among the many incidents and exciting scenes of four years passed in active service, none have left a more vivid impression than my experience as a prisoner. You all remember, comrades, that during the year or more previous to the close of the war, the position of a soldier, either as a private or commissioned officer, was one of doubtful honor; and I only refer to this in order that due credit may be given to the heroic sufferers of whom I am about to speak. When the signs upon the horizon of our beloved Republic indicated her dismemberment, men thought not of toil, danger and privation; but sprang to her rescue with one consent, cheerfully giving all that life could afford as their individual offering upon a common altar as the price of her salvation. The best and noblest of the land, the pride of homes, the first-born of families, the beloved of households, stepped into line, actuated only by motives of the purest patriotism. As time rolled on and our people became more acquainted with the privations and calamities incident to a protracted struggle, patriotism declined, and mercenary inducements were held out, which drew from the ranks of the people many who were *not solely* inspired by a love of country or pride in her honor; hence the position of the soldier was rendered more or less humiliating to those who enlisted at the outbreak, and served to the close of the war.

"But the record of the sufferings of the true soldier is eternal. The story of rebel prison pens is one which every true lover of our country might well wish were never written, and yet I make no apology for discussing it, for it is a part of human history—half written upon earth because humanity has no language to express, or pen to paint its horrors. Like some hideous nightmare transporting the imagination to the abode of the damned, do the recollections of this period of my life pass in review. Although nearly twenty years spent in peaceful civil life, have elapsed since the date of the events I am about to relate, I can only look back upon them to-day as a long, dark night of lingering horror—a fierce protracted struggle with a bitter, relentless, though unseen enemy, unmarked in its intensity by the roar of cannon or rattle of musketry, but in the slow, sure wasting away of mind and body; as though one were cast into a deep, dark pit, surrounded by dead and dying victims, whose emaciated bodies, despairing countenances, decaying forms and grinning skeletons marked the progress of death's victory. As has been repeatedly expressed by the survivors of some of these prisons, 'Words are totally inadequate to the task of a description of their horrors.' Without attempting the impossibility of conveying to the mind of the hearer a full comprehension of the unhappy situation of Union prisoners confined in these living hells, I will endeavor to give a simple narrative of what I, in common with others, saw and experienced. It may be deemed impossible for one who was a sufferer to give a faithful account of a portion of the proceedings which form a black page in the history of our country. I can say with all sincerity that I have no other than the kindest feelings toward those who were our contestants on many a hard-fought field, and if there be any stigma attached for barbarities to Union prisoners it must not fall upon those who crossed swords with us in the front; men who daily tested each other's fidelity, bravery and courage, learned to respect such enemies too well to be guilty of a breach of humanity toward their fellow-men.

"In connection with the circumstances which led to our capture, it may not be out of place to say that the Pennsylvania Reserves, to which division I belonged, claimed that their time had expired. The company with which I went out enlisted on the 22d day of April, 1861, but the division was not sworn into the United States service until July 27, of the same year. We claimed the right to count our term of service from the date of our enlistment; the government claiming from the date on which we were sworn in, a difference of three months. This was compromised by promising our muster out on the 30th of May, 1864. I merely mention this to show the fidelity of old soldiers, inasmuch as the date of the capture of a large number of us occurred on that afternoon, within a few hours of the time agreed upon for our final discharge. And you will pardon my digression in saying that the grand old division, composed entirely of Pennsylvanians, after serving more than a month over time, and that period spent in almost daily battle, in the front ranks of the Army of the Potomac, was finally relieved at midnight, while upon the picket line, on the field where they had fought for several hours previous.

"After the ten days' Battle of the Wilderness, second battle of Spottsylvania Court House, North Anna River, and the series of engagements ending in flank movements, which occurred in the spring of 1864, we were brought to a point about two miles from Bethesda Church, situated on the Mechanicsville plank road, distant about nine miles from Richmond. On the 30th day of May, 1864, the regiment to which I belonged (the 6th Pennsylvania Reserves), in connection with the original Bucktail Regiment, numbering in all about 700 men, were deployed as skirmishers in the woods in which we lay, with orders to move to the road mentioned, and hold it. The Confederate pickets were soon encountered, who fell back as we advanced. After driving them from the woods, we came to an open clearing about half a mile across to another woods. This we crossed on the double-quick, two companies on the left of our line crossing the road which was our objective point, and nearly a mile in advance of our regular line of battle. We were ordered to halt and entrench, which we immediately proceeded to do by tearing down the rail fences from both sides of the road, and piling up the rails preparatory to covering them with earth. At this moment we were joined on the left by one of the heavy artillery regiments, fresh from the fortifications about Washington, and utterly ignorant of infantry duty in the field. In the short interval the rebel skirmishers had fallen back to a point where their spent balls just reached us, leaving us under the impression that we were masters of the situation. But soldiers, like other people, are often the victims of misplaced confidence. We were totally ignorant of the fact that General Ewell's Confederate corps of about fifteen hundred fresh troops were lying concealed in the woods a few rods ahead of us, and had been busily occupying the time in surrounding our flanks, which being completed, they suddenly emerged from the woods in front of us, in a heavy line of battle, pouring in a volley upon us at a distance of less than ten rods. Surprised, and almost entirely surrounded by a force of ten to one, a large number were killed and wounded, and over three hundred captured, among whom was myself, wounded in the foot and leg. Previous to this time, Libby prison, Belle Isle, and Castle Thunder had already established reputations throughout the North for unwarranted and cruel treatment of their prisoners. The prison pen at Andersonville was yet in its infancy, and its world-wide fame was then confined within its silent walls. The pens at Florence and Cahawba were not established, but enough was known to inspire one with dread at the thought of falling into the enemy's hands. In fact, the idea of being taken prisoner had entirely escaped my notice until this moment. All the reports current in relation to rebel prison pens, which I had heretofore given but a passing thought, became unusually vivid. I endeavored to console myself with the reflection that I should see Richmond, which for three years we had so much desired to possess,—and probably much of the enemy's country. The first attraction I possessed in the eyes of my captors was an old silver watch. The colonel of the 43d North Carolina wanted just such a watch, and gave me all the scrip he had, $75 Confederate money, in exchange for it. Nothing but our swords, fire-arms and ammunition were taken from us by our captors. It being late in the afternoon, the able-bodied prisoners were sent back to the Provost Marshal, while the wounded were taken to about a mile in the rear of the rebel line, and kept under guard all night. As my foot, which had now swollen to double its ordinary size, and my leg gave me considerable pain, I could not sleep, but sat by a camp-fire, drawing consolation from the steady stream of ambulances conveying wounded to the rear, all night long. I knew our

LIBBY PRISON.

boys in blue had done their best to avenge us, and many a traitor to his country had been sent to his long home.

"The following morning we were marched to the headquarters of the Provost Marshal, an interesting place in all armies. In a large field, surrounded by guards, were grouped Union prisoners, rebel deserters, spies, citizens who were forcibly impressed into the rebel service, many of whom entertained strong Union sentiments, and refused to take arms, called conscripts,—a regular heterogeneous mixture of offenders. Here the first process of 'skinning' was performed. All equipments serviceable in the field, such as blankets, haversacks, canteens, shelter tents, rubber blankets, etc., etc., were taken from us.

"On our way to the Provost Marshal's, I had an opportunity to learn for myself that some, at least, of the Southern people believed that Yankees had horns. On account of my disability, I was unable to keep pace with the other prisoners, and a comrade was detailed to help me along, and a guard to keep us company. Before reaching our destination, we made a detour from the main road to a dwelling house, for the purpose of getting a drink of water, and, if possible, procuring something to eat. We secured a drink at the spring in the rear of the house, and passing to the front, encountered a middle-aged and two younger ladies sitting on the porch. Our guard, who acted as spokesman, asked for something to eat, telling them at the same time that we were Yankee prisoners. One of the young ladies, in all sincerity, immediately asked the guard:

"'Where are their horns?'

"Upon which we all commenced to laugh, when the young lady innocently replied that she had been told that all the Yankees had horns on their heads like cows. I hardly need say that we got nothing to eat, and doubt if we would, even if we had had horns.

"During the afternoon we were placed in cars and taken to Richmond, a distance of five miles from the Provost Marshal's. It was the custom of the authorities, upon receiving a number of Union prisoners to parade them through the streets, to encourage the people, and buoy up the hopes of the Confederates stationed about the capital. Our squad was accordingly marched from the depot to the War Department, and thence to the well-known warehouse used in times of peace by Libby & Co., whose sign was still suspended above the door, and gave a name to this prison which will endure for generations. It was with considerable difficulty that I performed this part of the programme, but by the assistance of a comrade I was enabled to walk through the city, fully as much to my own satisfaction as that of the enemy. I was struck with the appearance of both the city and the people as compared with the cities of the North. A miserable scantiness seemed to be almost universal. The shops and stores were poorly stocked. Ragged and threadbare clothing covered the wretched specimens of humanity whom the strictly enforced Conscription Act had left behind as home guards. Disappointment at the results of the war was visible on every countenance, and intense hatred for 'the Yankees brought forth loudly-expressed denunciations and epithets from the citizens who lined the sidewalks. One could hardly help realizing that the ashes of the angry Vesuvius outside the fortifications were settling over the doomed city. It was nearly dark when we reached the prison, and we were quartered for the first night on the first floor of the warehouse.

"Early next morning the officer in charge, Maj. Richard Turner, commonly known as Dick Turner, accompanied by an armed squad and two clerks, entered the apartment. The prisoners were ordered into line and a request politely made that all who had any United States money in their possession should come forward and give it up. (This was the first, last, and only *politely* expressed request or command ever addressed to us while prisoners.) They told us that all who would thus voluntarily give up their money should have their names recorded in a book, and when exchanged it would be returned to them. Our boys displayed a great lack of faith in the solvency of this bank *for deposits only*, as but two or three responded to the invitation. One of the clerks actually performed the farce of recording their names and amounts. The voluntary subscription to the fund being exhausted, and a further display of humanity on the part of our captors being superfluous, the rest of us were told that our money and valuables would be taken from us anyhow.

"The 'skinning' process resorted to was sufficient to satisfy any one that there was not much left in our possession. Each prisoner was called up singly and ordered to strip, which was done to the last stitch. Clothing was turned wrong side out and thoroughly searched in the pockets and between the linings, plugs of tobacco were cut open, daguerreotypes taken out of their cases, fingers were run through the hair, the mouth ordered to be opened, arms raised, and every imaginable means employed to thwart Yankee ingenuity in secreting valuables. Many of the old soldiers understand a disease known in the army as the 'green piles.' The rebels had heard of it, and no prisoner was permitted to pass without a careful examination on this point. Knives, rings, paper, envelopes, extra clothing of all kinds, was confiscated, pictures of friends were torn up or stamped under feet, for no other purpose than lest they might prove a comfort to the prisoners. In spite of the strict search I succeeded in retaining a part of the money I had, together with a gold locket containing a picture of my father and mother, which I still have in my possession. My comparatively helpless condition caused them to pay less attention to my movements than they otherwise would, and while the 350 prisoners who preceded me were being gone through with, I succeeded in placing the things mentioned between the linings in the legs of my boots, one of which I had been compelled to cut over the instep in order to get it off my foot when first wounded. The fact of my boots being cut proved fortunate, as I was enabled to keep them also—boots being a prize among the rebels.

"When the process of searching was finished we were taken up to the second floor, in a large room where were confined a number of other prisoners. The windows of the room were secured by iron bars, such as adorn prison cells. The building was surrounded by sentinels, whose beats were on the pavement below. No one was allowed to put his head close enough to the bars to look down on the street, under penalty of being shot. In the afternoon, this being the third day after our capture, we drew our first rations from the Confederacy, consisting of four or five ounces of corn bread, two spoonfuls of cooked rice, and two ounces of boiled bacon. This, once a day, constituted our rations while in Libby prison. What it lacked in quantity was made up in strength, the rice bugs and old bacon being abundantly able to satisfy our appetites and sustain our bodily wants.

"Here many of us for the first time contracted an intimate acquaintance with the prisoners' closest companion. When in after days hope grew faint and we seemed left to our fate, deserted by the country we loved, our little friend stuck to us closer than a brother. In sickness or health, rain or shine, through evil report or good report, he never deserted us. Twice each day he helped us by his presence to while away a portion of the long dreary hours, and we even took off our clothing to catch sight of him. I refer to the festive louse.

"We remained in Libby prison only ten days, it not being deemed safe by the authorities to accumulate too many prisoners in Richmond at one time, as fighting was in progress outside the city continually, and fresh batches were being brought in every few days. Our lot at that time seemed very hard to us, fully confirming all the reports we had heard, but future experience proved that this was a paradise compared with what was to follow. It was positively asserted by the older prisoners that Libby prison was at that time mined, and it was the intention of the rebels, if the Northern army was successful in penetrating the lines around Richmond, to blow up the building and destroy the contents. This information was obtained from the negroes, who were sent in every morning to sweep the floor of our room. These negroes were inclined to be very friendly to us, and many a loaf of bread was smuggled into the prisoners' room; but the greatest caution was needed, as the slightest attention shown us would have subjected them to the severest punishment, if detected.

"Prices of everything in the rebel capital were enormous. A uniform of gray for a Confederate officer cost $1,200; a good pair of boots, $900. Salt was scarce at any price. A loaf of bread but little larger than a baker's bun sold for $2.00. One greenback dollar was rated equal to six of Confederate scrip. Their reason for this was that the United States money would be good whatever the result of the war, while theirs would be valuable only in case of success, which many of them doubted, even at that time. They displayed great desire to get possession of all the greenbacks they could, notwithstanding the stringent laws in vogue against a discrimination in favor of United States money.

"In a few days we were told that we would be taken to a military camp which had lately been established at Andersonville, Ga., for the benefit of prisoners, and that our condition would be much improved. The camp at Andersonville was painted in glowing colors, and the advantages so well represented, that we were eager for the change. They told us it was beautifully situated in a meadow, cleared out from the woods, where we could be sheltered by the trees from the sun; also that a fine stream of water ran through it, in which we could fish and swim—in fact, that we could spend our time in any way to suit ourselves, as very much more freedom would be allowed us than could be permitted at Richmond.

"Accordingly, on the 9th of June, we were aroused at early dawn, marched to the depot, and placed on cars destined for Andersonville. The cars were of the most miserable description, for freight and cattle, some of them being open, such as we use on our construction trains, without seats. We were packed in so close that we could neither sit nor stand with any comfort. We slept somewhat after the style of sardines in a box, though not quite so sound. As we were carted along at the convenience of the various roads over which we passed, our trip consumed eight days. During this period we drew rations only four times, very small rations for a day each time. Once we were fed dry corn on the cob, which, though unpalatable, we were glad to get. Want of water added very much to our discomfort. At Danville, Va., I paid fifty cents for a pint of water, and at a station in North Carolina I procured half a pound of corn bread and three-quarters of a pound of bacon for the modest sum of $5. Another serious loss befell me on the second day of our trip, which added one more cause of destitution. I was trying to sleep, by way of passing away time on the uncomfortable cars, but was aroused by some unusual movements about my head, and raised up just in time to discover the rebel captain in charge of the train putting on my hat and traveling off with it. I called out to him, demanding my hat, when he threw me his old gray headgear, remarking that it was good enough for any Yankee. Filled with indignation, I threw it out the car door, and was compelled in consequence to pass the next six months of my life without a hat.

"At Greensboro, N. C., we failed to secure a train to continue our journey, and were marched to a piece of woods near the town to pass the night; a severe thunderstorm came up, and the rain fell in torrents all night. Sleep was, of course, impossible, and we stood there in the rain until morning, making the woods ring with 'Rally Round the Flag, Boys,' and other patriotic songs, much to the annoyance of the guard, who threatened time and again to shoot the whole lot of us. The people all along the route displayed the most intense hatred for Yankees, and many were the denunciations heaped upon us. Hang 'em! Shoot 'em! Kill 'em! were the exclamations that greeted our cars at the different stations passed. The guards were very rigid, and being composed of troops who had never listened to the music in front, felt that they had a heavy responsibility attached to them in guarding a lot of unarmed prisoners through a peaceful section of their own country. At only one place along the route did we encounter anything approaching humanity of feeling, and that was at Augusta, Ga. The train stopped there for a few minutes, and a young lady, accompanied by two colored women bearing baskets of provisions, came to the cars and commenced distributing food to the prisoners. The guards undertook to stop her, but she gave them some reply which was satisfactory to them, and continued her labor of love unmolested, actuated by a feeling of humanity, if not of Union sentiment. The boys cheered her lustily, and I am positive that was the sweetest morsel of food ever offered to Union prisoners south of Mason and Dixon's line.

"We arrived at Andersonville on the 16th of June, and found this world-renowned place to consist of two houses, a railroad station, and a water tank. The situation of the place was one of utter isolation, surrounded as it was with a wilderness of pine woods, and was apparently intended by nature as an abode for owls and bats, the whistle of the locomotive seeming to be an intrusion upon the utter loneliness which the place inspired. The whole distance from Macon, which we left that morning, had been through a desolate, dreary part of the country, each mile more and more God-forsaken in appearance, until our destination was reached,—truly a fit place for the dark and cruel tragedy which paved earth six miles long and six feet wide with human victims. A weird spot, where the groans of the dying and shrieks of the maniac reverberated through the forest wilds, lost from human ear in the murmuring of the tree-tops, and wafted up to heaven by the swaying of the giant pines. The sense of novelty in being a prisoner of war diminished very rapidly as we marched to the pen designated for our future abode, which was situated about a half mile from the depot. Before entering the gate, we were again drawn up into line and searched, lest our Yankee ingenuity should succeed in procuring and concealing something in spite of the watchfulness of our guards. We were then divided into detachments of 270, sub-divided into nineties, and further into thirties, to facilitate the regular morning roll-call, and the not altogether regular drawing of rations, a captive non-commissioned officer being placed over each detachment and its divisions.

"The true inwardness of the situation was then made known to us in these words, uttered by the officer who commanded our escort from the cars:

"'You d——d Yankees, you will never come out of here as men; what we cannot kill of you, we will disable for life.' I shall never forget the effect these words produced upon my mind. I had seen three years of hard service, participated in fifteen pitched battles, and flattered myself that I knew something of the hardships and dangers of war. My twentieth birthday had been passed only the second day before, and life seemed large and full of hope before me. The truth of the awful situation fell upon me with full force. We were to suffer with exposure, neglect, starvation, insults and indignities, until our spirits were crushed out and bodies skeletonized, if we submitted to the will of our keepers; or be shot down if we rebelled. From that moment our imprisonment became a struggle between life and death. We knew that everything that could be devised would be done to end our lives.

"We then entered the prison, as many had done before us. Alas, we had little dreamed of the hardships we should here encounter; how few of us would ever come out alive! It is impossible to describe in words the living horrors presented to the eye. To think that human beings should be compelled to exist in such a place is a stain upon all record of human barbarity. The pen was built by clearing out the pine woods and inclosing about twenty acres within a stockade. The ground upon which the camp was built was rising on two sides of a mud bottom stream, the borders of which were swampy. The stockade was formed of logs set upright, reaching sixteen feet above ground, and about four feet below the surface, with sentry boxes on top at intervals of perhaps one hundred feet. Inside of this, and about twenty feet from its base, was a railing three feet high formed of stakes set upright about twelve feet apart, with a single rail extending across the top. This was the 'dead line,' and the prisoner who stepped over its bounds was not asked to retrace his steps; the unerring bullet promptly met him on the other side.

"No shelter of any description was provided for the prisoners; on the contrary, all our blankets and shelter tents had been taken from us. Sick and well alike were left exposed to the burning sun or drenching rain, to live as best they could upon the dry, barren, sandy soil, with only the canopy of heaven for protection. Within the inclosure we found 23,000 poor creatures, some of whom had scarce a trace of

ANDERSONVILLE PRISON AND STOCKADE. (See Page 352.)

manhood left in their appearance, some feeble and emaciated from starvation and disease, clothing worn to tatters, filthy rags, unwashed faces, uncombed hair, countenances indicative of utter despair, earthly hopes gone,—waiting only for death. The stream which ran through the camp and supplied us with water was rendered unfit for use before it reached us. Five regiments of rebel troops who guarded the prisoners had their quarters above us, and threw all their offal into it before it reached us. At least three acres on the borders of the stream were swampy, and was a living, surging mass of filth propelled by maggots. The stench which arose from the entire camp was beyond imagination, seeming to solidify the atmosphere. Three of our squad, in utter despair at such a prospect of existence, stepped over the 'dead line,' and received their call for another world, satisfied that death, with all its uncertainties, would not produce a worse place than this. To say that the bravest hearts quailed at the sight of these living horrors, coupled with the fact that we might be there until the close of the war, then an indefinite period, would but faintly express our feelings. Speaking for myself, I can only say that I was filled with a feeling of dogged determination to live it out to the bitter end. Every impulse in my nature seemed to rise in revolt against the idea of dying a victim to the machinations of our heartless enemies. I gloried in my hope to live as a witness to what I believe to be the *most barbarous treatment in human history!* I knew from the experience of others that upon this hope hung life itself, and I held to it with all the tenacity of a youthful and unconquered nature. Standing in that fated line where every second man was destined to fill a grave on the ground where he stood, my brave comrades upon my right hand and upon my left hand have gone down, and by the favor of Divine Providence I am left.

"The routine of prison life in this pen was as regular as

clock work in all respects, save in drawing rations. At 8 o'clock every morning each detachment was called into line and counted by a rebel sergeant. Every man had to be accounted for who was alive. No matter how sick, he was brought out and counted. Every morning, regularly, a circuit of the camp was made outside the stockade by the officer of the guard, accompanied by two or more bloodhounds, for the purpose of ascertaining whether any one had made his escape, either over or under the stockade. The rebel drum corps always played the one tune, 'Ain't I Glad I'm out of the Wilderness.' It is said that 'music hath charms to soothe the savage breast,' but after listening to that tune every day for three months, I am forced to the conclusion that rebel music had no power to soothe us. It may be, however, that they were unfortunate in their selection of a tune.

"At 10 o'clock in the morning we generally drew rations. The rations at Andersonville consisted of one and one-half pints of corn meal and three ounces of old bacon per day. The quantity was sufficient to subsist upon, but unfortunately for our stomachs, the meal was often cobs and corn ground together. Fresh beef was sometimes substituted for bacon, and rice for meal. The rations were issued from wagons driven into camp to the sergeants of detachments, by them to the sergeants of thirties, who divided it as nearly as possible into thirty portions. One of the squad would then turn his back, and as the sergeant placed his hand upon a morsel, would call out to whom it should belong. Bones were considered equal to meat in the division of the rations, and the man who drew a shin bone with every particle of meat stripped from it, was considered the fortunate man for that day, as the bone was broken to pieces and boiled for broth, after which it was burned almost to a cinder and eaten. One of the greatest difficulties we experienced was in cooking our food. The utensils we used for that purpose in the army had been taken from us. Wood was very sparsely issued to us, although surrounded by woods. A piece as large as an arm sold for twenty-five cents. We cut it into splinters with the aid of beef ribs. The lucky possessor of a case or pocket knife picked up many quarters by manufacturing wooden dishes, plates, spoons, pails, etc. With these we could mix our meal to the proper consistency, put it into a wooden plate, and stand it before the fire until it was browned, or at least smoked with pitch pine until it had the appearance of being cooked. From some pieces of tin and sheet iron torn from the roof of the cars on our way from Richmond, some were enabled to make pails or cups in which to boil mush. Occasionally our rations would be stopped for a day or two, upon some trifling pretext. The prisoners suffered very much, not from the quantity of our allowance of food, but from the quality and kind, as well as constant exposure and general surroundings.

"Want of vegetables made scurvy very prevalent in camp. A small potato sold for twenty-five cents, and whoever could raise the cash generally had a potato which he carried with him to rub his teeth and gums.

"It must not be supposed, although destitution reached a low point, that there were no speculators in Andersonville. There were several booths stocked with a few articles, such as tobacco, potatoes, flour, etc., at enormous prices, and a small traffic was carried on by some enterprising Yankee who divided his profits with some reliable rebel outside the camp who furnished him the merchandise. Others, on a smaller scale, who possessed enough of the 'ready John' to get a pound of flour, a stick of wood, and a piece of sheet iron, were found making slap-jacks about the size of a trade dollar, calling out, 'Here's your hot cakes, only twenty-five cents each.' It was a godsend to many of us that the garrison of Union troops, numbering about 4,000 men, stationed at

Plymouth, N. C., had surrendered conditionally, and were confined at Andersonville. These men retained everything except arms and munitions of war, and freely shared their shelter and conveniences with those of their friends who were less fortunate. It was my good luck to find a company from my old home among them, and I was not slow in accepting an invitation to make my quarters with them.

"During the month of July the stockade was enlarged, six acres being added to it. We were fortunate enough to be moved on the new and higher ground inclosed by the addition, as the old portion of the camp had been literally catacombed for the convenience of the sick. The number of prisoners was increased to 32,000—a motley mass—composed of almost every nationality under the sun, and it was not long before the new portion of the camp had become almost as bad as the old. The filthy swamp enlarged its borders, and daily became more abominable. The situation grew worse each day. Rumors of exchange or of a cavalry raid for our release were daily gossiped through the camp, and served to inspire hope. It was well, perhaps, that no raid was ever attempted. Our guards told us repeatedly that if such an effort was made they would open fire on the camp from the four batteries which were situated so as to sweep the entire surface of it; and we had no doubt they would have been highly gratified to have done so, as they never neglected an opportunity to kill a prisoner upon the slightest pretext. A furlough of thirty days was granted to any guard who killed a Yankee. Deaths increased to a frightful extent, numbering from sixty to two hundred per day during the hot months. Hundreds of poor creatures, weakened by hunger and sickness, gave up hope, lay down, and died miserable deaths, lonely in the midst of thousands almost as badly off as themselves; each engaged in a struggle for life, and powerless to help a fellow man. Early every morning on my trip for water, of which we endeavored to lay in the day's supply before the camp was aroused, and while the miserable stream was comparatively clear, I would encounter a score or more of poor creatures who had crawled down to get a drink during the night and were unable to get back, covered with vermin and filth, maggots filling up the nose, eyes and mouth, while the breath of life still lingered in their emaciated bodies—some whose eyes were already set in death, others too far gone to speak or move—sights like these language cannot describe. Here were men of intelligence and affluence who had surrendered the comforts of life, leaving everything behind to answer their country's call, with wives and little ones at home unconscious of their awful sufferings, waiting anxiously some tidings of the missing one. Mothers, sisters, fathers and brothers in their Northern homes were expecting the return of loved sons and brothers; yet here they lay strewn along the filthy swamp, dead and dying. No word of comfort reached their ear. No mother, wife, or little ones to gather around them in this their last hour; not even a stranger to speak a word of cheer, or point them to that 'far away home of the soul.' No, shut out from all earthly sympathy, surrounded by scenes of horror and disgust, in the hands of merciless, unrelenting captors, they died like dogs.

"Life at Andersonville was necessarily selfish. True, as in civil life, bullies had their followers and great minds their worshipers, but in the struggle for existence every man stood alone. Life was the prize fought for. Every ounce of food parted with to help a fellow-man was a drop of blood from the giver, that could poorly be spared. No matter how the heart was wrung with sympathy for others, no material help could be imparted. That which was necessary to relieve want and suffering was not ours to give. Day after day we were compelled to see a friend, old schoolmate or stranger, sink under the awful pressure, and be drawn closer and closer to a cruel death, without power to alleviate their sufferings. To abandon the dead and dying and inspire hope in the living, was all that was left us.

"I will relate a couple of interesting incidents which occurred during my imprisonment in this horrible pen, one of which was a remarkable display of Divine Providence, and if the time of miracles had not long since passed, might properly be classed among the catalogue of wonders justly ascribed to supernatural causes. Both of these incidents have been published in leading newspapers, and I as an eye-witness of the facts, and because they justly form a part of every man's experience who was confined in Andersonville at that time, reproduce them here. I have previously told you of the bad condition of the stream that supplied us with water. This was our only drink until about the 1st of August. One hot afternoon, after a heavy shower of rain, just outside the 'dead line,' where we were not allowed to go, on the descent of the hill where the camp was situated, there suddenly appeared a jet of pure cold water, as large as a man's thumb, springing out of the hitherto dry, sandy, barren earth, and describing an arch of about a foot in length until it reached the ground again. A cup was fastened to a stick, reached over the 'dead line,' and good water procured. It did not flow fast enough to supply the camp, but hundreds, even thousands, enjoyed its refreshing draughts, the priceless gift of One from whose fevered lips had once burst the cry, 'I thirst!' who saw and knew our sufferings, and in His infinite wisdom placed it where improvident humanity could not trample it out of existence. I do not know whether it flows to this day or not, but it was still performing its mission of mercy when I left the camp.

"When so large and so miscellaneous a body of men as were those confined in Andersonville, are freed from the restrictions imposed for the better government of society, a great deal of the worst side of human nature becomes visible. The weak were a prey to the strong, stealing was carried on without limit, and deeds of lawlessness were of hourly occurrence. No fear of law stood in the way of any act of depredation. Very severe methods were resorted to by the order-loving part of the camp to curtail the evil propensities of the malicious. During the latter part of June, the camp was infested by a gang of desperadoes, composed of our own men, who did not hesitate in the dead hour of night to murder any one who might have succeeded in retaining money or valuables in their possession, burying their bodies in the swamp. For protection, a police force of 500 men was organized, which was ever after retained in camp to preserve order. The perpetrators of these outrages were ferreted out, and brought before a self-constituted court-martial. It was discovered that an organized gang of eighty lawless characters had banded themselves together for the purpose of plunder, who hesitated at no deed to accomplish their object. Seven of these men were found guilty, and sentenced to be hung, the rebels consenting to keep them safely under guard till the day of execution. A scaffold was erected inside the stockade, and on the 11th day of July, six of the condemned men were brought in and hung in the presence of all the prisoners and 4,000 of the rebel guards, as a warning to lawless characters. One of the men had been previously shot by the guard while in the act of trying to escape. This prompt treatment put a stop to such lawlessness.

"As an incident of this remarkable execution, and to show the power of one desperate man over an unorganized body of men, while the prisoners were being led to the scaffold, one of them, the acknowledged leader of the gang, who had assumed the name of Mosby, broke from his guard and ran. The immense crowd of prisoners involuntarily parted, making a clear pathway for him, and it was with considerable difficulty that he was recaptured and brought to the gallows. As the drop fell, and the unfortunate wretches were launched in mid air, one of the ropes broke, and its victim fell with a dull thud to the ground; but he was promptly taken up and hung again.

"The question has often been asked why we did not try to escape. The reason is that at no time while I was at Andersonville were over one-third of the prisoners capable of active exertion, and any effort on the part of those able to make the attempt, would have brought on a wholesale slaughter of helpless, unarmed men. Artillery was planted so as to sweep every inch of the camp. Thousands would have been killed or wounded, and most of the others recaptured, and, if possible, treated worse than before. Our only chance of escape was in tunneling under the stockade, which was slow work, and very uncertain. Many attempts were made in this direction, only a few of which ever proved successful. The distance from the 'dead line' to the stockade was about sixteen feet, and it certainly was not safe to emerge from the ground nearer than the same distance from the other side. The ground was loose and sandy on top, and a tunnel necessarily had to be deep in the center and narrow all the way through to prevent the earth from caving in. In addition to the great labor of the undertaking was the constant danger of detection. The Confederate officer of the guard patroled the camp outside the stockade every morning with a pack of bloodhounds; besides which, spies were in our midst all the time, as well as some of our own men employed to watch our movements.

"Some idea of the labor, difficulties and disappointments of tunneling may be gathered from one of our attempts. Three of us at one time started a tunnel as close as possible to the 'dead line.' We carefully hid it from view by putting up an old piece of shelter tent possessed by one of the party.

Under this tent, one of us was ostensibly sick, and lay during the daytime directly over the hole on a board purchased from one of the speculators. At night we dug out the dirt with a piece of tin taken from an old canteen, and carried it off in our clothes, first tying our pant-legs tight around our ankles and coat-sleeves around our wrists, then filling these with dirt as well as our pockets, besides what we could stuff inside the bodies of our shirts. After being thus loaded, we started for the swamp, where we buried the fresh dirt, carefully covering each deposit with the filthy surface of the swamp. The utmost caution was necessary, not only to escape the suspicion of the guard, whose beat ran past the scene of our operations, but also to keep our work hidden from the other prisoners around us. In this slow way we worked for over two weeks, and calculated we had got about under the stockade. We worked with a will, animated by a hope of liberty, and imagined we could almost sniff the pure free air outside. Our venture was a profound secret, though we determined when the work was accomplished, to give several of our friends the opportunity to get out after we were gone. This determination was not altogether freed from selfishness on our part, as we knew the bloodhounds would probably follow the freshest trails, and the last ones out would be more likely to attract the attention of the guard than the first. Poor human hopes! In spite of our well-laid plans, our house was veritably built upon the sand. Our disappointment can possibly be better imagined than described when, one afternoon, a rebel sergeant and four guards with shovels, came into camp, and marched directly to the tent, took off the board, and commenced to fill up our tunnel. Our 'sick' comrade had by the merest chance crawled out after a drink of water, and the other two of us were spending the time with acquaintances. We had the mortification of seeing the fruits of our toil vanish before our eyes, and our hopes once more laid lower than ever.

Some treacherous prisoner or rebel spy had discovered our work and betrayed us. We were only too glad that we all escaped detection, though the rebels made no effort to find us beyond asking the prisoners in the immediate vicinity. Any of the prisoners who were found guilty of betraying their fellows in an attempt to escape, were in great danger of lynch law. I have witnessed several in the act of having one-half their head shaved, and a letter ' T ' branded on with a hot iron.

"At one time a plot was on foot to hoist the Stars and Stripes, a small flag which had been preserved by a soldier, raise an insurrection, capture the batteries, and turn them on the guards—the 4th of July, 1864, being set as the day for its execution. Through the perfidy of some of our own men, or by the aid of spies, it was made known to the enemy, who made the necessary preparations to resist it, and gave us notice that upon the first attempt on our part to carry out such a scheme, they would open fire and keep it up while there was a prisoner left alive. This fact, coupled with the fearful slaughter of the sick and helpless, as well as of the ablebodied, which would be the inevitable result, caused us to abandon the enterprise. The rebels contented themselves with firing blank cartridges over the camp at intervals during the day, as a means of intimidation.

"After the 20th of July very few prisoners were brought to Andersonville—none at all from the Army of the Potomac, and but few from Sherman's army. News was consequently scarce. An occasional rebel sheet fell into some one's possession, which was eagerly scanned by all who could get a chance at it. The sufferings were on the increase. Thousands were prostrated by scurvy and diarrhœa. Hopes of exchange or chances of escape grew less day by day. The poor men were carried off to the dead house by scores, weakened and dispirited by 'hope deferred,' added to disease, exposure, and extreme heat. Nothing served to break the monotony made up of continual suffering and scenes of horror, for even the excitement of such a life, death, murder, thefts, and the ravings of lunatics crazed by suffering, became wearisome monotony to those whose vitals were pierced by the pangs of starvation and sensibilities blunted by contact with the unspeakable horrors of a living death. Captain Wirz, the subordinate commander, was daily seen riding through camp in his shirt sleeves on an old gray horse, like an emissary of Satan, inspecting the work of human destruction. Brigadier-General Winder, commander of the post, never entered the camp, and is said never to have seen the inside of the stockade. The utter want of all feeling of humanity in these two men, as brought out at the trial of Captain Wirz in Washington, shows how well they were chosen to carry out the intentions of the authorities at Richmond. It almost surpasses belief that these men, instead of endeavoring to relieve, studied ways and means to add to the awful character of the situation. It is a matter of record that the authorities at the Confederate capital were cognizant of the situation. It is a matter of record that General Winder was acquainted with the condition of the prisoners; and to the everlasting dishonor of the men who held the reins of the rebel government, it is also a matter of record that nothing was done to relieve our sufferings. It is urged by some that the South was unable to do better by us. Granting that such was the case, we were guilty of no other crime than defending our country, and common humanity would have demanded our parole. To do battle for our flag and country is the least that any man can do, and is an honor rather than a crime punishable by slow torture and lingering death. But there is not even this poor excuse left, for it has been abundantly proven that they did not do what they could, and that proof has come from Confederate sources. The official report of Col. D. T. Chandler, an inspector-general in the rebel service, found on file in the archives of the Confederacy, dated August 5, 1864, in the time of our extreme suffering, forever silences all attempts to palliate this gigantic crime. At the trial of Captain Wirz, Colonel Chandler entirely verified this report, and stated that he had remonstrated with General Winder, suggested better food, draining the swamps, and other sanitary measures. To these humane suggestions Winder replied, ' Better let one-half die, so that we can take care of the remainder.' I am giving a personal sketch for the benefit of the Society for the Preservation of Unpublished History, and let the society record that now, after more than nineteen years from the date of these events, my ingenuity fails to suggest anything that could be done that was not done to render our lives as prisoners and human beings most miserable.

" During the hot months of July and August the sufferings were horrible to contemplate. The death-rate increased to 1 for every 6⅝. In August it stood 1 out of 10⅓, while in September it increased again to *one out of every three!* The latter rate is accounted for, however, by the fact that all but 10,000 of the prisoners, and those the worst cases, were sent to other points during this month, thus making a larger ratio of deaths in proportion to the number of prisoners than in any previous month, there being 31,693 prisoners in camp in August, and 8,218 in September. The total number of deaths in July was 4,742, an average of 154 per day. It always seemed to me providential that no contagious disease ever broke out in camp. Every death that occurred there was a monument to rebel barbarity. Great inducements were held out to our men to save their lives by taking the oath of allegiance to the rebels. They repeatedly told us that our government had deserted us and refused to exchange prisoners, thus practically abandoning us to our fate. In the midst of our sufferings, with death staring us in the face on every side in its most horrible form, they held out for us our salvation—dishonor; but, thank God, the suffering boys preferred death, and the rebel ranks were not augmented by recruits from Andersonville."

This was greeted with applause and exclamations of "Three cheers for the Andersonville boys!"

"The reputation of Andersonville as a place of cruelty," continued Mr. Bailey, "is world-renowned. Perhaps no place in history achieved a more unenviable name in the short period of fourteen months, than this insignificant spot. Its history from the 15th of February, 1864, when the first Union prisoner was received within its hated walls, to the 10th of April, 1865, can never be justly written by pen, or told in language. The unfolding of the chapter of atrocities at the trial of Captain Wirz, was but a page. The 14,461 names inscribed upon as many rude head-boards in the Andersonville cemetery, are significant of as many unwritten chapters of awful suffering and death. The 451 graves marked 'UNKNOWN' tell a fearful story,—names and resting-places blotted out of existence;—no, shut out from human vision only, not from the All-Seeing Eye of the Great Commander. Cruelties were perpetrated and sufferings endured, unparalleled in the history of civilization, and unapproached in the annals of barbarism, save by the bitter persecution of the early Christians, or the sufferings of the unfortunate Waldenses, in their Alpine retreats. Not less unrelenting in cruelty were these twin tyrants of modern times, Winder and Wirz, than the silver-veiled Prophet of the East, who held his victims by an oath imposed in the charnel-vault, and pledged in the blood of the dead."

The camp-fire was adjourned, and the soldiers went quietly away, some of them shadowed by this appalling memory, while, with the others, for once hilarity was a foreign thing.

CAMP-FIRE IX.

THE FLORENCE PRISON—HOMEWARD BOUND—PATHETIC INCIDENTS.

BUSINESS being resumed Mr. Bailey continued his experience:

"About the middle of September Sherman's army having pressed the forces of General Hood back too far for the safe keeping of prisoners at Andersonville, the camp was partially broken up, and most of the prisoners distributed between Milan, Ga., Cahawba, Ala., and Florence, S. C. About 10,000 were retained at the old camp. It was my ill-fortune to be among those who were taken to Florence, where our sufferings were greatly increased by starvation and exposure to cold weather, as well as the unexampled brutality of our commanding officer.

"On the 12th day of September, 1864, several thousand of the prisoners who had been confined at Andersonville were placed in cattle cars, destined for some point then unknown, —anywhere to escape Sherman. It was evident to us that it was something of a question in the minds of our captors just where we should be taken for safe keeping. On the 15th of the month we were unloaded at Florence, S. C., a town 106 miles north of Charleston. No preparations had been made for our reception, and we were turned loose in open field, with a double chain of sentinels around us. Rations were not issued regularly for some time. Meal and rice were dealt out to us in a table-spoon, not exceeding three spoonfuls on some days. During the first three weeks of our stay at

Florence, the post was commanded by a lieutenant-colonel whose name I cannot now recall. He was a very humane man, and was often moved to tears by the suffering and destitution amongst the prisoners. He told me upon one occasion, just previous to leaving us, that he could not stay there and witness such suffering,—he would rather turn the prisoners all loose. He had no heart for this phase of civil war. He had the kindness to tell the prisoners that, if any of them wanted to write home, he would himself deliver the letters on board the Union flag-of-truce boat. The Confederate postage was ten cents in silver, and as there were very few dimes among the prisoners, he paid the postage himself. My letter reached home in Pennsylvania about two weeks afterward, but as all our letters were examined before passing the rebel lines, we were instructed to write nothing but pleasing news to our Northern friends. A letter I mailed at Andersonville July 4, I took from the post-office at Williamsport, Pa., myself in the following March.

"Meanwhile a stockade was being erected in a neighboring wood, which, being completed, we entered October 2. We were formed into thousands, sub-divided into hundreds, instead of detachments of nineties and thirties, as at Andersonville. The camp was designated by the first, second, or third thousand, and so on. A stream also ran through this pen, but it was deeper and more rapid than the one at Andersonville, and gave us much better water. Soon came a change in commanding officers. One Lieutenant Barrett, formerly of General Morgan's staff, it was said, whose natural ferocity and brutal cruelty I have never seen equaled, was placed in charge of the camp. He was employed previous to the war as a slave driver, and was a better tool in the hands of leading authorities for the handling of prisoners according to the code than the gentleman whom he succeeded. His 'culcha' and early training eminently qualified him for the position of a human butcher. For trivial causes he would 'Tannerize' the entire camp for two or three days in succession. This was bad enough for well-fed men, but for half-starved wretches it was simply horrible. I have seen him, for punishment to a man trying to escape, tie up the poor unfortunate by the thumbs, his toes just reaching the ground, and kick his feet from under him, laughing at his shrieks of pain as his whole weight was suspended on his thumbs. He would continue this amusement until the poor fellow's thumbs would burst open from the pressure. I have also seen him take a club in hand, and walk through camp, swinging it right and left, hitting any who were too weak to get out of his way. I have seen him stand on the rail over the gate leading into camp, and fire his revolver at random amongst the prisoners. These few instances of the brutal character of Lieutenant Barrett, to which I might add many more, will show you how well the men were selected for the accomplishment of the purposes intended toward Union prisoners.

"The pen at Florence was modeled very much after the style of the one at Andersonville, only much smaller in extent. The 'dead line' was not forgotten. It offered too good an opportunity to shoot prisoners to be omitted. Many a man went to his long home who accidentally passed its boundaries, for in many places the railing would get torn down, and the line between life and death could only be distinguished by the fact that no footprints were visible on the other side. The commissary building was just outside the gate leading from the camp, and was generally well-stocked with provisions which, however, were dealt out sparingly enough to us. The weather was now getting colder, and the fall rains added much to our discomfort. Meat was left out of our rations altogether, and our meal or rice was reduced to one pint per day, and a half teaspoonful of salt every second day, varied occasionally with beans instead of meal. Clothing was worn threadbare; our knees and elbows began to be visible through well-worn holes. Affairs looked dismal. The change of camp had deprived me of my Plymouth friends, they having been sent to Milan. Fortunately the new stockade had been erected on the site of a piece of woods, and the brush and limbs trimmed off the logs used in its construction had been left stacked up in heaps on the ground. I joined in with eight others, belonging to the old Bucktail regiment, and confiscated a pile of this brush and limbs, and commenced the erection of a shelter, which, by great labor under difficulties, we accomplished. We first dug down about two feet in the earth, and stood up the limbs like the roof of a house, or after the style of an 'A' tent. We then covered the limbs with a light brush, and on top of that put the earth which we had dug out. Our only tool for this purpose was a half canteen. It was slow work, weak and hungry as we were, but we finished in about ten days, and from that time had a partial shelter from the weather. This effort on our part undoubtedly went far toward the preservation of our lives, and it was needed, as we began to be much reduced by short rations and want of meat. We took the precaution to bury all the surplus wood we could get to prevent it from being stolen, for wood soon became as scarce as at Andersonville. The majority of prisoners were less fortunate in this respect, than we. Many poor wretches burrowed in the earth to gain shelter from wind and rain, and soon lost all appearance of human beings. Scarcely had our shelter been completed, when a calamity happened to one of our number, which shed a dark cloud over our household. One of our comrades had gone down to the brook to procure water, which we were in the habit of getting by walking out on a log across the stream close to the ' dead line.' The morning was wet and muddy, and the log was in consequence very slippery. While in the act of reaching down for water, he slipped and fell off the log over the 'dead line' into the water, about two feet deep. The guard immediately shot him. Some of us hearing the shot ran down, half suspecting the state of affairs, and implored the guard to let us take him out, but not until the officer of the guard with a squad of men came to the spot and covered us with their rifles, were we permitted to lift out our friend, who breathed his last as we laid him on the bank. Such cold-blooded murder of Union prisoners under circumstances without a shadow of justification were of daily occurrence, and we felt our manhood crushed to the very earth, being powerless to resist such atrocities.

"The police system established at Andersonville became the ruling power at Florence. While it was far from perfect, it was better than no control at all, and although the bounds of justice were frequently passed in the display of self-constituted authority, yet life and rights were comparatively safe to the mass. The ordinary punishment of criminals consisted of a prescribed number of lashes on the bare back, or running the gauntlet and dodging what blows the prisoner's tactics and ability would permit. I am satisfied that the trial of Guiteau at the police court of either Andersonville or Florence, would have been conducted without the aid of red tape, and ended entirely to the satisfaction of the American people in less than two hours.

"During the month of November we passed our darkest days of misery and distress. We got up hungry and cold in the morning, and laid down at night the same. The rations were again reduced in quantity, and men were brought to the direst extremities. I have seen men, impelled by hunger, accomplish feats which cannot be described here.

"Even the rumors of exchange, which had been put in circulation from time to time to raise the drooping spirits of the despondent, died out. The brave hearts who dared to hope against hope were daily growing fewer, so utterly deserted did we seem to be by the outer world. For simple pretexts our poor food was often denied us, and many men were rendered insane by the pangs of hunger. Many a long night we lay sleepless from cold, wet and hunger, when it seemed as though one were in the regions of the damned. Men crazed and idiotic from starvation rambled by scores and hundreds through camp, raving lunatics, muttering their unintelligible moanings, their eye-balls protruding with a wild, unearthly glare, faces and bodies thin and emaciated—they seemed like ghostly apparitions from the unknown world, making night frightful with groans of terror, and wails of despair. Many were in this condition who were men of education and ability, and had been reared in refined and comfortable homes. The only hope of escape from this awful state of affairs held out to us, was the oath of allegiance to the Confederacy. Their recruiting officers were daily in camp, and some were induced, as the only means of preserving their lives, to take the oath and join the rebel army, resolving to escape at the first opportunity. A Canadian by the name of Haley, with whom I was acquainted, was among those who took the oath and went out. He had belonged to the English army in Canada, and, deserting it, joined the Union army; then deserting our side, joined the rebels, and when I arrived at parole camp, Annapolis, a month later, his was the first familiar face I saw. He had been placed on picket guard, and deserted the rebels within a week after he got out of Florence. But to the majority of us, the idea was worse than death. They might torture us with cruelty, they might kill us with starvation; but compel us to swear allegiance to a band of traitors whose purpose it was to destroy the best government God ever gave to man, they could not.

"During the first of this month our government succeeded in sending through the lines a quantity of blankets for our use, but very few of them ever got into our possession. We were drawn up into line by hundreds, and marched single file past a bag containing six black beans and ninety-four white ones. Each prisoner drew out a bean; those who held black beans got blankets,—six to cover a hundred men. The remainder of the blankets were confiscated by the rebels. The number of sick and helpless increased so fast that a hospital was formed in a corner of the stockade, attended by two or three rebel surgeons. Not the least of the dangers to be avoided was gangrene. One of our comrades named Roberts, a very promising young man, had hurt his foot slightly before leaving Andersonville. From a minute scratch it developed into a serious wound, until finally he was taken to the hospital and had his foot amputated. But it was too late —the virulent poison had penetrated his entire system. He used to come from the hospital to see us as long as he could, but his visits ceased, and, as we were not permitted to go and see him, his light went out alone and among strangers. These were our darkest hours. The sands in the hour glass were running low. Day by day we grew weaker and more helpless, and yet the time of deliverance seemed no nearer than at first.

"Daily we visited among our friends and acquaintances to see how each was getting along—to learn who had been touched by the death messenger, and who were left; to receive and impart messages to be carried by the survivors to far-off friends whom we might not see again; to exchange farewells with the dying; to look at the living with the mute inquiry, Who among us will be the next? I remember, as if but yesterday, sitting by the side of a dying comrade, who said, ' Frank, we were boys together, living as neighbors; we went to school together (and here the tears rolled down his cheeks), but I am going fast, and all that is left of Oscar

Henry will soon be carried to the deadhouse. When you go back I want you to go and see my poor old mother—tell her that I died like a man.' Such were the messages which weighed down our already heavy hearts. It seemed to us then that if we could be permitted to take one more look at home and friends, and a hearty meal around the family table, our fondest expectations on this earth would be fully realized.

"But 'tis well that the sun does not always remain below the horizon. With what delight we hailed the first rays of morning light! On the morning of November 27 the first thousand was marched outside the stockade, and the sickest and most destitute ones selected for parole and taken to Savannah. The next morning the second thousand, to which I belonged, was called out. As the examining surgeon passed down the lines, selecting the worst cases, for once in my life I desired to look sick. He stopped before me, and asked a few questions, which I answered as well as my throbbing heart and the lump in my throat would allow. He then said, '*You may go!*' Controlling my emotions as best I could, I went forward and signed the parole. Those of us who had signed the parole were permitted to sleep outside the stockade that night, though well guarded; while those less fortunate were marched back to the bull pen. Early next morning we got on freight cars destined for Charleston, where we arrived in the evening. But alas! we learned to our sorrow that the Union General Foster had intercepted communications to Savannah, whither we were going for exchange. This is the only instance I can think of when a Union victory was unwelcome news. This one was ill-timed and out of place. We remained in Charleston three days, waiting to go through. Our forces were shelling the city all the time, and no arrangements could be effected for our transfer to the Union lines. We were again placed on cars and our faces turned toward the 'bull pen' at Florence. Many desperate efforts were made to escape that day by jumping from the cars. The guards kept up a desultory fire from the roofs of the cars to show that they were on the alert. Our aspect was sorrowful and our hearts sad as we once more entered that hated, dreaded place; it seemed as if fate had conspired against us.

"Once more our drooping spirits were revived. On the 5th of December we were again called out, and taken back to Charleston that night. It was a ride long to be remembered. The cars were not only filled inside but on top. We traveled all night, over a hundred miles, with a strong, cold, December wind in our faces. I crouched behind a large man with an overcoat on, who had laid down on the car roof, to shield, if possible, my bare knees and elbows from the pitiless storm. When morning came and our destination was reached, we were ordered to get off and embark on a steamer lying at the wharf. I tried to arouse my strange friend whom I had used as a fortification during the night, but he was *dead!*—paroled with us, but gone home before us. About 9 o'clock in the morning the rebel steamer started for Fort Sumter, where me met our own boat, to which we were transferred, within a mile of its battered walls. The emotions that filled our hearts at the sight of the old Stars and Stripes waving above our heads, it is impossible to describe. It was like a dream. The tears would come from very joy—a joy that will endure while life lasts, for I can never refer to that moment of supreme relief, without a full heart. As soon as we were on board our steamer, we received a new suit of clothes and a clean meal. We laid down that night with lighter hearts than we had had for many a long month. The next day we were transferred to an ocean steamer, and sailed 'homeward-bound' from Charleston harbor.

"A few months later, on the field of Appomattox, some of us were permitted to step across the 'bloody chasm,' and receive the stacked arms and drooping battle-flags which denoted the downfall of rebellion, and assured us that our sufferings had not been in vain.

"The incidents I have related form but an individual experience, the half untold, in a chapter which one might almost wish had never been written. When I look back and review my experience as a prisoner, I am, at times, disposed to doubt my own senses, or the soundness of my mind—so incredible does it appear that such barbarities would be allowed within the pale of civilization. But the world will not suffer the memory of such atrocities to die. How well they carried out their threats of extermination is proved by testimony more conclusive than was ever brought to bear on a similar case.

"The time has passed to inquire whether punishment has been meted out to the authors of this suffering, but there will come a day when the angel of justice will uncover the silent mounds of earth, and bid the scores of thousands of ghastly, emaciated victims of Southern prison pens come forth and confront the keepers at the bar of the great Unerring Judge, indicting them with blacker crimes than the world will ever know, because it is impossible for human mind to comprehend, or words borne on human tongue to tell, the suffering prescribed to Union prisoners; and though the full extent will ever remain an unwritten chapter of the war, I am pleased to know that the Society for the Preservation of Unpublished History has heard what remarks I myself have made."

CAMP-FIRE X.

WAR ON THE WATER—DARING DEEDS—HOW MANY REGIMENTS EACH MAN CAPTURED—REMARKABLE ESCAPES—THE BIGGEST LIAR IN THE WAR.

"WILL the Society for the Preservation of Unpublished History be pleased to hear of a romance on a river?" inquired Mr. L. D. Simonds, late acting master-mate of the United States Steamer *General Thomas*.

"No!" said the temperate S. P. U. H. "Water is foreign to our nature. Away back in the reign of Abraham I, sixteenth adviser-general to Uncle Sam, when we were but a few years old, our mother was accustomed to wash our fevered cheeks with the hated fluid. Thence to now be it known that eternal total abstinence is sworn. Never mention that name to us again."

But for the benefit of posterity, which argument always hits a weak side of the S. P. U. H., the Society was persuaded to listen, and Mr. Simonds proceeded:

"When General Hood, on his march to Nashville, Tenn., halted his command at Decatur, Ala., he threw out his skirmishers, and placed his artillery in position on the river bank, expecting to capture the pontoon bridge, cross over his army, march on to Nashville, and then make a bold strike to save the Confederacy. But the sequel proved that he counted without his host.

"The U. S. Steamer *General Thomas* at this time was stationed at Decatur, with orders to patrol the river to a point about thirty miles above Decatur, reserving what coal we had to bank the fires, and to confiscate rails along the river for fuel while under way, as the river at that time was so low that we could not get to Bridgeport to lay in a supply of coal.

"At the time mentioned, the *General Thomas* was some twelve or fifteen miles above Decatur. Captain Morton was pacing the hurricane deck, enjoying a good smoke from his meerschaum pipe, when all of a sudden he stopped, turned around, took his pipe from his mouth, and listened for several seconds. Then he resumed his pacing, but presently halted again in his reverie—listened, turned, and called out to Mr. Johnson, the pilot:

"'Did you hear anything, sir?'

"Mr. Johnson replied that he did not. The captain once more resumed his pacing the deck. Some seconds elapsed, when the captain suddenly stopped again.

"'There, sir!' said he, 'did you not hear that?'

"'Well, captain, I believe I did hear something that sounded like a cannon shot.'

"Once more the same distant rumbling sound echoed up and down the valley. There was no mistaking it—it was a sound that had become familiar to every veteran of the war, the noise of artillery. Immediately the orders were given to round to and steam down the river. The engines were reversed, and down the river we went. Hammocks were taken out of the nettings and stowed around the boilers, and every precaution was taken to prevent any disaster to the boat. The men were beat to quarters, the guns run in, and port holes closed. We soon neared a small creek running into the Tennessee, about five miles above Decatur. We landed, and all hands were piped ashore to rail up. Some two hours were thus consumed.

"Opposite to us and in the middle of the river, lay an army gunboat at anchor, manned by an Indiana battery, which was commanded by Captain Naylor. The captain had gone to Decatur, to confer with General Granger, and left the boat in charge of the first lieutenant, with only twenty-three pounds of steam—almost in sight of, and in range of the rebel batteries. All hands were aboard, lines were cast off, the gang-plank hauled in, and orders given to back out, and steam down the river to the scene of action, when a cloud of dust was seen in the distance. As it came nearer, the clatter of horses' feet were heard. A little nearer, a squad of cavalry were seen. Nearer and nearer they approached, until a bend in the road hid the horsemen from view. Suddenly an officer dashed down to the river side, who proved to be Captain Naylor, of the army gunboat, returning from Decatur, with an escort of cavalry. The cutter of the *General Thomas* was called away to bring the captain on board. It came alongside, and Captain Naylor was met at the gangway by the captain, boatswain, and two other men.

"By the way, Captain Morton was what was termed an *old salter*. As brave a man as ever trod a deck, and a strict disciplinarian, though he was kind and courteous to the officers and men under him; but like other men, he had his faults, the principal one of which was profanity.

"'Well, Captain Morton,' said Captain Naylor, as he entered the gangway, 'Hood has twenty-three pieces of artillery stationed on the river bank to prevent us from coming down to help General Granger.'

"'I don't care a —— if they have 200 pieces,' returned Morton.

"'Well, they'll blow us clear out of the water if we undertake to run by—that's all there is of that,' replied Captain Naylor.

"'I don't give a ——; I might as well be blown out of the water here as any other place, and by —— I am goin' down to help that fort out, if I get blowed to h—l. You can follow me or stay where you are.'

"'Well, captain, wherever you go, you can depend upon my following, let the consequences be what they may,' said Captain Naylor, resigned to his fate.

"'All right—get up steam and follow me. Signal, when you have steam enough.'

"Captain Naylor then stepped into his own cutter, which by this time had come alongside, and was rowed to his own boat. In about fifteen minutes afterward, he signaled the *General Thomas*, 'All ready!' and we rounded to and sped on our way down the river.

"The first intimation we had of the presence of the enemy, was about one mile below the mouth of the creek, when a shot from the gun of a sharpshooter struck the casemate, just above the port-hole abaft the larboard wheelhouse, which instantly caused me to take my head out of the way. Immediately after came several shots from the same direction, and from equally as good marksmen. Orders came from the pilot-house through the trumpet, to shift the starboard guns to the larboard side, and prepare for action. This was done in the twinkling of an eye, and a shot from one of our bow guns went crashing, tearing, and plowing its way through the timber, on and on, until it exploded in the midst of Stuart's cavalry, which was massed about three-quarters of a mile back from the river, and caused considerable commotion in their ranks. Another, and another followed its predecessor, when presently the rebel batteries opened fire, making it lively for us the rest of our way. Things began to be a little dangerous. A shot came plowing its way abaft the larboard wheel-house, carrying with it a piece of the inner casemate, striking one of the men at the gun on the head, and knocking him senseless. The same shot struck a stanchion, just forward of the magazine hatchway, knocking the captain's cook over, and maiming him for life, then passed out through the starboard wheel-house. Another came through the hull of the boat, about two feet forward of the magazine; another still further forward, two inches above the water line; another passed through the upper and after part of the larboard wheel-house, thence through the pilot's stateroom, carrying with it one-half of the pilot's dress coat-tail, and came out through the second assistant engineer's room, taking with it a feather pillow; another found its way through, and exploded in our pantry, breaking every dish we had, scattering the beans, flour, and dishes in all directions. At this time the captain's steward was passing through the wood-room on his way to the captain's cabin, and a piece of the shell struck him on the back, tearing a fearful gash. He afterward died in hospital.

"About two miles above Decatur there is a bend in the river, and as our boat came into view, both sides ceased fighting, to witness a beautiful river sight, for it was supposed that our boat was on fire, as nothing could be seen of it, save one massive sheet of flame and smoke—so rapid was the firing. Had we hugged the north shore as was supposed by the Johnnies, the probabilities are that there would have been but few of us left. Instead of this, the captain hugged the south shore, right under the very muzzle of the enemy's guns, which saved us. As we passed the batteries and came opposite the fort, we rounded to, and gave them a parting salute with our two bow guns, and such a cheer as rent the air from our boys in the fort, only those who heard it know.

"Hostilities ceased, and the enemy withdrew, leaving us in our glory. That night they moved farther down the river, where they succeeded in making a crossing, and marched on to Nashville.

"I must not forget Captain Naylor and the brave boys under his command, who so gallantly followed us in running the gauntlet. No one but a *brave* man would have followed us, knowing the position and strength of the enemy, as he did; and, above all, his boat was not even protected by a casemate. He fared, however, even better than we did, for he lost only one man, whose head was taken off by a shot, and rolled out into the river; and, I believe, one or two slightly wounded.

"The following day Captain Naylor, our executive officer, second assistant engineer, another officer, and myself went ashore, and procuring a horse each from the quartermaster, rode over the field of action. As we neared the river bank, we could see coat sleeves torn to shreds, a man's arm here, a leg there, and pieces of ammunition chests and caisson wheels scattered in all directions. All over the field could be seen what death and destruction we had dealt out to the enemy. In our ride over the field, we came to a planter's house, dismounted and went in, and from the planter's wife we learned that General Stuart had massed his cavalry on their plantation. When our first shot was fired, it came tearing its way through the woods, exploded in their midst, killed several, and wounded quite a number of others. One shot from our guns blew up a caisson and killed fifty men. Another dismounted one of their guns, and tore the gun carriage to pieces.

"The day following, the troops commenced to evacuate Decatur, and fall back toward Nashville. The orders from General Granger were to destroy the pontoons after the troops had all passed over, which destruction was placed under my charge. Through much tribulation, and receiving a good many shots from the rebel sharpshooters, I succeeded, with the assistance of some of the troops, in accomplishing this, and we went on down the river."

"Speaking of throwing shells into the woods," said Mr. C. E. Harden, of Co. F, 26th Illinois, "reminds me of a peculiar little anecdote:

"On the day previous to the evacuation of Charleston,

PONTOON BRIDGE.

S. C., a shot was fired from one of the Island batteries (I think Morris Island), marked with chalk or paint, ' *Good for James Street*,' and strange as it may appear, it dropped in James Street, and was pointed out to me by an old citizen, in the last of February, 1864, who remarked that no other shot had come near as far, and he knew it was a bad omen, for that night the city was evacuated. I would like for the comrade who fired that shot to know that it fulfilled its mission."

In behalf of posterity, the S. P. U. H. took due note of this.

"That reminds me of a strange occurrence," said the colonel of the 40th Ohio, " about the most curious incident that I met with during the war.

" In February, 1864, our brigade was encamped at Blue Springs, Tenn. Sherman, who was with his forces then at or near Vicksburg, intended to make an advance upon the rebels at Jackson, Miss. In order that Joe Johnston should not go to the relief of the Jackson forces, we, with the other troops, were ordered to make a demonstration in his front, and for that purpose moved down toward Dalton, Ga., before and around which place his troops were located. It was not the design, apparently, to do much fighting, but to make a pretence of it, and to engage his troops so completely that they could not be withdrawn. We marched and counter-marched, and fired our guns, and set fire to the leaves and woods, and made the rebels believe we were going to devour them bodily. After three or four days of this kind of manœuvering, our object was accomplished, and we withdrew and went back to camp.

"The incident I refer to occurred just as we were withdrawing our skirmish line. I went along the skirmish line of our brigade, to withdraw the men as quietly as possible. The line was stretched along the north side of a gorge, or deep ravine, which was some two hundred yards wide. The rebel skirmish line was posted along the south side of this ravine, so that between the two lines there was clear space, and the men on either side were plainly discernible to each other, when they exposed themselves by leaving their cover.

"As I withdrew man after man, I finally came to a member of Company C, who was standing behind a tree, and who, at the instant I stepped up to him, had just fired, and was taking his gun down. He looked curiously at the muzzle of it, and I asked him what was the matter, when he pointed to the gun, and said:

"'Look there! That rebel's bullet went square into that barrel!'

"And sure enough, the rebel ball had gone directly into the barrel, just as he had fired. It met his own ball about five inches from the muzzle, and the concussion of the two burst the barrel, making an opening some three inches long, and about half an inch wide. The muzzle of the gun was unbroken and not abraded. Both the balls were flattened and welded together. The rebel ball, just as the Company C man fired, had gone straight into his gun barrel, and met his own ball, which was on its way to pay its respects to the fellow across the ravine. The Company C man said that he and that Johnny had been firing at each other for some time.

"If our man had held his gun one thirty-second part of an inch up or down, to the right or to the left, from the position in which he did hold it, the rebel ball would have crashed into his brain, instead of going into the barrel of his gun, and I would have found a corpse at that tree, instead of a man wondering at the incident that had occurred."

Doctor Watson, of Company B, 53d Illinois, then related this remarkable experience, which shows how many regiments one man can sometimes capture:

"On the 24th of February, 1864, sixteen men and myself

were detailed to go out foraging to procure meat, meal and flour for our regiment. At this time, we had a large foraging party detailed from each regiment in the corps, as we had started from the rear of Vicksburg for Meridian, Miss., with quarter rations for ten days, and had been out some twenty-five days; so that we had to subsist off the country. Subsequently we were detailed from the foraging party to act as alarm guard, with orders to join the main squad at Willis' plantation, near Katley's Ferry, on Pearl River.

"At 4 o'clcock in the afternoon, after staying on post, and running around over the surrounding country all day, we started to join the main squad at the appointed rendezvous. On coming out from some timber to the main Canton road,— we were twelve miles from Canton, Miss.,—and looking up the road toward Willis' place, we saw a body of men. We supposed, of course, that they were our own squad, when behold! they ran up their colors (detailed foraging parties never carry colors), and so we saw at once that we were facing the Johnnies, the first we had seen on our trip, and now were nearly back to Vicksburg, after going to Meridian, Miss., and accomplishing that for which we went,—tearing up railroads. It seemed to me, as I sat on my horse there, and looked at those Johnnies, as if there were a whole division of them.

"While we remained in the timber, looking at the Johnnies and debating what to do, another regiment went by us on the road, not over twenty rods from where we were. We concluded that the regiment that had passed us were our own men, and decided to give the enemy the best we had, and then vamoose; so we rode up to the fence and fired all at once. I tell you we shook them up terribly.

"We kept up a lively fire for a time, and then became bold. With a dash we rode up to the Johnnies,—about four or five regiments,—and demanded their surrender, telling them that our troops were just coming out of the woods. One of our boys, Dan Buckley, of the 14th Iowa, was especially bold. Riding up to an Alabama colonel, he placed a revolver to the colonel's head, and said:

"'Surrender, you rascal!'

"Of course the colonel accepted the inevitable and surrendered. We were just thinking what we would do with our prey until we could get assistance,—sixteen men against 6,000,—when to our mortification the supposed Federal troops which passed us in the woods came up, proving to be the 56th Alabama Johnnies.

"'Now, then,' said our Alabama colonel, whom we had just taken prisoner, 'who has the trump card? No more of your Yankee tomfoolery,—give us your guns.'

"'I—I—beg your pardon, colonel,' said Buckley.

"'Not much; there's no pardon for audacity of your kind,' returned the colonel. 'I guess you're destined for Andersonville, where, sure enough, we *did* go, and thence to Florence, where we remained over nine months.''

"The bursting of that gun, in the incident previous to the last," said Mr. H. H. Armstead, "has called up an incident at the battle of Nashville, where we dispersed Hood's army.

"The Johnnies had been throwing shells into our vicinity, and it began to be somewhat dangerous where I was. The boys had been very fortunate in dodging shells, but finally one of the cavalrymen near us,—his name was J. M. A.—became separated from his company, and his horse began to plunge and rear. The horse had just avoided two or three shells, but finally he turned his head to the left and one struck him in the shoulder, plowing clear through him, and taking him with great force from under the rider, who was left uninjured, except that his clothes were torn, and he received a few slight bruises from the saddle, as it passed from under him."

"Huh! dat's nuffin'," said Mr. Jehosaphat Alexander (colored), "you know de battle ob Vicksburg?"

"The *siege* of Vicksburg, you mean," answered the commander.

"Well, de *siege* den," said Jehosaphat, "no dif'runce,—same ting."

"Yes, go ahead."

"Well, sah, you know how many defs wuz occasioned by de great display ob artil'ry fire dar, an' how many died from eatin' ole mules. Well, sah, I 'scaped all dat—all dem defs—I 'scaped 'fo' de battle commenced."

But perhaps the most remarkable escape during the whole Civil War was that of Mr. Aldrich, private of Company K, in a certain Wisconsin regiment; and as it is now so very seldom that we meet a private of the war of 1861-'65, since almost every soldier has become a "colonel," or a "captain" at least, the S. P. U. H. deliberated that it might be interesting to posterity to learn of this most wonderful escape.

Mr. Aldrich's station in life would never be guessed from his personal appearance. Ordinarily he looked very much like a colonel—in his every-day clothes; but what with his kinky, iron-grey, wedge-shaped beard, moderately long hair, with a slight curl at the ends, his six-foot, arrow-like form, his military nose, that far-off look in his eye, that apparent reticence of speech, he seemed not unlike the historic "Suthun brigadeah,"—when he was on dress parade.

Also, Mr. Aldrich differed in two other very marked particulars from the rest of the soldiers, and from mankind in general,—he did not pride himself on having a "keen sense of the ludicrous," or that other worst form of egotism—ability to read and understand human nature. To *study* human nature is a very laudable occupation; but when a person boasts of having mastered the subject to any degree of certainty, his mental condition is too disgusting for classification.

Mr. Aldrich, then, was one of those fellows who rarely laugh; and, with the exception of an occasional inconsistent twinkle in his eye, he seemed like other men. But beneath the prettiest flower there may a muttering mountain sleep. It was not expected when Mr. Aldrich arose that he would tell of a remarkable escape. However, suffice it to say that, as he stood before the camp-fire in all his ingloriousness, the S. P. U. H. could not forgive him for being so glaring a breach of nature, in that he had no sense of the ludicrous, when his outward appearance and seeming inward reality were so directly opposed. But it's just like her—Nature is always fixing up some such specimen; there would be no dime museums if she didn't.

Said he, "It was near the west end of Mason and Dixon's Line. [See Webster's Unabridged Dictionary, p. 1575, col. ii, edition of 1874.] Somehow it never occurred to me that a volley of musketry was a very palatable thing to swallow, and being conscious that I belonged to a higher order of life than a tree which stood a few rods to my rear, I naturally concluded to let the tree be killed first. But it seems that in those days a man was not permitted to hold conclusions of his own. And this was not the first time that I had suddenly arrived at such a conclusion when the firing began in front; so I was brought before a court-martial, tried, and it was found that I had been absent when needed. The verdict was that I should be shot out of a cannon. There was no use of resistance, and I rather hoped that it would be the last of me, so I walked up like a lamb to the slaughter.

"The gunners began to load the gun—a monster Rodman. [See Newman's "America," page 671.] I saw scoopful after scoopful of powder put into the cavern-mouthed thing, and thought that there would be power enough behind to place me safe across the Pacific Ocean. Finally the shell—a seven-hundred pounder—was put in, and then your humble servant. They put me in head first, in mercy, and when they thought I was comfortable, they asked:

"'Ready?'

"'Y-e-s,' I said; and while they were fixing the thing, I tell you I began to think. I thought of one other fellow who had been shot out of a cannon; I remembered he had a good deal of presence of mind, and ate nearly all the powder in the gun before it exploded, so that it did not hurt him much; but I did not have his advantage, for the seven-hundred pound shell was in my way. But even this would not have been a very great obstacle had it not been for one other disadvantage. Probably I could have devoured the metal and the powder too, but my teeth were all worn down, as I had been fed on 'hard-tack' for a few weeks previous.

"So I resigned myself to my fate, and made up my mind to see the thing through. Just then she went off. Of course I was pushed out first, but I raised my head to take notes of the scenery and the progress of the battle as I passed along, and found that the trip wasn't so bad after all. As I raised my head the shell passed under me and gained the center of my body. I then discovered that I was getting left behind, and clapped my right hand against the shell either to hold it back or myself up.

"In my excited state my fingers were spread out, and the nervous stroke was so strong that my fingers were pushed clear through the shell. I now had a good hold of my companion with my fingers clinched on the inside, and was going along as happy as before. But soon the thing began to go sidewise. So I clapped my left hand against the other side, and clinched it on the inside also.

"By this time I was about a mile and a half from the starting point. Other shells were flying on all sides of mine and me, and some of them were going ahead of us for

THE BIGGEST LIAR IN THE WAR SHOT OUT OF A CANNON.

awhile, because we were so heavy; but in the long range we made it up, for when the other shells began to sink into humiliation and roll along the ground, we were sailing on in the grace of a May-day queen.

"Presently I saw a brigade of Confederate cavalry a short distance in front. I knew that I must come back to the earth sometime, and just then my shell began to wend its downward course. So I worked my fingers around a little, made a larger hole in the side of the shell, got hold of an old piece of horse shoe, and selected my Johnny. When I was near enough I hurled the iron at him, he tumbled from the saddle, I jumped from the shell, straddled the horse, and dashed away from the dazed crowd, safe and sound."

Great applause; and when it had subsided one veteran inquired, "What became of the shell?"

"E-hic! That busted and (hic!) killed all the rest of the liars in the war," said Boozy Dick, who had again put in an appearance. With the impression that the last adventure was probably fiction, the camp-fire adjourned.

CAMP-FIRE XI.

SUTLERS—QUARTERMASTERS—MULES—HOW RICH A SOL-
DIER MUST BE TO BUY ANYTHING FROM A SUTLER—
THE PROFITS IN THE GOVERNMENT APPOINTMENT OF
QUARTERMASTER ON A REGULAR SALARY—EULOGY
ON THE SUTLER AND THE ARMY MULE.

IN this commercial age handsome returns are often realized from occupations where there has been very moderate investment, and apparently very little business transacted. There are also other instances in which a great amount of business is done on a regular salary, without any investment; but still these operatives become suddenly prosperous. And this latter condition of things has existed in other periods than the present. Mail routes have not been the only source of gain in the history of the United States patronage. Even the patriotism of twenty years ago was not unmixed with that enemy of human happiness—avarice.

The gallantry of the patriotic quartermasters who so bravely volunteered to *live* for their country and undergo all the privations necessitated by a full supply train, will ever be treasured in memory. There were also other patriots who, in the hour of the country's need, kindly consented to take government contracts for furnishing coffee and other articles of food. But alas! some accident must have occurred, especially to the coffee. While that was being ground, before the government took it in charge, it is probable that the section of floor in the room just above the hopper suddenly gave way and let down into the grinder a quantity of peas and chicory, which incidentally had been stored above it. Owing to the great demand for ground coffee there could be no time lost in stopping the mills to take out the peas and chicory. No one was to blame. The millers could not stop to repair the loss from the accident; the proprietors, who held the contracts, were too busy with something else—buying cotton in the South, and smuggling it through, purchasing and stocking Western farms at a million dollars apiece, and establishing extensive seed houses in the East. Truly they were men of great minds, and could not attend to details.

But it is the devotion of the quartermasters which is now to be lamented. Could the eloquent army mule get up from his grave and give forth his reminiscence, how many times would he say that he had been driven off, recaptured, and sold again to the government? Could each extra ration due the soldier speak, how far would it say that it missed its destination? However, the quartermasters were not responsible for the vagaries of the rations and of the mules; though in this connection it is a little difficult to see just why these officers were so prosperous after the war, when the majority of them were nearly penniless before; how a man with a family, in moderate circumstances, could accumulate a competence on a salary of $124.00 per month,* paying war prices for everything. It was no moral wrong to be a quartermaster, but the source of profit in the business was never accounted for until the Society for the Preservation of Unpublished History learned the following from one of them.

One evening after the adjournment of a camp-fire, the society was invited to become the guests of a qaurtermaster. Of course they accepted such a pleasure. From the campfire they were conveyed in an easy carriage to a fine portion

---

*Besides a liberal allowance of rations, etc. For pay-roll, uniforms, discipline, etc., and much interesting information concerning armies, see Revised Regulations of the United States Army, to be found in any well-appointed public library.

of a thriving city. They were driven up to a large brownstone front on the south side of the street, surrounded by a neat and spacious lawn, with an aristocratic air about the whole home. As the society advanced up the fashionable stone walk, and the bright moonlight outlined the mansion and its surroundings, and they beheld the sphinx-like figures crouching on the banister, in the dim gas-light from the hall, they almost wished *they* had been quartermasters.

In the morning after a rich breakfast, which made them feel that it was a decided advantage to accept invitations like the one of the previous evening,—they were shown about the premises. The house was furnished richly within, well-suiting its outward beauty; and when the society congratulated the quartermaster on his comfortable abode, he said:

"Come into my cellar," which was accordingly done, because the historians suspected something.

"Here," said the quartermaster, "is some that is twenty years old—fine old Bourbon. Smack your lips on that."

With true historical skill, after a comparison of dates, which was not uttered, the S. P. U. H. simply, but forcibly replied:

"Well, we are total abstinence; but whenever we *do* take anything, it is invariably twenty-year-old Bourbon."

When the party were again in the open air, the society inquired of the quartermaster what he did to pass away his declining days.

"Oh!" he laughed, "I 'tend to the farm, and look after my place here, and loan a little money once in awhile."

If the S. P. U. H. had been a little better acquainted, and could have given security, they would probably have asked the good quartermaster to loan them a little "for a few days," as they were no richer than other historians and penny-a-liners; but as it was, they concluded to keep up their accustomed dignity, and only interrogated:

"How did you get your start, Mr. Quartermaster?" as they felt a sudden desire to have a similiar experience.

"Oh!" said he, " I am getting old now (forty-eight years) and I have been a good while at it—every old man ought to be rich in this country; and then I have a very economical wife."

"Ah, yes!" said the S. P. U. H., glad to note the solution of quartermasters' post-bellum prosperity; and with the reflection that nearly all of the economical women in the country must have married quartermasters or government contractors, the society took its leave.

Curiously enough, the subject of quartermasters was brought up that evening at the camp-fire, and also that other similar object of sympathy, the sutler, who was the only man of a regiment permitted to buy goods from the outside world, and retail them to the soldiers at his own price. He was guaranteed the miscellaneous and exclusive patronage of from six hundred to a thousand soldiers, being the poor storekeeper of the regiment, and deserves much pity and memorial.

In connection with the subject, Mr. A. Lammey, of Company C, 2d Chicago Board of Trade Regiment, said:

" I was on detached service for a time—in the secret military police force, or detective service, which was a part of the provost marshal's department. Our work was confined to cities, and we were for sometime in the city of Nashville. We generally knew what was going on 'behind the scenes,' and often had considerable sport seeking out offenders, arresting them, and putting them into prison. At one time we caught the post quartermaster, Capt. Charles Irwin. I do not remember who was the special plaintiff, but I know that Irwin was sued by the government for $2,000,000. His trial did not come off for two or three years, and I think it was compromised, as I never heard or read anything of it afterward, though I watched for it.

"But that was not what I was going to say. We had communication with the quartermaster's department, and being a branch of the provost guard, we sometimes did special duty, adjusted adverse claims, and settled disputes by arresting suspicious parties, and bringing them to justice. So I came to know of a case where a sutler was punished for the exorbitant prices he charged.

"This was at the battle of Stone River. Lager beer had been pretty scarce for sometime, and the sutler had not been able to furnish it. Finally he succeeded in getting twenty kegs, and began to retail it out to the boys at ten cents a glass. The boys were all thirsty for the beverage, and the result was that the sutler had to have two or three assistants. Half the beer was soon gone, and it was evident that the remainder would not last long.

"To save the beer and still make a good profit, the sutler put up the price to twenty cents a glass. But this did not seem to check the demand, and the beer flowed as fast as ever. Then the sutler concluded to make the price be felt, as he knew the difficulty of getting any more beer at any price, so he raised the price to *thirty* cents per glass. Some of the boys now stopped drinking, and the others remonstrated at the price, but still kept buying. There were now only six kegs left, and this being deemed insufficient for the demand, the sutler raised the price this time to forty cents per glass. But it seemed that the boys were determined to drink up all that beer, though the majority had given up the luxury. Then the price was again raised. It took *fifty cents to purchase a glass* of that beer! Then came the *finale*.

"The boys at once held an indignation meeting, and demanded the sutler to lower the price of his goods. This the merchant man refused to do, saying that he would get fifty cents per glass for what beer he had left, or he would drink it all himself.

"'All right,' said one of the boys, 'if you don't come to reasonable terms, you will soon wish you had. We will give you twenty-five cents a glass for what beer you have left.'

"'Not much!' replied the sutler—'I'll have fifty cents a glass for that beer, or I'll not sell you a drop.'

"This settled it. Night soon came on. The boys were already decided as to their course of action. When all was quiet around the camp, one of them took the end of a long rope which the rest had provided for him, and crawling quietly down toward the sutler's tent, fixed it to the end of the wagon tongue. The other boys then began to pull quietly, but surely, and soon the wagon began to move mysteriously up a high hill near by. The soldier who fastened the rope to the wagon, then crept into it, took out the rear end-gate, and as the wagon moved up the hill, he threw out a keg of beer here, and a box of provisions, candies or tobacco there, and a barrel of crackers a little further on, until the entire contents, about $1,500 worth of goods in all, were scattered along the hillside When the wagon reached the crest of the hill, it was empty. The soldiers then started it down the other side, and it did not stop for half a mile.

"It did not require a great deal of time for the goods to disappear, and after a general jollification and distribution of the sutler's effects, the soldiers turned in to their tents, but not before they had taken a liberal amount to the colonel's tent, including half a barrel of fine butter crackers.

"In the morning the unfortunate sutler made a wonderfully close search for his goods, but of course found nothing. He at once appealed to the colonel, and demanded the arrest of the whole regiment. But before he finished speaking, he noticed the crackers in the colonel's tent.

"'Yes,' he said, 'and here you have half a barrel of my crackers,' and the sutler undertook to take possession of them.

"'Drop that barrel this very second,' interfered the colonel, 'or I'll put a bullet right through your stingy carcass!' and he drew his revolver to show that he meant business.

"The sutler dropped the crackers, but began:

"'Well, I'll have my own property, or have you all arrested.'

"'That is not *your* property,' returned the colonel. 'Those crackers were a present to me, and I mean to keep them. Hands off!'

"'No they ain't,' the sutler replied,—'the cussed thieves stole 'em from me last night.'

"'That makes no difference to me—these crackers were given to me with the compliments of my regiment, and I mean to keep them. I don't care where they came from.'

"'You're all a set of d——d robbers,' said the sutler—'take a poor man's property away from him, and then shoot him if he tries to get it back.'

"'Silence!' roared the colonel, 'or I'll fill you full of cold lead, you avaricious hound! Out with you, and never show your stingy face again at headquarters! Charge ten prices for your goods, cheat all you can, and squeeze every cent from the soldiers, and then complain if they retaliate! Consider your commission withdrawn, and never show yourself here again!'

"It is needless to say that the sutler did not set up another stock with that regiment, and he was not the first sutler who was served in a similar way by oppressed soldiers."

There were three cheers for the Stone River colonel after this story, and then Capt. John O. Pullen delivered the following grandiloquent eulogium on the sutler and the army mule:

"Comrades, you have heard in every Fourth-of-July oration of the 'Volunteer Soldiery,' the 'Loyal Women,' 'Veterans of the Grand Army,' of the 'Rank and File,' and obituaries to the 'Unknown' who were left, bearing their insignia of rank across the river—only their valiant deeds their vouchers.

"But, comrades, it is for me to tell to-night of the truly loyal sutler and the patriotism of the army mule; and I am glad that the Society for the Preservation of Unpublished History is here to chronicle my remarks. The sutler, unlike Artemus Ward, who was 'willing to sacrifice all his wife's relations for his country'—took his own life in his — pocket, and went forth to dare or die, that he might live.

"It is fitting, my comrades, that the sutler should be placed first in this sentiment, as his loyalty— heretofore unappreciated by those learned in the art of war—is demonstrated by his valorous chivalry in always being at the front in the grand charge—for canned fruit and 'Scheidam Schnapps.'

"Who so loyal as our sutler, when he met us at the paymaster's table, and there by written testimonials convinced us of his willingness to take charge of all the pay Uncle Samuel had so liberally donated to us, and send the same home to *his* little ones! Who so loyal, as when our sutler, at the sound of the retreat, would appropriate all the contrabands, and press into service all stragglers, for the removal of his stores to a place of safety—thereby demonstrating that it was for Uncle Sam's volunteer soldiery that *his* loyal heart was beating? Who so loyal as the sutler, when the Southern Confederacy acknowledged the collapse, and by his counsel, and on the stump, and through the public press he denounced the squandering of the nation's wealth, either as bounty or pensions upon the 'hirelings' who had taken their lives in their hands, 'and gone forth to battle, that a nation might live?'

"Truly, the loyalty of the sutler of the volunteer army shines equal to the electric light of the present times, and while the brilliancy of the loyalty of the sutler is so transcendent, that pure sparkle in the eye of our army mule, with its liquid fire of loving patriotism, surmounts the illuminating deeds of 'Sherman's Bummers.'

"Our army mule's patriotism far exceeded that of the human race; an animal with no ancestors to vindicate, or posterity to protect; an individuality unknown in civilized warfare until the 'late unpleasantness'! The first we learn of this purely patriotic beast is in divine history, when the great-great-great-grand-dam of his step-brother's sire is recorded as saving the life of one of the great leaders of the warfare of that day, by holding a conversation with an authorized agent from the Great Commander of the Universe, in a walled lane, whereby she saved her master from the sword by her perceptive faculty and vocal ability.

"Our patriotic mule's only *quasi* paternity known to fame is that of the great-great-grand-sire of his step-sister, when, as also recorded in divine history, an eminent warrior took the musical portion of his anatomy, and slew a thousand Philistines.

"It is quite probable that these two demonstrations of the vocal ability of these senior kindred ancestors so discouraged this race by non-appreciation, that they were lost to history until there came the call for volunteer soldiery. Then the commotion commenced, and the cry went forth for transportation.

"Down in the 'blue grass' region, from that soil upon which the great commander-in-chief of all the American armies first saw the light of life, came forth also Balaam's faithful servant of yore,—this patriotic volunteer, ready to bear the greatest burdens and support a tottering nation in its trying ordeal for life.

"When this demonstrative patriot came forth, bestrided by the 'great mogul' of the army, that talented linguist,—he to whom all of the army were subservient, the Jehu,—as he threw his leg over the 'off cuss,' and pulled the check line; do you remember, comrades, how those little fellows in the lead who had known no service, twinkled their eyes and wriggled their ears in anticipation of becoming a prominent force in maintaining the dignity of this great republic; and then when the welcome sound was vibrated from hill top to hill top, and came rushing through the valleys, 'I'se coming!! I'se coming!!!' and the cracker line was opened? And do you likewise remember, as in the exuberance of joy you caressed this patriot, how he, with his pathetic acknowledgement, winked and blinked his eye and wagged his ear? I tell you, comrades, such history must and will be preserved.

"But the order of 'About—face!' came,—then the trouble commenced. Our mule was *par excellence*, the true ideal of independence, of pluck, of endurance, and of power; always ready to advance with the usual speed as dictated by *his* judgment, but always adverse to a retreat, as requiring too much haste and accompanying excitement, which caused a contraction of the nerves along the spinal column, and made a rear view a decidedly precarious position to maintain. It was clearly demonstrated that his majesty, the army mule, instead of the cowardly eagle, should have been selected as our national bird of freedom.

"While with the critical judge he would hardly compare with the king of the forest, or 'Mary's little lamb,' nevertheless he is an animal of imposing presence and commanding great respect from the rear.

"When at the close of the war at the grand review in Washington, who demonstrated his patriotism *so loudly* as the veteran army mule?—standing at the street corners, and nodding his head from left to right, calling your attention to the scars of war from collar-gall to breeching-blister, and articulating in his sadly musical voice:

"'Good-bye, my lover, good-bye.'"

CAMP-FIRE XII.

BUSHWHACKING—WHAT CIRCUMSTANCES DO WITH CASES
—A JEST ON GEN. A. J. SMITH—FORAGING.

PERHAPS the most inexcusable practice in all the Civil War was that of "bushwhacking." The " bushwhacker" was not a soldier, but a cowardly, contemptible battleman who never carried on hostilities unless he was unopposed. His name portrays his true character. He generally prided himself on his skill in playing his *role*. Around the flanks of armies, on the march and in the camp, could be seen his suspicious figure peddling sundry goods to the soldiers during the day,—much to the disgust of the sutler,—and at night he would lie in ambush to kill some unguarded traveler, simply for the plunder he could obtain.

The " bushwhacker " was somewhat similar to the guerilla, except that he sometimes had a smooth side to his character, which would permit him to walk among the soldiers in daylight, and acquire such information as would aid his despicable designs at night. Again, he never grew bold, like the guerilla, but generally perambulated alone in thickets and obscure places, invariably keeping near a safe retreat. However, there is one consolation in the recollection of him, even though it was the result of selfishness; he was broad-minded in his theft, stealing from all armies alike, yet like the mountaineers of old, he " never took anything which he could not carry off."

But his marksmanship was good. Many a poor sentinel who went forth to die in the front ranks of a great battle in the war, found an unprovoked and untimely death at the instance of a "bushwhacker's" musket, with nothing but the quiet stars to witness the atrocity.

It is beneath the dignity of the Society for the Preservation of Unpublished History to place in its honored annals any panegyric on the "bushwhacker"; but he was a part of the war, just as vermin were a part of prison pens, and for once the S. P. U. H. felt like calling itself the "Society for the Persecution of Unhung Heroes." However, an incident by Mr. S. W. Rodgers of the 113th Ohio Volunteer Infantry will show how the "bushwhacker" sometimes received his desert:

"While a portion of the army was lying at Franklin, Tenn., in the spring of 1863, a number of Johnnies were encamped at Spring Hill, only six miles distant. There had been considerable skirmishing between the two armies, and bushwhacking on all sides; and a certain picket post in Grass Creek valley, just where the skirmish line crossed the stream, was being molested continually.

"Accordingly one night, a brave, stout young fellow was posted there, who was thought equal to any emergency. He kept quiet for a time, but finally perfected a scheme in his mind to entrap the wary bushwhacker who disturbed the place. He made the outline of a man with some sticks, then threw an old coat over the frame, and with a long stick as a substitute for a gun at support, the bogus sentinel was ready to receive the bushwhacker's bullet.

"There were two or three other boys besides the sentinel waiting to assist in capturing the bushwhacker, if their aid should be needed. All hands were not much more than well hidden before 'Whang!' went the bushwhacker's bullet through the supposed sentinel at his post. At the crack of the gun, the young fellow who had been ordered to the post started on a lively race through the brush, and before he had gone many yards he succeeded in overtaking the bushwhacker, and laid his strong arm on him.

"'Come on, boys,' called the sentinel to his comrades 'I've caught the rascal!'

"The bushwhacker had not a word to say. He was taken to a spot where the moonlight could shine full in his face, and was found to be a person who lived near the camp, and had peddled pies, milk, bread and cakes to the soldiers that very day. He had preached sometimes in the neighborhood, and pretended to cover his dark career with the meek and lowly garb of Christianity. But alas!

> "'Truth, crush'd to earth, shall rise again:
> The eternal years of God are hers;
> But Error, wounded, writhes with pain,
> And dies among his worshipers.'

"The result was that summary punishment was meted out to this despicable man at the hands of the outraged soldiers."

There was another class of preachers with the army, however, who were somewhat more sincere in their duties, as the following will show:

"There were but few comrades in Kilpatrick's cavalry who did not know Chaplain Cartwright, of the 92d Illinois, for he was one of those men who are always doing something to help the condition of the boys. I remember when he first joined the regiment at Franklin, Tenn. He seemed to be boiling over to assist the boys, and many a surviving comrade can testify to the untiring efforts of Father Cartwright in alleviating their sufferings while lying in a hospital tent, or upon the march.

"The first march we took after he joined us was from Franklin, Tenn., to Triune. It was in the spring of the year. The sun shone brightly, and the boys were loaded down with winter clothing, which they soon threw by the roadside, some casting off everything except their ponchos. The good old chaplain came riding along, and seeing so many blankets, blouses, shirts, etc., jumped off his horse and began to pack the animal with these various articles of clothing, saying to himself, 'My boys will be glad to get these articles when they go into camp to-night. If I only knew to whom they belonged, I would take them to their tents.'

"The aged man trudged along all day, leading his horse, and when he came into camp that night, his old horse looked like a traveling pawnshop. It is needless to say that the faithful chaplain had no trouble whatever in finding owners for every article of value,—in fact, he could have disposed of an army wagon load. A smile lit up his countenance while the boys were unloading the horse, and he remarked that he wished he had a cargo to give them, for he found the reward for his labor in the gratitude that was visible on every face."

A soldier in the (late) command of Gen. A. J. Smith, who well understood the General's character, then told this:

"In December, 1862, while Sherman's army was moving down the Mississippi River on transports to attack the Confederate stronghold at Vicksburg, the supply of fuel became somewhat limited, and we were obliged to obtain that necessary article wherever opportunity offered, sometimes at a deserted wood-yard, at other times from the dry rail fences of the rich plantations which were too tempting for the pilots to pass by.

"These occasions were hailed with joy by the men, as they were enabled to leave the close quarters on board for a ramble upon *terra firma;* and although they were required to assist in 'toting' the wood or rails to the steamer, few, if any, held back, but all were anxious to get what little exercise such occasions afforded.

"On one of these halts, the steamboat which was partly occupied as the headquarters of Gen. A. J. Smith, whose many eccentricities were widely known throughout the division, effected a landing immediately in front of a beautiful plantation, upon the right bank of the river. The plantation house, one of those grand old Southern homes, was situated about forty rods back from the river, with a beautiful lawn gently sloping down to the bank, studded with semi-tropical trees and foliage plants, while at one side in the rear of the house were the outbuildings, around which were plainly seen a large number of chickens and larger poultry, which were the only animate objects to be seen upon the premises.

"I presume that every old soldier will bear me witness that there is nothing in their experience which so sharpens a man's appetite for chicken as a few days' steady diet of hard tack and bacon, and the men upon the General's boat were no exception to the rule; hence as they filed off the boat after rails, occasionally a man was seen to visit the neighborhood of the above-mentioned out-buildings, and when he returned with several rails upon his shoulder, a large protuberance was noticeable under the breast of his overcoat.

"While standing upon the upper deck of the boat, General Smith had noticed a commotion among the chickens, and immediately his ire was aroused to a towering height. He descended to the boiler deck with all promptness and gusto, and with drawn sword in his hand, required the men as they came on board to unbutton their overcoats and surrender their coveted plunder. In a very few minutes there were lying at the General's feet some dozens of chickens, while his eye showed that he keenly enjoyed the disappointment of the men who reluctantly relinquished their prizes at his stern command.

' Presently a man came on board, bringing an unusually large load of rails, whose coat had the appearance of the others who had come to grief.

"' What have you under your coat?' gruffly demanded the General.

"'Well, General, if it makes no difference to you, I had rather not tell.'

"'*Unbutton your coat, sir!*'

"'I had rather not, General.'

"Raising his sword in a threatening attitude, the General yelled at the top of his voice:

"'UNBUTTON YOUR COAT! d——n you, or I'll open it for you!'

"The soldier now saw that the General meant business, and in all meekness replied:

"'Well, General, if I must I *must*,' and in a hesitating manner he slowly unbuttoned his coat, when, to the General's surprise and great disgust, there dropped down a huge billet of stove wood.

"'Sold, *by G——d!*' said the General, and he turned on his heel, walked up into his cabin, and left the boys to enjoy their chickens as best they could."

[It was with some hesitation and considerable disturbance of the finer feelings of the Society for the Preservation of Unpublished History, that they consented to place any profanity upon their sacred scroll; but it was argued that this dialect was so very characteristic of *some* soldiers and officers that their quoted language would be incomplete without it. When, however, in the course of human events it becomes necessary for the society in its diction to contend with these useless expressions, their historic minds revert to a lecture once given by a prominent but profane general in the war, who was indeed superabundant in his profanity. The general was a very interesting speaker, and proceeded to the delight of the audience until near the close. He related many humorous incidents in the earlier part of his discourse, and finally came to the pathetic side of army life. He told of the sufferings in the prison pens, and of the touching experiences there. Then he came to "homesickness," and remembered an incident of a young soldier who had been in camp for some time along the malarial Chickahominy, and longed to return home. The soldier had fully realized the hardships of war, and could well repeat Longfellow's sweet "Psalm of Life." The general here thought he would give the words, and believing that he had the "Psalm of Life" so well committed to memory, he allowed his mind to wander on in the course of his lecture, while he trusted his vocal organs, unthoughtfully, to pronounce it.

"'Tell me not, in mournful numbers,
Life is but a d——d dream,'

said the vocal organs, much to the astonishment of the general's ears and all others who heard the mistaken utterance. Well understanding the general's character, the audience burst into applause. When the merriment subsided, the general apologized for his error, and though he had previously prided himself on the forcible and fearless language of his everyday life, he then and there declared that that was the last time he would ever use profane language.]

The following was then told before the camp-fire, by one of the boys who took part in the experience:

"On the night of Dec. 31, 1863, two members of our Company,—K, 92d Illinois,—passed the pickets at Huntsville, Ala., and started for the Matthews Plantation, to ascertain whether any forage was lying around loose. Upon entering the gate several shots were heard in the direction of the negro quarters, and we feared that bushwhackers were near, so we made a reconnoissance, and soon discovered that the darkeys had secured some of our metallic cartridges, and were celebrating New Year's eve by throwing them into a bonfire.

"This was a great relief to us, but while we were talking to the darkeys a new danger threatened. The old gate again swung upon its hinges, and eight mounted men came upon us. Of course we thought they were Johnnies, and they passed the same compliment upon us. It was quite dark, so we could not tell from the uniforms whom we were addressing. They asked us:

"'Who *are* you?'

"'Yanks,' we said.

"'Where do you belong?'

"'To the 92d Illinois Infantry;' then it was our turn, and we asked:

"'Who are *you?*—cavalry from the 1st Ohio?'

"'Mathematically correct,' they said; 'how did you know it?'

"'Oh!' we replied, 'your regiment went through Huntsville to-day.'

"Then they got off and felt us from head to foot to make sure that we had told them the truth. When they were convinced they asked us again:

"'Where are you bound for?'

"'Foragin',' we replied.

"'All right; let's proceed to business, boys,' they said; and in less time than it takes to tell it, we were making selections from a stock of well-cured hams which were stored in the smoke-house. From there we proceeded to the house, upon entering which the Ohio boys began to pillage. I protested; and, being the only person in the crowd who wore a blue overcoat, the folks thought I was an officer, and appealed to me:

"'Do you allow your men to commit depredations of this kind?'

"'No,' I returned, 'I would not if I had any control over them.'

"'Are you an officer?'

"'No,' I answered.

"'Well, will you regard a protection?'

"'It depends upon who gives the protection,' I said.

"'Colonel Alexander,' they replied.

"By this time the boys were up-stairs, ransacking the house, and I told the folks that I would go up and use my influence to have them stop; and here is how I succeeded:

"'Boys,' I said, 'this must be stopped; these folks have a protection from Colonel Alexander, commanding the post at Huntsville.'

"'Who in h—l is *he?*' asked one of the Ohio boys.

"'Say, 92d,' said another, 'don't you want some sugar?'

"'No, boys,' I replied, 'I don't want anything when we get it this way.'

"'Ha! ha! ha!' they laughed, 'you're no forager,' and just then one of them secured a pair of linen pantaloons, tied up the ends of the legs, told the boys to scoop in some sugar, and when it was well filled, he threw it across my shoulders with the remark:

"'Here, try some of our best brand of Southern sugar.'

"I confess that I did hump my shoulders a little to keep it from sliding off, and when I thought of taking to camp enough sugar for the whole company, my moral nature gave clear away, and I allowed the pantaloons full of sugar to remain around my neck.

"We began to depart, one by one. We filed down the stairs, while the family were at the bottom, anxiously awaiting the return of the supposed officer. They were in some distress, and as we passed out with our pillage, they began to cry. It was really pitiful, but nevertheless ludicrous, as they began to lament:

"'*Oh!* there goes poor uncle's boots!'

"'Yes, an' there goes poor uncle's coat,' said another.

"'An' there goes poor uncle's hat. *Oh! oh!*'

"'An' there goes poor uncle's pants,' they said, as I passed out. 'He's been dead five years, an' ef his sperit knowed what was goin' on, it 'd make him turn over in his grave. *Oh! oh!*'

"It is needless to say that I did not stop to report my success in persuading the boys to leave the premises.

"We now had meat, flour, sugar and coffee; and there were about 150 hives of bees in the yard, so we thought we would take along a little honey.

"The 1st Ohio boys were veterans at this business, and while I was using my thumb and finger trying to get the honey without being stung, they had filled their vessels. One of them grabbed my hand and said:

"'See here, 92d, I'll show you *how to take honey!*' and with that he smeared my hands all over with the sticky stuff, and continued:

"'Now go in for it.'

"My comrade and I had two vessels,—an eight-gallon jar and a long butter bowl. We very soon filled these, and were then ready to bid farewell to the Matthews Plantation. I took the jar of honey and 'poor uncle's pants' full of sugar, and my comrade had the butter bowl full of honey, and some other things.

"We then said 'Good-bye' to our Ohio companions, and started for Huntsville. The night was very dark. A drizzling rain set in, and in passing through the woods we lost our way. I got off my horse and felt around for the road, but could not find any. I told my comrade to follow me, and I believed I could come out of the woods all right. We had not gone far, however, before my comrade began to indulge in profanity to an alarming extent.

"'What's the matter?' I asked.

"'Matter! the pommel of my saddle has punched a hole in the bottom of this bowl, and this honey has run all over me! Why, blast my buttons! if the stuff hasn't glued me to my saddle!'

FORAGING.

"'Ha! ha! ha!' I laughed.

"'What shall I do?' he asked angrily

"'Why,' I told him, 'if you are glued to your saddle, the only thing you can do is to sit still until I can get you out.'

"'Curse this foragin' business, anyhow; curse war; curse everything; it all goes wrong,' he said.

"'Throw the stuff away,' I suggested; and with many regrets he flung it against a tree, but this left us eight gallons still.

"We passed on through the woods, and finally reached the picket, who asked us who we were. We told him where we belonged, and that we had been out that day scouting and picking up salt (which was true); that we had got lost from our command. He let us pass, and we reached camp at 4 o'clock A. M. We learned that the orders were to march at 6 o'clock; but we treated the whole company to the honey and sugar, and I shall never forget how the boys cheered us on the success of our first lesson in foraging."

"Son J. H." then contended that soldiers were "creatures of circumstance," in the following language:

"I believe that we are in a very large degree creatures governed by circumstances. This was plainly demonstrated to my mind while I was in the army. I was a boy of but nineteen when I enlisted. My parents very much disliked to have me go, but finally gave their consent if I would go with Mr. S.

"This Mr. S. had been my school teacher the year before, and I very readily agreed to that; so we went off together with sixteen of the neighborhood boys.

"The object my parents had in wanting me to go with Mr. S. was two-fold: (1) he was a near neighbor, and (2) they thought his influence would help to keep their son J. in the path of right doing. All was very well until we were on the march with General Fremont in Missouri. Provisions became very short, and then it was that this son J. (with others) thought about the wicked practice of foraging. For this purpose we visited a hen-house one evening, but alas! how circumstances were against us. We found the door barred, and two large Southern hounds tied on the inside. But, determined not to be outdone, we changed our plan of attack. We concluded for the time to be honest, and go in and ask for some of the chickens. We did so. The old man was very kind and glad to give us two as a reward of merit for being honest and asking for them.

"Now we went from that hen-house across the way to another where the circumstances were different,—no dogs on the inside, but plenty of fat chickens. We mounted a rail fence which joined the hen-house, and slipping the boards to one side, we put in our honest hand and it brought out eight nice ones. We then went back after the ninth, but an old hen that had been trained gave the alarm, and the circumstances were such just then that we were obliged to make a hasty departure.

"From these and other incidents which passed under my observation, I am inclined to believe that we were governed by our circumstances; at least, we rarely attempted to rob a hen-roost when it was guarded by bushwhackers and bloodhounds."

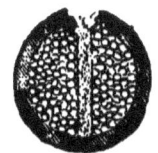

CAMP-FIRE XIII.

BATTLES UNSUNG BY THE MUSE OF HISTORY—ORIGIN OF THE STARS AND STRIPES—GENEALOGY OF GEORGE WASHINGTON.

CAMP-FIRE Thirteen had for its subject the most pathetic part, perhaps, of the whole purpose of the S. P. U. H.—to place garlands of fame upon the brows of unflattered heroes. Accordingly, all who had participated in battles which had never been chronicled upon the papyrus of history were invited to relieve their minds of any unwritten conflicts which they might remember.

Thereupon there was at once great confusion in the assembly. It almost seemed as though, instead of simply relating accounts of these heretofore unheard of battles, the veterans were attempting *to act them out!* But the discipline of the camp was most perfect; and to reduce the chaos to system it was only necessary for the commander, after he secured attention, to suggest that the veterans talk by companies and regiments—one company at a time. Immediately there was harmony, and the accustomed good feeling at once returned.

But the relief was only temporary. It was like a flag of truce or a lull in a great battle in order to bring heavy reserve forces forward for more regular and telling blows. When this reflection presented itself to the ambassadors from the throne of history, their stock of long-suffering was at once exhausted. They suddenly recalled the close of the first camp-fire, when all the veterans present were talked to sleep by *one* man. What would it be now with the oratorical force so multiplied? Truly, Camp-fire Thirteen was an unlucky number. But the lamb submitted to the slaughter. Lighting a fresh " Havana," which the commissary of subsistence had thoughtfully provided in plenty, the historical visitors arranged their dignity for the night, while the commander bade his followers begin their work.

The first step was a motion. It was seconded, whereupon came the resolution:

Whereas, We, the veterans here in camp-fire assembled, desire to preserve for the benefit of posterity the memoirs of our most manifest feats in the " late unpleasantness;" and,

Whereas, There were many battles in said unpleasantness which have been heretofore unrecorded; therefore,

Resolved, That the Society for the Preservation of Unpublished History be hereby petitioned to place the same in its annals.

The same was thereby placed in the said annals, after the several records were related, and the aforesaid memoirs were duly contributed to the society's collection of curiosities.

The first speaker tried his memory, and related an account of a mountain skirmish; but this was found in the official reports published by the Government. In like manner the discussions proceeded until the camp-fire embers were nearly all consumed, and the evening had grown late. Nevertheless, the representatives of the S. P. U. H. noted the minutes of the meeting literally, in accordance with the hereinbeforementioned resolution, until finally one veteran from a Kansas regiment remembered a battle which he was sure had not been recorded in history.

"On the Fourth of July, 1863," said he, " was, indeed, one of the grandest climaxes of the war. The haughty city of Vicksburg fell, and was allowed to come up out of the ground. The bloody battle of Gettysburg was fought, with which two battles the public mind was so occupied that it could not notice the rest of the carnage. But there were other mighty battles fought at that time, one of which was in the midst of a large Western city.

"However, the preliminary to this must be understood. Of course people all over the country were celebrating the day, and our city, in which I had been confined in L——'s general hospital for six weeks, was no exception to the rule.

"To entertain the wounded soldiers, and fill his own purse, an ingenious Frenchman obtained permission from the city authorities to give a balloon ascension at one of the large parks. It was expected to be a grand affair. There were to be other performances in a tent near by, and some rockets were to be sent up, with a further display of fireworks. All soldiers who had enough money bought their tickets at fifty cents apiece, and also those who could borrow money.

"The morning came, and we all went up to the park. On arriving, we found a man there to take our tickets, but very meager preparations had been made to entertain us. The old balloon was torn, and there were holes in it in some places two feet in diameter. The rest of the programme was in a similar dilapidated state of rehearsal. Soldiers are not the people to be deceived or cheated in such a manner, so the boys determined to have the fireworks, at any rate, and they took the thing into their own hands. They tore up things generally around there, and when they left there was not a piece of that balloon large enough for a Comanche Indian's pocket handkerchief. But they kept the rockets for future use.

"We returned to the hospital to rest after our sport, much disappointed. But we had the rockets on hand and a few Roman candles which must be disposed of in some way.

"Just across from the hospital was the Fifth Street market, which we could see from our side of the building that fronted on Broadway. The hospital was located in the worst part of the city, as far as the sentiments of the people were taken into account, for on every side our neighbors were the most bitter 'copperheads.' Some of them had gone to the would-be balloon ascension in the afternoon, and they, too, had Roman candles and sky-rockets. The possession of these suggested to them a new method of tormenting the sick and wounded soldiers in the hospital, so they gathered at dark in the Fifth Street market, together with many other Confederate sympathizers from various parts of the city, and began to bombard us with the rockets.

"Our windows were open, as the evening was very warm, and it seemed as if every rocket that was fired was aimed straight for a window of the hospital. One came square into my window, and would have set my bed on fire had I not been there to extinguish it; and I suppose that it was the same with the other rooms on that side of the building, for I could hear the boys above and below me cursing the 'copperheads' over in the market. Verily, the martial music on this occasion was a prolonged fantasia of profanity. When some of our boys would swear exceptionally loud the bogus Confederates would applaud. This only enraged our boys the more, and they at once declared *war!*

"One of the boys, by the name of Slaughterback, had the courage to call the boys together to materialize their desires, and the lines were formed immediately.

"Our ire was aroused. We determined to vanquish the enemy as quickly as we had the balloon. All who were able to walk came to join our ranks. Some of the boys hobbled out on their crutches, some with one arm in a sling, and others with so high a fever that they could not have rallied from their prostration under any other circumstances. Each one took it upon himself to resent what he considered almost a personal insult. I was so sick that I could not have raised my head on ordinary occasions, but the stimulus to my weakened nerves was so great that I crawled out of my bed to the window just in time to see a battle which seemed to me more magnificent than the 'battle above the clouds.' It was the grandest display of fireworks that I ever witnessed. The Roman candles, with their irregular flashes, gave a glorious effect to a charge at night by men so weakened that in many cases they were scarcely able to stand, while the rockets well represented the 'sky-scraping shells.'

"There were forty of the boys in all who were able to 'rally round the flag.' They had no guns—they were armed with nothing except bravery and Roman candles. But the enemy were still worse off—*they* were armed with only Roman candles! Of course bricks or clubs and many other things were picked up by our boys as they advanced in regular line of battle eager in their obedience to 'Forward—March!' from Commander Slaughterback. On they went, this formidable phalanx of forty! The enemy were greatly superior in numbers; but, alas! they were men who had run from even the draft, much less then, a body of forty trained soldiers on crutches! A few hurled sticks and stones at the regulars as they advanced to the attack, but they kept a steady step, unmindful of the contemptuous thrusts from these 'smaller fry.'

"The main line of the enemy stood nobly, in the hope that they might rout the disabled Federals by a flank movement, for the latter were not reinforced. But the regular step of the Federals seemed so grand and undaunted that, it being their first battle, the overwhelming numbers of the enemy stood aghast; and when the Federals hurled their first volley of miscellaneous ammunition at them it was the 'most unkindest cut of all,' and they fled in dismay.

"So closed, simultaneously with Gettysburg and Vicksburg, the only battle of the war which heretofore has not been described.

INCIDENTS OF THE BATTLE.

"The hero of the battle was Commander Slaughterback. With one arm in a sling, and his whole body weakened from suffering, he kept well forward, and was the first to engage the enemy. As he came near the scene of the encounter one of the enemy bravely advanced to meet him, and with a contemptuous look said:

"'If your arm was not in that sling, sir, I'd thrash your cursed impudence out of you.'

"Come on,' said Slaughterback, clapping his other arm behind his back; 'tie my other arm where it is, and then I'll kick you clear across the street at the first blow, you insignificant coward!' Immediately after which, the fellow beat a precipitate retreat.

"As I beheld in my admiration the grand charge of our boys along the whole line, being too weak to give the old army yell of triumph, I eagerly grabbed my crutch and hammered on the window-frame with all my might. A similar noise came from several of the windows on the front and side of the building, while the forty who had gone forth and conquered the enemy responded with a prolonged cheer."

"As the battle just related occurred on a very proud day for the old flag," said Dr. A.W. Gray, late Adjutant of the 51st Illinois Infantry, " let me give the result, in a few words, of considerable research for the true origin of our flag, and also some points in regard to Washington's ancestors, which may be of interest:

" How often has the American citizen thought whether the design of the United States flag signified anything of itself, or was simply an artistic accident? Some have one explanation, others another. The common one is, that the white bars typify purity; the red, the blood shed for our nationality; the stars, the individual States, each shedding luster one upon another; the blue, faith in the strength and perpetuity of our government, and, like the azure blue of the sky, overshadowing the entire land.

"But the true origin, and the one now generally accepted is, that it was a design offered by Gen. George Washington himself, and was simply a modification and enlargement of his own coat-of-arms. It is a well-known fact that Washington prided himself upon being a gentleman, as the term is understood in the old country; and that he had a coat-of-arms emblazoned upon the panels of his carriage, embroidered upon his book-mark, and engraved upon his watch seal.

"The first Washington of whom we have any record was one John Washington, of Warton, Lancashire, England, who had a son, Laurence Washington, a London lawyer, who was a partisan and favorite of King Henry VIII.; who moved to Solgrave, County of North England, and was Mayor of Northampton in 1533, and again in 1546; whose epitaph and coat-of-arms may still be seen engraved on a brass plate in the village church at Solgrave.

"When King Henry VIII. seceded from Popish rule and established the Church of England, he confiscated the landed property of the Catholic Church throughout England, and divided it among his favorite followers. To Laurence Washington he gave in 1538 the 'Manor of Solgrave,' formerly the property of the 'Monastery of Saint Andrews,' Northampton. He also gave to him a coat-of-arms, which is thus recorded in the College of Heraldry in London:

"'Arms—Argent, two bars gules; in chief, three mulletts of the second.'

"'Crest—A raven, with wings indorsed proper, issuing out of a ducal coronet.'

"Which being explained means: *Arms*, a shield; *argent*, silver; *bars gules*, red bars; *in chief*, the top part of the shield; *mulletts*, rowels or spurs of knighthood, and are represented by several *five*-pointed stars; *crest*, the ornament that surmounts the shield; *coronet*, a crown.

"This coat-of-arms can yet be seen engraved on the stone over the gateway of the 'Solgrave manor house,' on the brass plate which marks the grave of Laurence Washington and his wife, and also on the plate over the grave of his grandson, Robert Washington, in the church at Brington.

"So much for the coat-of-arms; and now a few words as to how the Washingtons happened to emigrate to America. As before stated, the family were pronounced loyalists, and when Cromwell was made Protector of England he beheaded Charles I., the King. He then persecuted the royal followers, among whom was John Washington, a great-grandson of Laurence Washington; who, to save his life, fled to America in the year 1659 and settled in Virginia, where he died in 1675. John Washington left a son, Laurence, who died in 1697, leaving a son, Augustine, who was the father of George Washington, the first President of the United States—born in 1732 and died in 1799.

When Congress discussed the question of adopting a national flag various designs were submitted for adoption. Washington drew a design of a flag which embodied the essential features of his family coat-of-arms, and had a Mrs. Ross, who kept an upholstery establishment in Philadelphia, make a flag in accordance therewith. The raven was changed to an eagle; the stars and bars were increased in number to one for each of the thirteen colonies, and the blue was inserted as the natural contrast of red. The crown or coronet, emblematic of royalty, was dropped. This flag was the one adopted by Congress, and is the same flag that waves in triumph at Yorktown, New Orleans, the City of Mexico, and Appomattox, and that to-day still waves 'o'er the land of the free, and the home of the brave.'

"And here is the genealogy of the 'Father of his Country': (1) George Washington—the first President of the United States—son of (2) Augustine, son of (3) Laurence, son of (4) John (knighted by King James I., and who came to America in 1659), son of (5) Laurence, son of (6) Robert, son of (7) Laurence, who was twice Mayor of Northampton, and to whom, in 1538, King Henry VIII., granted the coat-of-arms, which, 240 years later, broadened out into the national flag of the United States of America.

"In this connection another interesting fact is discovered: Ferdinand and Isabella of Spain aided Columbus to discover the continent of America; Katharine of Arragon was their daughter, and was also the wife of Henry VIII. King of England, who gave the coat-of-arms to Laurence Washington. So that Spain has the honor of not only discovering America, but also of having a son-in-law who gave her a flag."

CAMP-FIRE XIV.

A ROLLICKING RECRUIT—LOVE AND WAR—THE S. P. U. H. SUTLER—"WHEN GABRIEL BLOWS HIS TRUMPET IN THE MORNING."

HOWEVER lamentable the fact may seem to the self-styled philosophers, the chroniclers of these chats have the cool reflection that this is about the best world they ever lived in. There is sufficient evil to test the energies of the good; plenty of black clouds to make the sunshine all the more enjoyable, and almost enough smiles—those beautiful triumphs of good will toward men—to cheer the melancholy.

And what a blissful thing it was that, notwithstanding the soldiers were all selected, this state of things existed in the army!

Humanity was pretty well represented there, abounding in over a million distinct specimens all told; but none was more praiseworthy than the "funny man" of each company. He was just as necessary as the chaplain; for, while the latter buoyed up the sunken spirits of the soldiers by urging an unfaltering trust, the joker played upon the said spirits latterally by keeping up the ridiculous end of the programme.

Nothing could have been received with more gratitude, in the dull hours of the winter camp, than the exhilarating effect of a real, wholesome, rib-shaking joke; and, though it was a little severe on the boys sometimes, yet they usually recovered and felt well over it, as is illustrated by Mr. Wm. A. Crawley's recollection of a comrade:

"I was fortunate enough to belong to the 10th Illinois Cavalry, and not having to trudge along on foot like the poor infantry men, we seemed never to grow weary, and were standing candidates for anything that promised entertainment for man or beast, while our opportunities and desires for general deviltry and wholesale 'cussedness,' were without any discoverable limit.

"There was one other fellow in our regiment—a pale, slim youth, who enlisted as a recruit in 1862. He had a sad expression of countenance, but, indeed, he was not sad—he was only meditating on some new invention for the production of mischief.

"Crawford was his name, and as soon after entering the service as he became acquainted, he took another young recruit by the name of Boyd 'snipe hunting.' While Boyd held the sack in one hand and the lighted candle in the other, Crawford made a circuit to drive in the snipe.

"Five minutes later Crawford, having put on a Confederate uniform, charged upon Boyd and demanded his surrender. But alas! Crawford had mischosen his man. Boyd was a fellow who would have had no more sense than to fight a whole regiment, and was not the soldier to be intimidated by any *one* opponent. No sooner had Crawford made the demand than Boyd stepped up to him, pulled him from his horse, and began beating him with all his power. However, Crawford finally succeeded, by a great amount of 'moral suasion' and apology, in persuading Boyd to 'let up,' which was done after the latter thought that he had punished his inveigler sufficiently, and peace reigned once more, the two returning to camp together.

"Crawford felt rather sore over the ill success of his first trick, and still sorer over the beating Boyd had given him. He tried to bribe Boyd into silence, but the fellow could not be bought, and the truth soon leaked out. After the facts had become known about the camp, the adventure furnished sport for the boys for a week or more, or until something else took its place, which was not long; for, notwithstanding the severe pounding he had received, which kept him in his tent for a few days, Crawford was not in the least discouraged; and while he was recovering was just the most opportune time to concoct another trick.

"But before he regained sufficient stiength to carry out his project he received a letter from his sweetheart, which moderated his immediate plan of action somewhat. I called on him while he was yet convalescent:

"'Bill,' he said, 'I want you to go to the sutler's and get me a ream of fool's-cap paper.'

"'Why, what can you possibly do with so much paper?' I asked, knowing that his family were all dead, and that he seldom wrote a letter. With a solemn and aggrieved expression on his face he asked again, in reply:

"'Will you go if I tell you what I want with it?'

"'Yes,' I said, 'I'll go; but it's folly to have so much paper lying around. You don't expect to write for the press, do you?'

"'No,' he said, holding his sides, and with great effort suppressing a convulsion of laughter, 'don't make me laugh; I am so lame yet.'

"'Well, what is it?'

"'I'll tell you. I have been writing to a young lady in Peoria, Illinois—as fine a girl as ever admired a brave soldier—and she complains that my letters are *too short*. I mean to write her one that will satisfy her, if it takes all the paper the old sutler has.'

"'Oh, well, now Crawford, don't be silly; don't put butter on bacon. Write her a reasonable letter, and let that settle it.'

"'No, sir, I'll string it out; if *you* can't get me the paper, some one else will.'

"'Oh, I'll get you the paper; but, boy alive! it will cost you ten dollars the way the sutler charges!'

"'I don't care if it costs the next year's wages! I'll write the whole ream full to her,' he concluded.

"'All right,' I replied; 'I'll go for the paper.'

"'Well, here's the money,' he said, giving me a ten-dollar bill; 'and keep quiet about it—the boys have one too many jokes on me now.'

"'All right,' I said, and started off for the sutler's place, feeling confident that Crawford had given me sufficient money to buy the ream of paper and to spare, and that I would soon return. But, to my surprise, I had not over-estimated the sutler's price; on the other hand, I had come considerably below it. The miserly old sutler wanted *fifteen dollars* for that ream of fool's-cap! I succeeded in getting him to reduce the price to twelve dollars, but was unfortunate enough to drop some remark which informed him that it was absolutely necessary for me to have that paper. This settled the matter in the sutler's mind. He would not fall a cent from twelve dollars. So I paid him the price and took the paper, making up the additional two dollars from my own pocket, but said nothing about it to Crawford."

[The narration of this transaction is probably the only proceeding in the history of the chats that was attended by misfortune; and the error was, indeed, practical in its application, for, very unkindly, it directly affected the S. P. U. H. in their paper supply. The society's own, true, integrant, reliable, upright, incorruptible, open-hearted, tender-conscienced sutler, caught an idea from this story; and, spurred on by the promptings of avarice in the human heart, he concluded to increase the cost of the stationery—he, whose fortune they had cherished from its infancy! whose welfare they had spared nothing to look after (when it occasioned no expense)! whose success up to date they had smiled upon with pride!—he, the one whom from all the wide circle of the business world they had chosen for commercial virtue! Verily, Ingratitude has a stone heart, and Mis-Fortune is often clad in gold. It was not the extravagant price per ream that the society must pay for their paper—current price of which is $2.00@$3.00—which now appalled them, but their annoyance was that they must hereafter acknowledge their non-infallibility in judging human nature. Alas! "how much the heart can bear, and yet not break!" But, thankfully, their presence of mind returned, after which the society bore no ill will toward their sutler, for it was not their policy to allow the phenomenon of bad feeling in their existence; and then the sutler was a good sutler—he sold many good things, great among which was bottled good humor. So that the stationery question was the only one to be dealt with now. The society once more reverted to history, and read how Sharon Turner "wrote the third volume of his 'Sacred History of the World' upon paper which did not cost him a farthing," though he drew annually a literary pension of three hundred pounds. His paper consisted of "torn and angular fragments of letters and notes; of covers of periodicals—gray, drab, or green —written in thick, round hand over a small print; of shreds of curling-paper unctuous with pomatum or bear's grease; and of the white wrappers in which his proofs were sent from the printers. The paper, sometimes as thin as a bank-note, was written on both sides; and was so sodden with ink, plastered on with a pen worn to a stump, that hours were frequently wasted in discovering on which side of it certain sentences were written." The S. P. U. H. remembered all this, and concluded that they had read history to too good a purpose not to "wring victory from defeat" in the present emergency. At once they hit upon a plan which possessed two advantages: One in giving discipline to the sutler by withdrawing their patronage; the other in becoming even more historic than the hereinbefore mentioned lord, by using anything which could be written upon, whether paper or not. Of course this scheme gave considerable variety to the material of which the manuscript should be composed, the same including collars, cuffs, shirt fronts,—a practice held over from college examinations, when the students were accustomed to write the answers to all hard questions upon their cuffs beforehand,—boot soles, leather hat-bands, the smooth side of bark from neighboring trees—anything to keep from buying paper of the sutler. Finally the crisis came. One veteran arose, and spoke loud and long. The society's notes were being made very full and complete. The speaker grew more eloquent, and his words fell faster than ever. Every pencil was being pushed to its full capacity. The manuscript now consisted largely of sticks and stones. How the report of the speech was to be kept together could not be considered in the present state of high nervous tension. Not a word must be lost. Then rolled forth with great force the burning syllables of the peroration, at a terrible velocity. What could be done? Everything available for stationery had been used—even the beautiful hands of the members were covered with notes! But, ah! the society must not be overcome by circumstances; hence they hurriedly called up the camp-dog, turned up the inside of one of his ears, and went rapidly on with their labor of love. But from this proceeding another difficulty arose— misfortunes again came in a pair. Everything went on smoothly enough until the society began to collect and arrange their minutes of this unfortunate camp-fire, when alas! the canine had fled, with the notes still untranscribed from his ear; hence if these chats seem incomplete, the cause is hereby made apparent. Then it was, to be sure, that the society began to feel some sympathy for the poor printers who must needs "follow copy."—Furthermore, notice is hereby given that, if any one may find a camp-dog with "page 184" written upon the inside of his left ear, a favor will be conferred upon suffering posterity by returning the same to this camp-fire. No questions will be asked, nor any reward paid, as that would tend to accumulate a stock of dogs around the fire, which proceeding would be unhistoric, inglorious and undesirable, except when rations were short. And, still further, be it known that not only his left ear, but also the entire lost dog is copyrighted, and therefore cannot be used for anything else until the expiration of twenty-eight (28) years, at which time, it is thought, he will be valuable only as a relic for the museum of the S. P. U. H., since he had already reached the age of discretion.]

"As soon as I returned," continued Mr. Crawley, "Crawford began to cut each leaf of 'fools-cap' lengthwise in the center, pasting the two strips thus obtained together, then combining the double strips until he had a string of paper seven hundred forty-six yards, two feet long, when he began to write." [This letter is in the society's collection.]

"The letter discussed a great variety of topics, and was embellished with numerous original pen etchings intended to more fully elucidate the various subjects discussed. While he was at work on this lengthy epistle I frequently visited him in his tent at night. One evening I asked:

"'What do you think the postage will be on your stack of nonsense?'

"Upon which he burst into an uncontrollable fit of laughter, replying that he would not allow that to keep him from sending the letter now, after he had spent so much time in writing it, and preparing the illustrations. He paid the postage on the letter, but would never tell me how much it was.

"Well,' said I, " I must be going back to my tent—I also must write home to-night.'

"'If you'll wait a minute I'll read you the last *sentence* of the letter.'

"'All right,' I replied.

"'Well, here it is.' Then he read:

"* * * 'And now, my dear Angelica, I can tell you that I am very happy, because the assurance dawns upon me that I am near the end of my paper; and I have only to say that, after I have been through the usual number of pitched battles, long, weary marches, and narrow escapes; and have at last completed this letter,—the climax of all my toil and hardship,—if you are not satisfied with the length of it, I will come home as soon as our business at the front is finished, and, trusting that my affection for you will have increased sufficiently to warrant our marriage, will have the ceremony performed; and then you shall obey me when I order you to assist me in writing you a letter of sufficient length.

'Wearily yours, C.'"

Mr. Crawley resumed: "Sometimes, when we were making a forced march, day and night, with trouble ahead of us, the column would halt for a few minutes, to allow our trains and howitzers to 'close up.' We generally dismounted to rest ourselves and horses, when some of the men would throw themselves upon the ground; or, sitting with their backs against a tree, with rein in hand, would endeavor to catch a moment's sleep before the shrill notes of the bugle sounded the advance.

"This was Crawford's opportunity. With a large tree branch under his arm he would rush across the body of some sleeper, stamping his heels in the earth, and crying:

"'Whoa! Whoa!'

"Supposing that a horse with something tied to his halter had broken loose and was running over him, the awakened soldier would jump up, throw his arms wildly about him, and sometimes run several yards, joining in the cry, before realizing the farcical situation, when he would return rubbing his eyes, with chagrin, discomfiture and rage depicted on his countenance.

HALT ON THE MARCH.

"Of course this made some sport for the comrades, and was not always consonant with the feelings of the victimized soldier; but pouting in the army, as elsewhere, proved very unprofitable, so that serenity soon prevailed again."

Mr. C. F. Matteson then related this:

"The regiment to which I belonged (17th Illinois Infantry) spent part of the summer and most of the fall of 1861 in tramping over the hills and through the swamps of Southeastern Missouri; and it is hardly necessary to say that to an Illinois boy, this part of the State did not appear quite as near to Paradise as to the other place. The regiment was finally stationed at Cape Girardeau for winter quarters. During the winter many of the boys fell sick with that greatest scourge of the army, the measles. Among the sick was one 'Bob,' full of the dryest wit imaginable. Bob was *very* sick; so much so, that we thought he would 'turn up his toes to the daisies'—a poetic form of saying that one was going to the Great Hereafter. I was a sergeant in his company, and as such it was one of my duties to visit the boys, and in cases like his to learn, if possible, what disposition they wished made of their personal property; also to take any last message for their friends at home, and to say to those friends that Johnnie or Jimmie was the 'best, most faithful, honest and obedient soldier in the company,' and that since he was gone we did not know how we should get along without him, etc., etc. As Mark Twain says, 'It soothed them,' and did not hurt us at all. Well I had received Bob's 'last will and testament,' what I was to say to the boys for him, bade him good-bye, telling him to keep a stiff upper lip, that I would have the whole company come down when we 'planted' him, which should be done in the best style, and started for the door, when the nurse called me back, saying, 'Bob wants to tell you something else.' I returned to the cot, and inquired,

"'Well, Bob, what is it? Is there anything else?'

"'Yes, Charlie, I wish'—and he spoke very slow and labored, with a pause after almost every word;—'I wish—you—would tell—one thing more for me.'

"'Of course I will,' I said; 'what is it?'

"'I wish you would tell 'em, when they *plant* me, to place me with my face down, my head to the east, and a clam shell in each hand.'

"'All right,' said I, 'I'll do it.' Now I knew if I did not ask him why he wanted to be buried so, it would be the death of him in less than an hour, as there is nothing more fatal than an undeveloped joke. 'But why so, Bob?' I asked.

"'Well, I think, Charlie, if old Gabe would put off that horn business of his a reasonable length of time, I could tunnel through under the Mississippi, and come up from Illinois, for I'd hate like h—l to rise from Missouri.'

"The relieved and satisfied smile that crept over his tired face, and the merry twinkle of his eye, satisfied me that Bob's request would not be complied with then. He served out his full term of enlistment, and still lives in the State that he was so anxious to rise from. I think that the effort saved his life."

CAMP-FIRE XV.

THE RACE FOR COLUMBIA—"TO AMPUTATE, OR NOT TO AMPUTATE?"

"OF all the various organizations," said Mr. F. Y. Hedley, Adjutant 32d Illinois Infantry, A. A. A. G., 2d Brigade, 4th Division, 17th Army Corps,—"whose united effort preserved to us nationality, none affiliated so heartily or trusted each other so completely, as did the 15th and 17th Corps. They were the Siamese Twins of the army. Together and at the same moment they came into being; side by side they grew to sturdy manhood, and marched and fought until peace smiled approval upon them, and fame proclaimed their glory. Their regiments had gathered at Cairo in the early days of the struggle; as divisions they had fought at Donelson and Shiloh; and when they came to be army corps they bore their full share of the hard struggle at Vicksburg. In the grand movements about Atlanta they were the whip-lash of the army—snapped hither and thither, from flank to flank, marching by night to reach a new vantage ground, whereon to fight by day. In the memorable March to the Sea, and the raid through the Carolinas, their services were most conspicuous. And then the end came, and they marched proudly side by side down the streets of the national capital, cheered by all Christendom.

"The dramatic brilliancy of the achievements of these superb commands had a fitting counterpart in the phenomenal ability of their chiefs. Grant had personally commanded these troops before their organization as corps. He it was who gave them their identity, and selected their commanders. At first, the 15th Corps was led by the brilliant Sherman, and the 17th by the peerless McPherson, both of whom were speedily promoted, giving place respectively to Logan and Blair, who were regarded by their troops with admiration and affection. They were instinctively recognized as conspicuous types of the volunteer soldier whom too many of the West Point martinets affected to despise. Their men had heard them on the hustings in political campaigns, and knew them. Logan had fought with a musket at Bull Run; in turn he had commanded regiment, brigade and division, and his magnetic presence and soldierly bearing had given them confidence in many a struggle. Blair had organized the free soilers of St. Louis while Sumter was yet being fired on, throttling rebellion in Missouri, and saving Illinois and Indiana from the fate of Kentucky and Virginia, and afterward commanding in the field with courage and marked ability. The great prestige of their first chiefs, Sherman and McPherson; the conspicuous services and the similarity in the careers of their later commanders, and the coincidences of their own history in the field, gave to these commands an *esprit de corps* and a feeling of comradeship which was wonderful, provoking friendly rivalries which led to extraordinary effort in battle and march, and of which this sketch may serve as an example.

"Sherman's army lay grouped about Savannah from the occupation of the city a day or two before Christmas, 1864, until the middle of January, 1865, when a movement upon South Carolina began. The 14th and 20th Corps and a part of the 15th moved by land to the vicinity of Beaufort; the remander of the 15th and the entire 17th were transported from Thunderbolt Inlet by water. After a sharp engagement a lodgment upon the Charleston railroad was effected in the vicinity of Pocotaligo. January 30 the march for the interior commenced, and on February 3 Mower and Giles A.

Smith, with the 3d and 4th Divisions of the 17th Corps effected the passage of the Salkehatchie, wading and swimming that stream and its indescribable swamps, in the face of a fierce resistance by the enemy. On the 6th the 15th Corps was at Bamburg, on the railway between Augusta and Charleston, and the 17th Corps at Midway, a few miles further east. To this time, the objective point was unknown to the troops, and as the stations named were about equi-distant from Augusta and Columbia, there was much conjecture as to the route to be pursued. Four days later, the 17th Corps crossed the South Edisto after a brisk engagement, and on the 12th, after more sharp fighting, Orangeburg was occupied, the 15th and 17th Corps having crossed the main branch of the Edisto about the same time. Then it was realized that Columbia lay in the line of march, and the fact was regarded by the troops with unusual interest. They recognized Columbia as being of a verity ' the hot-bed of rebellion,' the birthplace of nullification and secession, and that its occupation was properly to be regarded as a triumph more significant than the capture of Richmond itself. These views were peculiarly current in these two corps, whose route was evidently nearest in line with the city; and the men of the two commands commenced to observe movements with a rare degree of interest and expectation. On the 13th all four columns, pursuing parallel roads, were headed toward Columbia, about forty miles distant. The 17th Corps had the inside line, on the right of Cawcaw Swamp. The 15th was to the left, and had a somewhat more direct route, but more difficult on account of the passage of several small streams. On the 14th but little distance was made, both these columns meeting with stout opposition. The 15th, however, managed to forge ahead a little, and reached a point about twelve miles below Columbia. On the 15th, that corps was sharply engaged, while the 17th had less trouble and made a march of fourteen miles, getting well in line with its rival. That night the enemy fiercely shelled the camp of the 15th Corps, wounding a few men.

"The next day, February 16, both corps broke camp early and after making a march of twelve miles drew up on the west bank of the Congaree River, just below the confluence of Saluda and Broad Rivers. On the opposite side, on ground gently sloping to the river, lay Columbia, its wide streets and beautiful buildings making a handsome picture. The imposing walls of the new capitol, yet unfinished, rose in massive beauty, and near it stood its less conspicuous neighbor, the old capitol. Up the river a short distance, and on the same side, was a water-mill, which proved to be full of rebel riflemen, who, finding a conspicuous mark in a large gray horse upon which the adjutant of the 32d Illinois regiment was mounted, fired a volley at that officer while he was engaged in forming a color-line. Three men in his vicinity were wounded by this fire. A few shots from one of the famous little Rodman guns of Clayton's 1st Minnesota Battery knocked the water-wheel to pieces and set timbers a-flying at so lively a rate that the riflemen tumbled out and scampered away like rats from a burning barn. About the same time a battery of Parrott guns threw a few shells into the city, and dispersed a crowd of people plundering the rebel commissariat. It was while these events were transpiring that General Sherman rode up and examined the city through his glass, then remarking to General Belknap, afterward (Secretary of War) commanding the 3d Brigade, 4th Division, 17th Corps, that he 'would appreciate the men who first made a lodgment in Columbia.' That night the 15th Corps passed to the left of the 17th, under orders from General Sherman to effect a crossing of Broad River, three miles above, and enter the city from the north; and while this movement was in progress General Belknap was devising a plan for carrying into effect the hint let drop by General Sherman.

"After a conference with Lieut.-Colonel Kennedy, of the 13th Iowa, the regiment formerly commanded by himself, General Belknap dispatched a party to search for a boat. They were so fortunate as to find a leaky, rickety old scow, and by dint of all-night hard work, under the superintendence of Capt. H. C. McArthur, who had at one time been a carpenter, they succeeded in repairing it to such an extent as to make it tolerably seaworthy. About 10 o'clock on the morning of the 17th, Lieut.-Colonel Kennedy, with twenty men from his color company, and accompanied by Captain McArthur and Lieutenant Goodell, of General Belknap's staff, embarked, and essayed the passage of the stream. It was a desperate undertaking. The current of the Congaree was inconceivably swift, and the route lay across dangerous rapids which would have deterred less determined spirits. But energy and courage were strong in these gallant men, and after several narrow escapes from wreck on the rocks, they landed in safety. Ascending the slope to the town at a double-quick, at a distance of a couple of squares from the river they intercepted a rebel officer making off in a buggy. The officers of the party and their color-bearer took possession of the vehicle and drove rapidly toward the capitol buildings, directing the squad to follow at the double-quick. When within two squares of their destination, Lieut.-Colonel Kennedy and party were fired upon by a squad of Wheeler's Cavalry. Seizing the only gun in the party, Captain McArthur jumped from the buggy and fired at the enemy, now in retreat, unhorsing one of their number. Waiting until the arrival of the remainder of the 13th Iowa squad, Lieut.-Colonel Kennedy went on to the capitol buildings, and displayed his national flag from the old State House, and his regimental banner from the new one. He had been in possession about an hour when an officer of the 9th Iowa from the 15th Corps, rushed up, colors in hand, and breathlessly asked the way to the dome of the old building.

"'You're too late!' hallooed Captain McArthur; 'the 17th Corps has been here more than three-quarters of an hour!'

"An expressive but impolite ejaculation was the only response. A short time afterward, Lieut.-Colonel Kennedy missed his national flag. It had been taken by a member of the 15th Corps, but was restored to its proper owners about a month later.

"To return to the narrative. After Lieut.-Colonel Kennedy's party had accomplished the passage of the river, a party of the 32d Illinois Regiment, also from General Belknap's brigade, boated across, and proceeded on the double-quick to the city hall. The color-bearer was sent to the summit of the tower to display his flag, and the officers in charge, Adjutant Hedley and Captain Richardson, remained in the mayor's office, having been accosted by a citizen there who said that he was a councilman, and that the mayor had gone out to meet the advancing troops and surrender the city. In the mayor's office were found two flags—the rebel stars and bars, made of some coarse woolen stuff, now in the possession of Adjutant Hedley; the other a silk State flag. Captain Richardson tendered the latter to General Belknap, who desired him to retain it, which he does to this day.

"While there is no question of the first occupation of Columbia by General Belknap's command (3d Brigade, 4th Division, 17th Corps) the truth of history demands the statement that the formal surrender of the city was made to Colonel Stone, of the 15th Corps. Major Cramer, of the 30th Iowa, of that command, had rafted five companies of his regiment across the river above the city early that morning, under a heavy fire. He drove the enemy from the outset, capturing several prisoners; and when near the city met a carriage bearing a white flag and conveying the mayor and marshal of Columbia, who tendered a surrender of the city. Colonel

Stone soon came up, and a formal surrender was made to him. He, with Major Cramer, then entered the mayor's carriage, drove to the city, and established a provost guard.

"The part taken by the 13th Iowa was suitably recognized by Gen. Giles A. Smith, commanding the 4th Division, 17th Corps, who issued an order reciting some of the incidents herein narrated, and congratulating Lieut.-Colonel Kennedy, and the men under his command, upon the successful accomplishment of their undertaking. General Sherman had, however, forgotten his remark that he 'would appreciate the men who first made a lodgment in Columbia.' His report acknowledged the formal surrender of the city to Colonel Stone, and only incidentally stated that 'about the same time a small party of the 17th Corps crossed the Congaree in a skiff and entered Columbia from a point immediately west.' But even this had escaped his memory when he wrote his 'memoirs,' ten years later, for he then said 'the 17th Corps did not enter the city at all!'"

Mr. Sol. R. Smith then remembered the following incident, and said:

"At the battle of Antietam, a colonel had his arm painfully shattered, and he was borne from the field of battle by his brothers and a private soldier. They carried him across the country a long and toilsome distance, to the house of a Maryland Union farmer. Every step of the journey was torture to the sufferer, who was indeed in great agony when the party reached the house. Then came the ubiquitous Yankee surgeon, with his glittering knives and cruel saws. and made hasty preparations to amputate the ailing member, The farmer protested vehemently, declaring that the man would die if the arm were cut off. The surgeon insisted, as usual:

"'The patient will be dead before to-morrow night,' said the surgeon.

"'No he'll *not*,' replied the farmer; 'I'll take care of him myself.'

"The surgeon again insisted, saying that he had no time to lose. The colonel's brothers agreed with the surgeon. There was about to be a small war. Again was agitated that great semi-suicidal question which was discussed so practically and tragically in nearly every floating hospital of the Civil War:

> To amputate, or not to amputate? that is the question:
> Whether 'tis nobler in the mind to suffer
> Th' unsymmetry of one-armed men, and draw
> A pension, thereby shuffling off a part
> Of mortal coil; or, trusting unhinged nature,
> Take arms against a cruel surgeon's knife,
> And, by opposing rusty theories,
> Risk a return to dust in the full shape
> Of man.   *   *   *   *   *

"But the determined old farmer dispatched his son on his fleetest horse across the fields to the other side of the mountain after a country physician, who was a friend and neighbor, but a rank rebel.

"When the rustic Esculapius arrived there followed a long contention with the Yankee hewer of bones, the result of which was that the arm was saved, and after some months of careful nursing, the colonel galloped off to join his regiment, a comparatively healthy man. He subsequently became Governor of Ohio, and was afterward elected President of the United States filling the office with credit."

CAMP-FIRE XVI.

"BRAZEN EFFRONTERY"—CORDUROY ROADS—LONG JOHN, THE DARKEY.

SOMETIMES the thread of human life is stretched across the edge of swords sharpened variously; sometimes it is sustained by very little more than the shadow of a circumstance; at other times it is held together by only a simple, single thought—unyielding determination, supported by irrepressible courage.

One incident was related at this camp-fire by Mr. James M. Allen, Company F, 2d Illinois Cavalry, in which "unbridled audacity" saved the lives of four soldiers:

"While Lee's Cavalry was in camp in advance of General Banks' army, at the commencement of his Red River campaign, four of us were very suddenly placed in a peculiar and dangerous situation, about ten miles west of the city of Alexandria, La. Like all the cavalry boys, we became uneasy and restless from our inactivity; so we took a scout on our own account, contrary to strict orders not to go beyond the picket line, as that part of the country was infested with guerillas, who took no prisoners, but shot men down without remorse. Hence, to accomplish our intent we evaded the pickets and went north toward Red River until we struck a corduroy road which ran parallel with the river, crossing a swamp and a bayou. When we reached this road we observed that a larger force of horsemen had recently passed over it going east, as the tracks were fresh. It is very natural to shrink from a mysterious danger, hence we concluded to turn

A CORDUROY ROAD.

back west, cross the swamp and return by another road, since we knew that no horse tracks in that vicinity could have been made by the horses of our boys. We rode up to within three hundred yards of the bridge, when we saw seven mounted rebs standing on picket duty at the further end. They had not seen us, and as we were not in search of either gore or glory, we concluded to retrace our steps to camp. But just as we had come back to the edge of the swamp we saw approaching at some distance a large force of either rebel cavalry or guerillas, who saw us at the same time. Then came the 'rub.' We were between two millstones, but, happily, the one stone was smaller than the other; yet they were both stones, and were rapidly coming together to crush us. To say the least, we were in a sorry plight; water and swamp on each side of us, guerillas and rebel cavalry at each end of us, while action on our part must be immediate and certain.

"I held the command, and of course the boys looked to me for direction. 'Of two evils, choose the lesser'—this flashed across my mind; seven rebel cavalry were less than over two hundred guerillas, so we wheeled around again, put spurs to our horses, and darted forward over the corduroy roads for the seven pickets at the other end of the bridge. The chances were desperate, but when *men* become desperate, *chances* soon yield to the superior force.

"On we went with the momentum of a whole regiment. The pickets at the end of the bridge saw us coming, and also saw us followed by two or three hundred other horsemen, whom they naturally concluded were our allies, judging from the bold front which we presented. We took advantage of this and felt, indeed, that 'fortune favors the brave.' We dashed forward, revolvers in hand ready for use, with a yell that echoed far up and down the cypress swamp. The terror we inspired by the rapidity of our motion, and the fierce determination which we carried with us, needed no additional elements to convince the pickets that we were just exactly what we appeared to be—four desperate men supported by nearly three hundred (enemies).

" The pickets were fierce-looking fellows, however they may have felt; and they seemed to have had no idea of being intimidated, so that immediately upon their discovery of us, which occurred when we were within about two hundred yards of them, they formed in line to resist our progress, and suddenly presented to our view seven of the ugliest double-barreled shot-guns that I ever saw.

" After this achievement any preference of the before-mentioned evils immediately vanished from our advantage. Now it was take the one evil or be taken by it.

" ' Boys, spur up,' I said ' we must go right through 'em, or they'll go through us.'

" ' On we go!' returned one of the boys, and forward we darted with a dash, a splutter and a splash.

" Our horses—trusty fellows—seemed to catch the spirit of the occasion, and as we glided along my voice seemed to become all-powerful as I gave out the solid command:

" ' Surrender! you black miscreants!'

" We were then at one end of the hundred and fifty foot bridge while they were at the other, raising their guns to fire. But our speed was unchecked, and on we went. When we had half crossed the bridge, we flourished our revolvers and I yelled again:

" ' Down with your guns!' and they obeyed. ' Into the river with them,' I continued, and this was also obeyed.

" What a relief it was to us as we saw those guns pitched into the water; and when the splash came I tell you it was the most welcome sound I ever heard!

" There was no time to lose, however, and since they were all mounted we ordered them to wheel about and put spurs to their horses. Two of our party followed close behind them, covering them with revolvers, while the other two rode among them and disarmed them of their sabers and revolvers.

"About the time we had taken the last revolver the guerillas behind us opened fire on us at long range. Then for the first time our captives realized that they had succumbed to a grand successful piece of their own strategy, and began to curse themselves for surrendering. After crossing the swamp we returned to camp with our prisoners, by another road. The rebs followed us hotly right up to our picket line, keeping a constant fire in our rear, but doing no damage; and we returned their fire with about the same effect. When we arrived in camp we turned the prisoners over to the provost marshal, related our experience and awaited the result, fully expecting to be put under arrest for going outside of the lines against orders. But we escaped punishment; I presume the general thought we had suffered sufficiently, and had learned a good lesson."

Gen. H. H. Thomas then said:

"A day or two before the battle of Kriston, N. C., our pickets near that place captured a suspicious darkey, who had been found lurking near our lines. He was an odd specimen, more than six feet tall, lean, 'lantern-jawed,' with a mouth of longitudinous dimensions. He was suspected of being sent out by the rebels to get information, and was kept at General Carter's headquarters, where he made no end of fun for us. Our talk was largely of General Sherman, whose advent was daily expected on his March from the Sea.

"'Long John,' as our captive had been christened by the Chicago member of the staff, was all ears; and we resolved to play a joke on him.

"A rather distinguished looking major, serving on Major-General Cox's staff, happening to drop in, we tipped him the wink and played him off for 'Old Cump,' asking a thousand questions about his march, etc. Long John's eyes protruded like huge saucers; and when we introduced him he struck a theatrical attitude, and saluted the supposed general thus:

" ' Why, bress de Lor', Mars' Sherman, I'se heerd a heap 'bout you! Dey done said you had hawns. Dey done said yo' berd come clar down to heer,' (placing an immense hand on his right hip). 'Dey so feered o' you, Mars' Sherman, if dey heer yo' name tree hundred mile off, dat town's done bin captured.'

" We all shouted, except our extemporized General Sherman, who took it all as stoically as the great chieftain himself would have done.

" We became satisfied of the loyalty of our altitudinous darkey, and released him. When General Sherman joined us at Goldsboro, we related the incident to him, and he was greatly amused, replying that it was the neatest compliment he had ever received."

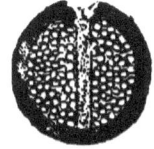

CAMP-FIRE XVII.

LAZY JIM'S STRATAGEM TO AVOID WALKING BACK TO CAMP—"THEY GOT OUR FLAG"—ANECDOTE OF GENERAL SHERMAN.

WITH the kindling of the fagots of this camp-fire the boys assembled in a goodly number, and, chatting with those he knew, the scribe of the S. P. U. H. appeared also, pencil in hand, as eager as ever for the spirit to startle the veterans into active endeavors. The social atmosphere was just as genial, pleasant, and unruffled as ever, save by the memory of the drum corps from the Freedmen's Exodus Society. It is an old saying that if you speak of a certain evil individual, some of his emissaries will appear. But, without even hinting that the application is practical to the case in hand, it may as well be acknowledged that, after the camp had received a communication announcing the return of the said corps, the commander suggested that a change of scenery might be pleasant, and even expedient. The suggestion was adopted without delay; and when the drum corps arrived they beheld, instead of the jolly camp-fire that had greeted them on their previous visit, a scene similar to the appearance of a camp that had been made by the almost traditional " Forty-Niners," on their way to the gold fields of the Pacific slope.

On the other hand, with their usually rapid method of doing things, the veterans and the S. P. U. H. accomplished the change of camp to a secret place in a very short while, and all fear was then allayed. Once more everybody lent a smile and a hearty hand clasp to his comrade, and amid the crackling óf the twigs and branches which the ruddy flames were devouring, many a jest caused a laugh to go round. It was pleasant enough to listen to the witticisms and jokes, but the aforesaid scribe greatly desired a longer story, and agreeably to a nudge, a veteran called on Leonard Oliver, 13th West Virginia Infantry, for a yarn. Taken somewhat aback at the invitation, he pleaded forgetfulness, but a comrade prodded his memory by saying, "Tell us about Jim Frye, Leonard!"

"Well, I can do that if you want to hear it."

"Why, of course," responded several.

"Here goes then. We were camped at Winfield, W. Va., and we had a fellow by the name of Jim Frye in our regiment, who was shiftless, good-natured, witty and — lazy. Partly because of his imperturbable good-nature and partly because he was too lazy to parry the attacks made upon him, Frye became the butt of all the raillery and fun abroad in camp.

"Well, one morning some of the boys were lounging in a store near the suburbs of the town, discussing the probability of the truth of certain rumors afloat to the effect that rebel spies had been seen about the outskirts of the camp, and that various depredations had been committed, in which small stock and poultry had suffered to an alarming extent.

"During the discussion, Frye, who sat astride of the coal box, whittling and spitting at the shavings he made, kept a remarkable silence, all the while eying the floor meditatively, as if he had never considered the fact that pork meant ham, sausages, 'fat, salt and unctuous,' and fowls meant savory stews, and gravy, and various other luxuries not always purchasable in camp—though seldom wanting.

"One of Jim's good qualities consisted of being a hunter. When he felt like it he would sally out with his gun, and seldom returned to camp without having bagged some game. The air had become thick with stories of the rebels and their misdoings in the country, and the people in the neighborhood were in a continual state of alarm, and the troops were kept wide awake, and on the alert.

"It was at this time that Jim announced his intention to his comrades in the store, to go out for a day's hunt.

"'You look out,' called one of the boys, 'or you'll get nabbed and hauled into camp here for a reb!'

"'Dunno as I'd object to that, seein' as the tramp back allers sets hard on me anyways,' answered Jim, as he sauntered off, and, as he went, a person of fine observation might have noted Jim's eyes light up as if the friendly admonition had suggested a brilliant idea to him.

"It was a bright day in February, and patches of snow gleamed and sparkled in the sunlight here and there upon the hills; the air was bracing and almost chilly, but the warmth of the sunshine bespoke soft ground and mud later in the day. Soft fleecy clouds, lovely in their white repose, floated in the blue heavens, and rested lovingly against the great silent hills.

"Jim had a great deal of what we fellows dubbed 'poetry of nature,' and he was not altogether blind as a bat to the beauty around him. Indeed, the day was so serene and delightful, the forest so quiet and restful, and he found the air so exhilarating that he wandered on many miles further than he usually did, in search of game. Once down to work, however, he had no end of luck in filling his game bag. True, the quails kept provokingly shy of him, but woe unto the unsuspecting chicken that came within range of his gun. No matter if the rabbits did go skurrying across the fields. Jim solaced himself with a ten-pound gobbler that strayed up to him. The day had worn pretty well along when the vivid question arose in his mind how to get his spoils into camp, for, as he had averred, the 'home stretch' bore hard on him, and his indolent nature recoiled from the exertion.

"At this juncture, an idea occurred to him, and he forthwith proceeded to put it into execution. The contents of the game bag he secured in a manner intended to disarm suspicion, and defy inspection. This done, he set out for the farmhouse nearest at hand. The worthy farmer and his boys were engaged in unloading a cart in the yard, and they eyed Jim's approach suspiciously, a fact which Jim noted as being propitious to the furtherance of his scheme.

"In accordance with his request, Jim was taken into the house and regaled with 'a cold bite,' after doing justice to which, he casually remarked that he was a rebel soldier, and supplemented his words with the startling announcement that the Confederate troops were within six hours' march of that locality. He also dwelt long and significantly upon the harrowing fact that the rebels were preparing to scatter ruin and desolation through the country and lay waste the farms, burn dwellings and make prisoners of the farmers themselves.

"Jim was not slow to discover that his words had not fallen unheeded. Fear and consternation were depicted upon the faces of those around him, mysterious glances were exchanged between members of the family, and faint whispers betokened suppressed excitement. Nothing loth, Jim seated himself before the fire and awaited results, which, as he fondly hoped, would complete his scheme. He fully expected the farmer and his sons would make a prisoner of him and take him to camp, and as hasty preparations of some kind began in other parts of the house, he felt certain of success.

"There was flitting here and there, and hurrying back and forth through the chambers overhead, and excited consultations were held by the family. He found it hard to repress a chuckle as he waited in momentary expectancy of the desired arrest. But the hours grew apace, and not a finger did the patriotic farmer raise toward making him a prisoner. The bustling and hurrying about ceased, and the house became suddenly and strangely quiet. It was unaccountable, and Jim concluded to investigate matters a little. He peeped into several rooms and finally discovered that the premises were deserted, and it dawned upon his mind that the whole family had given him the slip, and, somewhat crest-fallen, he shouldered his gun and weighty game bag, and set out for the next house to try his joke again.

"Upon arriving at the house he found its only occupant was a purring cat stretched on the carpet before the fire, while the disordered condition of things told him that his story about the rebs had preceded him. Jim began to think that his little plot was no good, and by the time he had gone into several houses along the road he was sure of it, and, tired of stalking from house to house, he set off for camp across the muddy fields, and reached there before 'drill.'

"It was about 4 o'clock in the afternoon that the country folk began to pour into the town of Winfield. By 6 o'clock the town was a stirring mass of anxious looking men, white faced women, and crying children.

"Our colonel was nonplussed. He had made several attempts to find the true cause for the existing state of alarm, but having failed, he took extra precautions and doubled the pickets, all of which had a tendency to augment the excitement. All that could be extracted from any of the coolest headed of the citizens was, that a suspicious looking character had been skulking about through the country, and that he had stopped at the farmhouses and warned the people of the dangerous proximity of the rebels. All the stories differed, but one fact was noticeable, and that was to the effect that the description of the suspicious person was about the same in every instance. The mention of a pair of new blue over-alls conjured in the Colonel's mind the image of 'Lazy Jim Frye.'

"Shortly before nightfall, unlucky Jim put in his appearance. He looked most 'æsthetically weary,' and his new blue over-alls were spattered with mud by his long and tiresome tramp; moreover, it needed no second glance at his habiliments and accoutrements to make sure that they were identical with those worn by the often described individual who had been the cause of the present alarm. A new light dawned upon the Colonel's mind. He ordered Jim to be put under arrest and brought before him. The farmer who had furnished Jim the 'cold bite' identified him as the self-avowed rebel who had frightened him and his family by his story about the rebels, and numerous others said that he was the same man whom they had seen in the woods.

"Jim, seeing that he was in for it, confessed the truth, and told the whole story.

"At 9 o'clock the detachment of cavalry sent out to reconnoiter, returned and reported the country quiet for miles around. The citizens, being assured there was no danger, soon wended their way to their respective homes, and by midnight order and quiet was obtained.

"And Jim! Well, Jim's trouble had just fairly begun. Colonel Brown was too vexed over the affair to allow the offense to pass unpunished, but bless you, you could *never* guess the manner of punishment! It was this: Every day for ten consecutive days, at dress parade, Jim was marched out, accompanied by fife and drum, and after being assisted to mount to his shoulder a hod full of bricks, he was required to carry it up and down before the line of men six times. Jim was an overly modest chap at the best, and to be so made the cynosure of all eyes was too much for him, and being born chronically tired, too, he was fearfully cut up about it.

"Even at this late day I can see poor old Jim's abashed countenance, red and streaming with perspiration as he carried his heavy load up and down, keeping step to the inspiring strains of the fife and beats of the drum, and I can almost hear the banter of his comrades and the laughter with which they assailed his ears.

"'There's nothing like serving yer country, old feller!' a rollicking friend would call out.

"'Well, 'taint all honey an' pie, mebbe, but Lordy, the glory of it!' Jim would reply, and so it went, day after day, until his time was out."

"That's one of the ways to punish a fellow that we had too, comrade Oliver," said one, who sat on the other side of the fire, "but its' nothing to being 'bucked and gagged' for taking a snooze while on duty, I can tell you!"

"By the by," said another veteran, "one of the most heart-touching incidents that occurred during my army life happened with a little drummer boy. There had been some sharp fighting and General McPherson, among others, had been killed. We had been hurried to the field expecting to take part in a great battle, but we didn't arrive in time to do much work, and in an hour or two we were ordered back to camp. While on our way, the captain and I turned off to visit an improvised field hospital which stood among some trees.

"We saw a great many of our boys who were wounded, and among them was a little drummer boy who had been in the fight and had had his leg amputated just above the knee. The chaplain dismounted, and expressed to him his sympathy for the loss of his leg, and tried to soothe the little fellow's feelings, as he was crying bitterly. In reply, the little hero sobbed out:

"'Oh! It isn't that—that's nothing—I—I—don't—I don't care so much about that—*they got our flag*! THAT's what hurts *me.*'"

As the last words of the speaker fell upon his hearers a quiet pervaded the circle about the fire, and more than one eye glistened with unshed tears, as the full force and power of the incident made its way into the hearts of those who heard its narration. It seemed as though a breath from the past had whispered into each ear a vivid recital of the fiendish carnage and brutal cruelty that, like a whirlwind from the innermost regions of hell, swept over our fair land; and each one held his peace and seemed conning the pages of memory where, inscribed in characters dimmed by the blotting fingers of time, were many a tale of bitterest suffering and keenest anguish—many an incident wherein the heroism, that only the love of country can excite, had figured in bold relief.

The silence, however, was soon broken by a battle-scarred individual who carried a musket throughout the entire "unpleasantness." He said, " The only time I saw General Sherman was after we had failed to break Joe Johnson's front at Kenesaw Mountain. It was plain that more flanking must be done, so the ' Great Flanker ' ordered General Cox's division of the 23d Corps to make a detour and threaten the enemy's left.

" This involved a long march, and General Sherman made his way to the top of a high hill, where we were lying, to enable him to overlook the country and see operations better. He sat on a stump with a map spread out on his knees, and was giving General Cox directions as to his line of march. After doing this, he mounted his horse and started away, but after having gone away a little distance he shouted back, ' See here, Cox, burn a few barns occasionally, as you go along. I can't understand those signal flags, but I know what smoke means.' "

CAMP-FIRE XVIII.

MANY WERE CALLED, BUT ONE WAS CHOSEN—A SAD OCCURRENCE — " LET THE DEAD AND THE BEAUTIFUL REST."

DISSOLUTION of the sacred ties of the family, the severe cutting apart of those tender affections which bind the child to the parent, and the life of woe and insatiable sorrow which follow, are among the almost insufferable results of the fierce cruelty of war. These results, too, endure, notwithstanding the benefits they may have, and their constancy does not cease when soulless governments make peace at the close of years of military operations. The sad effects are felt in, alas! too many American homes, even at the present time—now! twenty years since the war! Twenty summers have shed their glowing warmth over the old battle-fields! twenty autumns have shifted their melancholy smoke and sunshine above the sacred cemeteries! twenty winters, with their chilling snows and rains, have iced the tree boughs that droop over far away graves! twenty springs, with their cheering bird-calls, have spread their smiling floral covering, like Charity's peaceful mantle, over all the wide country where the campaigning was; and yet the heart strings then broken will remain unstrung until the soothing hand of death shall softly entwine them for all time.

The verification of this can be multiplied many times; but only one specification need be made here—an incident by Dr. A. Hard:

"The battle of Williamsburg, Va., was fought May 5,

1862. It was the first great battle in which our regiment (the 8th Illinois Cavalry) participated, and as we had never seen any engagement much heavier than a skirmish, of course we were very curious to observe the battle carefully, and also to go over the battle-field after the fight, and witness the desolation wrought. In going over the field an incident occurred which was of such touching interest that I, for my part, never tire of remembering it as among the pathetic incidents of the war.

"A Massachusetts chaplain who had just arrived was among the ones most anxious to go over the field, and in company with our chaplain, Reverend Matlock, soon reached the place where the dead were being arranged in rows for burial.

"A detail of soldiers were bringing the dead from the woods and 'slashings,' and laying them side by side to receive the last sad rite. Other soldiers were identifying and marking them by pinning a card or slip of paper on the breast of each corpse, while still others were digging the long trench in which to place the bodies that were to be covered from sight forever.

"The Massachusetts chaplain informed Mr. Matlock that upon leaving home he had promised Mrs. Benson, a widow lady, that he would look after her boy, Willie, an only son, beloved by a Christian mother and anxious friends, who were awaiting some tidings of his safety.

"'Can you tell me where I can find such a boy?' asked the Chaplain, after describing him.

"'What is his regiment?' asked Mr. Matlock in return.

"'I haven't been able to find out,' responded the Chaplain.

"'Perhaps the regiment you seek is burying the dead yonder,' suggested Mr. Matlock, knowing that it was a Massachusetts regiment then performing that office.

"The chaplain was now in a very trying position. He

hardly dared introduce the subject to the soldiers through fear that Willie had indeed met with some misfortune; but mustering courage, he asked of one soldier:

"'Was your regiment engaged in the fight?'

"'No,' was the gratifying intelligence received in reply; 'we came upon the field just as the battle closed.'

"'Well,' said he, 'I have promised a widow lady to look after her boy, her only support, and the comfort and the pride of her life. I almost feared to ask about him; but knowing that you have not been in the battle gives me relief and more grace to inquire further.'

"'Oh, we had just a little brush with the Johnnies,' returned the soldier.

"'The true presentiment came upon the Chaplain like a flash. He was a strong man and could bravely face the life-destroying fire of the enemy, and call it almost welcome when compared with the severe trial through which he must soon pass. He turned deathly pale as the soldier spoke, and it required a manly struggle to control his feelings. The knowledge that he must meet the anxious, waiting mother with sad news, was very vivid. How like a thunderbolt it would pierce her heart with a wound that could not be healed!

"As the Chaplain hesitated for a moment he attracted the attention of the by-standing comrades, who were also visibly affected; and as his cheeks flushed, and the tears glistened in his eyes, he inquired:

"'Then can you give me any information of Willie Benson? That was his name.'

"'Willie Benson? Yes. We have just buried Willie Benson; he *was the only one of our regiment who was killed or injured!*'"

For a reason which needs no interpreting, the chats suddenly ceased, after the above incident had been related; and all was quiet for several minutes, until a comrade from Company F, of the 78th New York, told this:

" The last incident has reminded me of one that occurred at the battle of Peach Tree Creek, July 19 and 20, 1864. Our regiment was in the fight, and about half an hour before the close of the firing a shot pierced the breast of J. W. Gould, one of my companions, and he fell, breathing his last in a few minutes. He had been a favorite, and of course we could not retreat or leave the spot until we had given him a fitting burial. So three of the boys and myself assumed the sad duty.

" We carried him to the bank of the stream, laid his body upon the grass, and dug him a neat grave. When all was ready a prayer was said, we lowered his body and shoveled in the earth. Then we placed a cypress board at the head and planted a weeping willow over the grave; and when this last rite was performed, we departed, after singing:

"'Let the dead and the beautiful rest;
Make his grave 'neath the willow by the stream,
Where the wind-harps shall whisper o'er the blest,
Like the song of some angel in our dream.

"Oh, so young and fair,
With his bright golden hair,
Let him sleep, let him sleep;
Let him sleep 'neath the willow by the stream.'"

CAMP-FIRE XIX.

A REMINISCENCE OF GENERAL NELSON—A SHAM BATTLE
DEMOLISHES A SUTLER'S STORE.

BRIGADIER-GENERAL I. C. B. SUMAN related an experience at this camp-fire which includes a reminiscence of General Nelson that well illustrates the private soldier's appreciation of the difference between the officer educated at West Point and the self-made commander of volunteers. Said he:

"I recollect an experience which may be of some use to the Society for the Preservation of Unpublished History. At the time of which I speak I was Lieutenant-Colonel of the 9th Indiana Infantry, a regiment as reliable, brave and prompt as was ever mustered into service.

"We had just come from the mountains of East Tennessee with the rest of the brigade,—the other regiments being the 6th and the 41st Ohio,—which was commanded by General Nelson.

"The General had left the navy to take command of this brigade; and, technically speaking, he was well fitted for his office, being thoroughly versed in military tactics, and he also had other qualifications. He was tall, handsome, with black moustache and beard, would weigh three hundred pounds; had a keen eye, and prided himself on his military bearing. Moreover, he was well educated, could speak seven different languages; but withal, he was arrogant, and especially overbearing when he was in liquor. He forgot, like many another officer in the Civil War, that he was commanding *Americans;* that his soldiers had *volunteered* to cast their lives into the balance, that the nation might be saved; that he was ordering around men who could think as well as himself, and that these men could not be lorded over like the regular soldiers who were compelled to serve out a certain term of enlistment.

"General Nelson was right in his purpose to enforce strictly the rules of war, but he often did it at the cost of respect from those who were to win his laurels for him. No doubt it made him angry to see the volunteer soldiers have so many privileges, but instead of submitting with at least an apparent good will, he attempted to ignore these by the strictest discipline.

"Yet he had his favorites, even in companies and regiments. He dressed well himself, prided himself somewhat on his fine personal appearance, and naturally had more admiration for those of the soldiers who kept themselves neat than those who were ragged from hard fighting and rough experience. It must not be understood that we do not like to see soldiers dress well (or anybody else, for that matter), but when cannon balls are cutting men down by the scores, and bullets are clipping off an ear here and a finger there, or breaking a bone in some other place, it is no time for a display of silks and satins.

"The 6th Ohio boys dressed well, and they were good fighters, too; but their good clothes had been furnished in part by contributions from their officers' pockets. It was not possible for all officers to do this, on account of not all having large bank accounts; and we did think that, after we had done our best and bravest on the field of battle, it was a little hard to be the subjects of untimely remarks because of our clothing, which *we* could not make better in any degree.

"We had no enmity toward the 6th Ohio boys, and they appreciated this; but when the superior officers would discriminate against us because we could not make as much display on dress parade, we thought it a little unjust."

General Suman was requested to go into detail somewhat, in order that the object of the incident might not be misunderstood; that it might be exemplary rather than personal.

"Well, to return, our regiment had just come from the mountains of East Tennessee, and indeed, were a pretty rough looking lot. In accurate observance of the laws of war, however, General Nelson prohibited all petty foraging for subsistence. So I told the boys to be cautious about violating the General's orders, but that they might steal all the chickens they could find, so long as they did not get caught at it, and you may know that my permission was more literally observed than were the General's orders, because hungry soldiers must be fed. I believed like Napoleon, that the quickest way to conquer the enemy was to live off of them, and the boys heartily agreed with me, because this was the most satisfactory and most practical.

"Nevertheless, the boys were conscientious, even though they were soldiers. It is not necessary for one to lay down his manhood when he takes up the dress and arms of war; and this sentiment was never better illustrated than in our Civil War. But for some reason the graduates of the military academy failed to appreciate this fact, General Nelson among the rest. He could hardly be taken as an accurate type of this class of officers, yet withal, his course of action, in many respects, made him a good illustration. One particular, however, is certain. General Nelson imposed a very severe discipline which was probably the result of his college training. But his object may have been to force his subordinates into winning greater laurels for himself. In this it would seem that he was ambitious, and that he forgot to pat men on the back instead of in the face. Although from the navy, he failed to realize that

> Ambition is a fearful ship to fight with;
> It tosses man's imagination up
> To the shaky pinnacle of his desires;
> Then lets him fall a flat, insipid thing,
> With only lax, low spirits in his frame.
> It takes away his sleep; it both consumes
> And quickens youthful hearts, which thus grow good,
> Then great.
>
> But still Ambition yields at times,
> And in that weakness is God-given; for,
> When Judgment's captain, and Obedience
> The helmsman, then Ambition is compelled
> To take that safe, though unsailed stream which flows
> In triumph through the ocean of the world—
> Clear of the rocks and reefs of circumstance.
> Then, with a virtuous, well-trained crew,
> She may at will seek her desired harbor.

" Also, General Nelson was very watchful to be sure that his orders were always carried out. Yet one incident occurred concerning which he took the wrong position. As we were marching by a farmhouse, about 4 o'clock one afternoon, two of the boys suddenly concluded to have chicken for supper that night, as there were a large number of fine ones in the barn-yard. The boys remembered my permission, and also remembered the caution about the General's orders. Hence they thought it best to *buy* the chickens this time, provided they could succeed in making the proper kind of bargain.

" Leaving the ranks, they approached the house and inquired of the lady who met them at the door:

"' Have you any chickens for sale?'

" The woman happened to be of Southern sympathy, and of course very radical; so she replied:

"' No! I don't sell no chickens to Yankees.'

"' Wait till Yankees try to buy 'em, madam,' returned

one of the boys; 'we simply wanted to know whether you wished to sell a few of your fowls.'

"'No! I don't sell no chickens to Yankees,' repeated the woman.

"Knowing that coffee was scarce, the soldier concluded to tempt the lady with some real genuine coffee in a trade. Hence he ventured:

"'Well, madam, how will you trade us some chickens for Lincoln coffee?'"

"'D-o-n-'t know,' she replied slowly, with a remarkable change of temper visible on her countenance.

"'We will give you two pounds of coffee for two chickens,' said the soldier.

"'I'll do 't if you'll give me three pounds,' replied she.

"'No, we can't do it; we have only two pounds with us.'

"'I'll do it fur three pounds,' she still insisted.

"'All right; we'll give you three pounds if you'll come down to the sutler's about 8 o'clock this evening,' he agreed, thinking that would be an effectual stop to any further parley.

"''Nuff said—the trade's done made. Whar'll I come?'

"This occurred about 4 o'clock in the afternoon, and knowing that the column would soon go into camp, the soldier answered:

"'We will probably go into camp in a short time, not more than a mile or two further on; and when you come down inquire for the sutler of the 9th Indiana Infantry. We will pay him for the other pound of coffee, so that it will be ready for you;' and with the last remark the boys took their leave and departed on their way.

"Prompted by a desire to make sure of her due, the lady came into camp some half hour or more before the appointed time—sometimes it happens that suspicion and distrust preclude honesty. So it was in this case. Hence the fear that she would not get her coffee made the lady very nervous; and after finding the sutler's place she concluded to satisfy her eagerness by demanding the coffee at once.

"The soldiers were delayed and did not get into camp as early as they expected, the result of which was that the sutler knew nothing of their agreement to have the pound of coffee delivered to the woman. Of course his stinginess would not allow him to part with a pound of his goods on any assurance that the woman could give, so that great disappointment took the place of her great expectations, which could not have been otherwise from hasty action; and she was so enraged by this state of affairs that she at once sought headquarters to have the soldiers arrested.

"The affair was reported to General Nelson, who was equally enraged at finding his orders apparently so grossly disregarded. He ordered the immediate arrest of the soldiers, who were soon found and brought before him. They were not allowed time to carry out their part of the agreement, or even to make restoration; but were then and there subjected to the discipline, being strung up by the thumbs.

"The general then sent for me, as the soldiers belonged to my regiment. He held me responsible for the disobedience, but I determined to have a fair hearing, so that when he informed me that the soldiers had been tied up by the thumbs, I at once protested.

"'I insist on their punishment,' said he, 'because my orders *must be obeyed.*'

"'I think there is some mistake, General,' I replied, 'and will presume to suggest that the boys be turned loose until we can inquire into the matter, at least.'

"'I insist that my orders shall be obeyed,' he returned.

"'Very well,' said I; 'but it will not do to forget that you are commanding volunteers, and I beg to warn you that it will be better for all concerned in this matter, if you release the soldiers at once.'

"But he would not, in his condition of mind at that time, consent to any concessions. I returned to my tent. It was not long before the situation of affairs was understood by nearly all the boys in the regiment, who were much irritated. They determined upon the release of their comrades, and it did not require much time for the practical demonstration of their wishes. A number of them quietly gathered near the general's tent, and each prepared to assist in requiring redress. One of the boys ascertained the general's exact position and reported to the rest immediately. He found that the general was lying down, so that a volley discharged at the top of the tent would do no damage to his person.

"To think was to act. The volley was discharged; and the boys were not careful to aim precisely at the extreme top part of the tent. As soon as the general comprehended the situation, to do which required no great extension of chronology, he cautiously slipped away.

"Not long after his departure three or four bullets pierced the tent at various points three or four feet from the ground; but as soon as it was found that the general had virtually surrendered, the firing ceased. Some explanations and retractions were made, after which the accustomed pomp and dignity of camp prevailed. The soldiers were unstrung 'as to their thumbs,' and were allowed to fulfill their agreement with the female poultry vender, who went joyfully homeward with her pound of coffee.

"We marched on to the field of Shiloh, where we arrived in time to be almost, if not quite, the first participants. The battle commenced early on the bright Sunday morning of April 6, 1862—a day too calm and bright, after the previous few days of very inclement weather, to be desecrated by the harsh sounds of war. But the armies did not stop for what they considered sentimentalism. The Johnnies came pouring right down upon us before we had been given time to make

THE MORNING REVEILLE.

our toilets, which consisted principally of shouldering arms.

"My regiment was in the front, and my original company, numbering sixty-three, were thrown still further forward as skirmishers. The first sharp contest had ended, and many of the boys lay around us wounded, dying and dead. Then the enemy came on again. We stood our ground. The 41st Ohio regiment was in our rear, and the 6th Ohio to our left. The shells were flying thick and fast, and the explosions were frequent. Things in front looked discouraging. But our boys had no thought of retreating, although the shrapnel shot would plow through us, creating real terror, and bursting among the 41st Ohio boys. Of course this compelled them to retreat, which left us without support.

"It was now only 8 o'clock in the morning, but the mortality in our regiment had been fearful. Thirty-four out of sixty in my old company had been killed. But the boys were still firm, staring death in the face. In this situation, General Nelson came riding by. He saw the boys standing like trees—some fallen, some shattered, some untouched and immovable; and he could also see the desperate expression on their countenances. Ordinarily this would have stimulated the general to anger; but this time he could do nothing more than admire the firmness of the boys who plainly showed an almost uncontrollable hatred for him. But the general pursued a different course from harshness. His heart seemed deeply touched, and, as the old man passed on down the line, the tears trickled down his cheek as he spoke:

"'Ah! volunteers *are* the men to fight after all. Believe me, my brave boys, I bear you no ill will.'

"'*Three cheers* for General Nelson!' called out the boys, after saluting him; and the chorus that went up was sufficient evidence that the general had been forgiven.

"'Hear! hear!' responded the general when he thought they had cheered sufficiently. 'I shall give the 9th Indiana as fine colors as any regiment *ever* had. I do this in order that your people at home may know of my good feeling for you, and that history may record this affair.'

" And true to promise," concluded General Suman, " after General Nelson's death, General Crittenden presented us our flag in behalf of General Nelson and the State of Kentucky."

" While listening to the previous narrative I was reminded of the funniest incident that came under my observation during the March to the Sea," said George Ellers, 113th Ohio Infantry.

" We will be delighted to have you relate the story," said one of the S. P. U. H.

" It was this," said comrade Ellers. " There had been a sutler following our brigade for some two or three months, and he was one of the most disagreeable men in camp. He used every artifice to take advantage of the boys, and never allowed an opportunity to escape by means of which he could rob them of their money. It was just after the battle of Goldsboro, back of Kenesaw Mountain, while we were in camp, that a plan was concocted to prevent the odious sutler from doing further mischief. The scheme was to have a sham battle, and in the melee stampede over his tent. Accordingly the 98th and 121st Ohio regiments were formed in line as adversaries near by the sutler's tent, and the rest of the brigade stood near at hand as spectators. After all was in readiness the 121st charged the 98th, and drove them back; then the 98th sallied and pressed their adversaries to their former position, after which the 98th reformed directly in front of the sutler's tent. Immediately the 121st charged again, and came down on the 98th like a whirlwind, all of them yelling like demons. The 98th broke and fell back, and as the laughing, yelling, howling mass swept along, some of the boys cut the ropes of the tent and in a trice the sutler's stock was scattered over half an acre of ground. Every man who could grabbed some article and made way with it, and in less time than it takes to tell it, over $3,000 worth of goods had vanished into the oblivion of haversacks and other secret places.

"The sutler fought like a wild-cat to save his property. He seized a cheese-knife and made savage attempts to mutilate some of the boys, but they were too many for him. They disarmed him, and pushed him about and fell on him so incessantly that he had no time to find another weapon, and when he came to himself he was five hundred yards from the site of his now ruined store.

"The shout of laughter and merriment that went up as the joke dawned upon the spectators, created a perfect bedlam. Everybody enjoyed the fun, and the boys of the 98th and 121st were richer by some thousands in the way of commodities and camp luxuries.

"The result of the sport was that a search was ordered from headquarters for the stolen goods, but not a dollar's worth was returned to the discomfited sutler. I never saw as much fun crowded into five minutes in my life, and many a time have I laughed over that day's sport with some comrade who participated in the charge upon our sutler.

"While I have the 'floor,'" continued comrade Ellers, "let me tell you a little anecdote of Capt. Chas. P. Gorman, of Co. A, and I will have done."

"All right," we exclaimed, and settled back into a comfortable position, and lighted a Key West with a burning brand from the fire.

"We were before Kenesaw Mountain," went on comrade Ellers, "and were on a charge against the enemy across an open field. The fire of musketry was sharp, and the bullets were whistling among us as thick and fast as raindrops. The boys were dropping, and the line was fast becoming broken. The situation was desperate. The field was fully a half mile in width and the chances of reaching the other side were decidedly against us.

"Captain Gorman was a German and as brave a man as there was in the army. His fund of humor was inexhaustible, and everybody in the company liked him.

"Just at the moment when the line faltered and was about to fall back, the captain shouted:

"'Vich vould you rather do or pe in yer Taddy's haymow, poys?'

"In an instant the humor of the remark was caught, and the self-possession of the boys returned, and with a hurrah the line rushed on until it occupied the position to which it had been ordered."

Another veteran, upon whose face the light of the flames fell in a pleasing way, remarked:

"I was told the following by General Scofield while we were on our way from Wilmington to Beaufort: 'A few days after our troops had taken possession of Wilmington, a large, good-looking negro made his way into my headquarters one morning, and asked:

"'Is you de gin'ral of dese people, sah?'

"'Yes,' I replied.

"'Is you de biggest ginral dat is heah, sah?'

"'Yes, I think so,' I answered, 'what do you wish?'

"'Well sah,' continued my sable inquisitor, 'when we black people hearn dat de Yankees was a comin', we knowed dey'd be a big racket, an' me an' de rest of us moved into de swamps, sah, an' dere dey all is, sah, 'bout fo' or five hundred of 'em. An' we hearn dat de Yankees had done tuk Wilmington, an' dat de ole flag was up!

"'We's mighty anxshus to know de troof an' I'se come in sah, to find out whether it's so, an' if it is so, an' you had come to stay, den I've to fiah a joy gun, sah!'

"'Well, we've taken Wilmington, Sambo, and the old

flag is up,' said I, 'and we have come to stay too, but what's that about a joy gun?'

"'Why, sah,' continued the negro, 'if eberything was all right an' de ole flag is up, den I was to fiah a joy gun, an' dey'd know all about it out in de swamps, sah, an den dey'd come in!'

"'I think I understand you now,' said I, 'and I will have a joy gun fired.'

"'So I went up to the fortifications and had one of the largest guns fired, and in the course of the afternoon, in came a great crowd of contrabands from the swamps, and every mother's son and daughter of them were shouting:

"'Glory!—glory! de ole flag is up—de ole flag is up!'"

CAMP-FIRE XX.

"WHEN THIS CRUEL WAR IS OVER"—A CONTINUATION OF CAMP-FIRE XVIII—A "MULEY" YOKE OF "MULEY" OXEN.

"AST evening but one," began Governor G., "the incidents of the camp-fire reminded me of a touching experience of which I omitted to speak at the time, but with permission, will give it now."

"Let us hear it," called out the commander.

"Well, to begin, I knew Dr. Hard, who related the occurrence, at the battle of Williamsburg. He was in our regiment, the 8th Illinois cavalry—which was the first to enter the village of Gettysburg, on the day previous to the first day's battle.

"The cavalry were always far ahead of the infantry, doing the advance skirmishing, and this time our regiment was in the extreme front. We were going into Gettysburg, and as we came nearer to the center of the town we could see the rebel cavalry receding. Many of them were yet scattered miscellaneously about the streets, but all were clearing themselves from the vicinity.

"We rode on, and as we passed the stores and shops we were greeted with a warm welcome on every hand. Women and children, and men and boys who were ineligible for soldiership, lined the streets and assured us of their most heartfelt joy, for we were the first Union soldiers they had seen for some time.

"Our attention was attracted to a number of school-girls

who apparently had just come together. There were perhaps fifteen or twenty of them, of ages ranging from ten to fifteen years. Many of them were beautiful, and all were good singers. It seemed to me as though they made not the least discord, and that the sweetest music I ever heard came from their lips as they sang—the first time we had ever heard the song:

> "'Dearest love, do you remember,
> When we last did meet,
> How you told me that you loved me,
> Kneeling at my feet?
> Oh! how proud you stood before me,
> In your suit of blue,
> When you vowed to me and country
> Ever to be true.
>
> CHORUS.
>
> "'Weeping sad and lonely,
> Hopes and fears how vain!
> When this cruel war is over,
> Praying that we meet again!'

"After passing through the city and going into camp, many of us returned again to the pleasing surroundings. The citizens threw open their houses and invited us in to enjoy the full privilege of their homes. On every hand we were met with the most cordial reception. Merchants would not even take pay for articles of limited value after we had bought them. Every one seemed heartily glad to assist the bold defenders of the Stars and Stripes.

"Indeed we appreciated this, for we had been deprived for a long time of many of the comforts of civilized life, and at times had wanted the necessities, not to say the delicacies; so that the enjoyment of all these, coupled with the earnest way in which we were received, could not fail to draw from us expressions of unalloyed gratitude. We felt that even in the midst of war there is tenderness; that, however fierce the battle may be, the heart which receives the blow and the one which gives it, may then or at any other time be the home of affection.

"Gratitude brought a tear to my own eye, and as I looked around to see the expression of other countenances, I beheld at my side an old, wicked, gray-haired man weeping from very joy—a man whose heart I had long since concluded had never held many feelings except those kindred to cruelty. This was only the day before the great battle, but I can tell you that even this short relief was welcome."

"Let me add another incident to those already given about Sherman's famous march," said Mr. C. E. Harden, addressing the commander.

"Proceed," responded His Dignity, and Mr. Harden did proceed thus:

"In the first place," said he, "the country through which we were passing produced only two staple commodities, to-wit: Bull-frogs and bad roads, the two being in almost equal abundance. There were also two other things similar in the purpose of holding food, namely, our stomachs and haversacks; and at this particular time they were exactly alike in one other respect—both were empty. Sometimes a man's appetite suggests a very sudden conclusion about going to work to obtain something eatable; and this was *our* exact condition. So comrade John Chandler and myself at once determined 'to see what we could see' in the way of forage.

"We left camp at day-break, and knowing the route which the column would take, kept well to the right. We tramped all day, and at night had succeeded in becoming the possessors of the following:

"One cart with one broken wheel.

"One and one-quarter bushels of potatoes; size of same, ½ to ¾ inches in diameter.

"One yoke of 'muley' oxen.

"One ox was red; the other brindle. One had lost its tail. The red ox, being the afflicted one, seemed to be favored by nature with a very small horn on the left side of its head, so that it was not entirely 'muley;' while on the other hand, brindle having no claim to a like favor from nature, had no horn, and was, therefore, entirely 'muley.'

"It was an odd-looking team; but we concluded to try its strength for a few miles, so we loaded our potatoes and continued our journey. The second day added the following to our store:

" 1. One rooster too old to crow.
" 2. One-half bushel wilted turnips.

"Late in the afternoon we began to hunt our command, and about sunset came to the road that the division had passed over, but found no other signs of a soldier. A short 'council of war' was held, after which the line of march was taken up and continued until daylight, when we came to a halt, fed the rooster and the oxen, and breakfasted ourselves on the 'pig-potatoes' and turnips. After a short rest we again proceeded, arriving in camp about 4 o'clock in the afternoon.

"As we approached, the cheering resembled the prolonged chirrup from an excited flock of geese. All kinds of exclamations were heard:

"'Hurrah for the muleys!'
"'Kill 'em! Kill 'em!'
"'Beefsteak for supper, boys!'
"'Give us some ox-tail soup!'
"'Old brindle's horns for powder flasks!' etc., etc.

"When the noise subsided, the commissary sergeant ordered us to report at headquarters with our team. We did this, received a reprimand for being absent from our command, and our oxen were inspected, and ordered slaughtered for the good of the regiment.

"Within fifteen minutes from that time the odor from fresh, tough beef emanated from numerous frying pans, and ascended to the evening sky; and in perhaps thirty minutes more no reminder of the oxen's sad fate could be seen, except the iron work of the wagon, the wood having been appropriated to replenish the various camp-fires."

CAMP-FIRE XXI.

THE GRAND ARMY OF THE REPUBLIC—NOT A POLITICAL OR-
GANIZATION—ITS PRINCIPLES: FRATERNITY, CHARITY,
LOYALTY—A COMPLETE, BRIEF RECORD OF ITS OR-
GANIZATION AND GROWTH TO THE PRESENT TIME.

HIS camp-fire was devoted to delineating the practical part of those magnificent memories which have resulted so happily from the comradeship which was begotten and made strong by the battles of the Civil War. Dr. A. W. Gray was the speaker, and said:

" At no time in the history of the world has there been an organization of such magnitude as this; which had such sudden growth and notoriety, and yet of which so little is known. As far as known there are no *official* records of any connected history of its origin, rise and progress.

" It is not strange that men who, for many weary months and years had shared the perils and fatigues, the weary marches and bivouacks of a soldier's life, —who together had breasted the storms of shot and shell, and shared the privation, suffering and hunger of the prison-pen—should desire to keep alive the memories and associations of their army life. History informs us that after great wars it has been in all ages customary for the surviving soldiers to form associations to preserve the memories of other days. We hear in our day of the associations of veterans of the Crimean war and of the French and German war; and in our own country of the 'Order of the Cincinnati,' an organization of commissioned officers of the American army who fought for national liberty during the Revolution, the organization to be perpetuated by the admission of the oldest sons of its members as the originators successively died. We have also the veteran associations of the war of 1812, and the war with Mexico; but none can compare with the G. A. R., whose posts may be found from the Atlantic to the Pacific, and from the St. Lawrence to the Gulf of Mexico.

"As to who first originated the 'Grand Army of the Republic,' no one man is entitled to the credit. There was nothing original in it. It had always been customary for surviving soldiers to organize, and for a long time many of the old soldiers had talked the matter over. The war was over. A *million* men—veterans of the greatest war of modern times—had stacked their arms, sheathed their swords, and returned to their homes and the pursuits of a civil life. What more natural than that these old comrades should enjoy each other's society, and should wish to preserve the 'memories of those hours of trial and danger' by banding themselves together, and talking over the old times?

"Although not a matter of record, it is an admitted fact that the State of Illinois has the honor of the G. A. R.'s birthplace; and that B. F. Stephenson, late surgeon of the 14th Illinois Infantry, was the first man to organize the veterans into an association. During the winter of 1865 and 1866, he, with other ex-soldiers of the late war, being at the time in the City of Springfield, Illinois, discussed the propriety of organizing the 'veteran' soldiers of the State into an association *for political purposes*—his idea being that the soldiers, having saved the country, were entitled *of right* to the offices of profit and trust. It was decided to form such an organization; that it should be a secret society, with signs, grips and password. The individuals present took an oath of secrecy. A ritual was prepared and adopted; also an initiation ceremony. It was also decided to go ahead and organize posts throughout the State.

"Immediately a difficulty presented itself; they had only one copy of the ritual. How to get it printed without publicity, was the question. But this was soon answered. The editor of the Decatur (Ill.) 'Tribune;' as well as all of the printers in the office, had served their time in the army, and were therefore eligible to membership in the new society. To each of these the obligation was administered, and they were admitted into full membership. Four hundred copies of the ritual were ordered printed and bound, and in a few days the rituals were ready for distribution. The organization was named,

"THE GRAND ARMY OF THE REPUBLIC."

"As yet not a single Post had been formed. On the night of April 6, 1866, in the Hall of the 'Sons of Malta' at Decatur, Illinois, was organized 'Post No. 1 of the Grand Army of the Republic.' It was late when the meeting adjourned, but, full of the spirit of the occasion, and determined to create a sensation, 'the Boys' went to the 'Tribune' office, and had a number of posters struck off, upon which was the following:

```
G. A. R.
POST NO. 1.
DECATUR,
APRIL 6, 1866.
```

"Armed with paste-pot and brush they patroled the city, and posted these dodgers in the most conspicuous places. Upon the following day they were the talk of the town; and such was the birth of the Grand Army of the Republic. The organization of other posts rapidly followed throughout the State. Eagerly the veterans enrolled themselves under the new banners. Dr. Stephenson announced himself as commander, and issued the following order:

"'Head Quarters Grand Army of the Republic,
   SPRINGFIELD, ILL., June —, 1866.
"'The undersigned hereby assumes command of the Grand Army of the Republic. Major Robert M. Woods is appointed Adjutant General; Colonel Julius C. Weber and Lieut. John S. Phelps are appointed A. D. C. They will be obeyed and respected accordingly.
   "'By order of   B. F. STEPHENSON,
   "'R. M. WOODS.   Adjutant General.'

"Soon the necessity of a State organization became apparrent; so Dr Stephenson issued an order calling a meeting of delegates from the different Posts to assemble at Springfield, Ill., *July 12, 1866.*

"At the meeting which followed, the Department of Illinois was organized and systematized. John M. Palmer was elected Department Commander. New Posts were organized in other States. Dr. Stephenson by common consent assumed the duties of ' Provisional commander-in-chief.'

"Observing the growing popularity of the organization, and the necessity of its becoming more national in character, Dr. Stephenson issued the following order:

"'Head Quarters Grand Army of the Republic,
   SPRINGFIELD, ILL., Oct. 31, 1866.
"'GENERAL ORDER NO. 13.
"'A National convention of the Grand Army of the Republic is hereby ordered to convene at Indianapolis, Indiana, at 10 o'clock on Tuesday, the twentieth day of November

next, for the purpose of perfecting the National organization, and the transaction of such other business as may come before the Convention.

"'The ratio of representation shall be as follows: Each Post shall be entitled to one representative, and when the membership exceeds one hundred, to one additional representative and in the same ratio for every additional one hundred, or every fractional part thereof.

"'All Department and District officers, *ex-officio*, shall be members of said convention. All honorably discharged soldiers and sailors, and those now serving in the army desirous of becoming members of the Grand Army of the Republic, are respectfully invited to attend the convention. All comrades are requested to wear the 'blue' with corps badges, etc.

"'Official: J. C. WEBBER,
        Adj't Gen., Dept. Illinois.
   "'B. F. STEPHENSON,
        Com.-in-chief, G. A. R. U. S.'

"In accordance with the call about two hundred and fifty members of the order from eleven different States assembled at Indianapolis, Indiana, on Nov. 20, 1866.

"The meeting was called to order by Dr. Stephenson, and John M. Palmer of Illinois was elected chairman. The business of organizing and adopting rules for the government of the order was gone through with in two days. Stephen A. Hurlbut, of Illinois, was elected as the first commander-in-chief, to serve for one year. Dr. Stephenson was appointed adjutant general.

"The convention adjourned to meet again at the call of the commander; but before adjourning the following 'Resolutions' and 'Platform of Principles' were adopted.

"'We, the representatives of the soldiers and sailors of the military and naval service of the United States during the late war against traitors, reaffirming our devotion to these States, the Constitution and the laws of our country, and our abhorrence of treason and oppression,—

"'*Resolved*, First: That the Grand Army or the Republic is organized to maintain in civil life, those great principles for which it stood in arms under the national flag; that it stands pledged to crush out active treason, to advance and support loyalty, to secure sound constitutional liberty to all men, and to vindicate everywhere and at all times the full and complete rights of every loyal American citizen,—against all combinations of force or fraud that may attempt to deny or deprive them of such rights;—

"'Second: That we pledge all the power and influence which, as individuals or as an association, we can wield legitimately, in the most especial manner to those gallant men who stood fast by the country in the hour of its agony, in the rebellious States, and who, through all manner of losses and injuries, persecutions by force and persecutions under color of law, maintained their integrity, and vindicated their loyalty; and we solemnly declare that no power that we can use shall be neglected until they are thoroughly and completely protected in the active exercise of every right of American freemen through the entire country over which our flag floats;—

"'Third: That Congress in justice and not in charity, should pass a law equalizing in a just manner, the bounties of all Union soldiers and sailors;—

"'Fourth: That we now, as heretofore, pledge ourselves to use our best endeavors to procure appropriate State and national legislation, for the education and maintenance of the orphans and widows of our deceased comrades and maimed brethren, and to enforce a speedy adjustment and payment of all lawful claims against the government, due soldiers and sailors, and their friends;—

"'Fifth: That, in our opinion, no man is worthy to be a free citizen of a free country who is not willing to bear arms in its defence, and we, therefore, suggest to Congress the passage of a law making it the inexorable duty of every citizen to defend his country in time of need, in person and not by substitute;—

"'Sixth: That as a matter of justice and right, and because the sacrifice made and dangers encountered by the Union soldiers and sailors who served in the late war for the preservation of the country, cannot ever be fully repaid, we respectfully ask that those in authority bestow upon needy and worthy soldiers and sailors such positions of honor and profit as they may be competent to fill; and while we seek nothing for ourselves, or those of our comrades who are able to maintain themselves, we do earnestly recommend this request to the consideration of those in authority. And we especially ask the attention of the President to his policy heretofore declared on this subject.'

" The *second* National Encampment was held at Philadelphia, Pa., Jan. 15, 16 and 17, 1868. Delegates from twenty-one States were present. John A. Logan, of Illinois, was elected commander-in-chief.

" At this session a resolution was adopted calling upon Congress to enact a law which should allow none but deceased *Union* soldiers and sailors of the late war to be buried in the National cemeteries; also, to enact a law whereby ex-Union soldiers and sailors should have the preference in appointment to positions of profit and trust.

"ORIGIN OF DECORATION DAY.

" It was at *this* encampment that 'Memorial Day' was instituted. A resolution was passed that the thirtieth day of May of each year be designated as 'Memorial' or 'Decoration Day," upon which day the members of the G. A. R. were to decorate the graves of their deceased comrades with flowers and evergreens; and General Logan, in an address to the encampment spoke as follows, concerning it:

"'To keep the scenes of war with all its horrors vivid before the mind, without some still more important motive, would hardly meet with the approval of this intelligent age. It was to keep constantly before the mind the *cost* of liberty, and the *price* paid for the suppression of rebellion, and the preservation of a free and independent Government; to keep forever green the hallowed memory of the heroic dead, who had fallen to save their country from disunion and dishonor. This ceremony is but an external expression of one of the great principles of our Order, and should the organization in coming years cease to exercise its functions,—I trust that the ceremony so happily coming from it, may never cease, for so long as it continues to be heartily observed, we will have the assurance that there are loyal hearts in the land that cling to the integrity of our Union, and condemn treason to our Government.'

"'The *third* National encampment was held at Cincinnati, Ohio, May 12 and 13, 1869. John A. Logan was re-elected commander-in-chief for another year.

" From the Adjutant General's report at this Encampment we learn that the order was rapidly dying out in the Western States, but was being kept alive in the East—Illinois, which at one time had three hundred and thirty Posts, reporting only *six*. On the other hand, Ohio reported three hundred and three Posts in good standing.

"Inquiry developed the fact that 'politics' was killing the order. The veterans were suspicious, and looked upon it as a huge political machine, used by unscrupulous office-seekers to further their own ends and aims. The people, taking the same view of the case, were also disgusted with it, and refused to countenance or help it along. Therefore this encampment voted to remodel the entire structure. A new set of Rules and Regulations was adopted, wherein politics especially was prohibited, viz: Article XI, Chapter V:

"'No officer or comrade of the Grand Army of the Republic shall *in any manner* use this organization for partisan purposes, and no discussion of partisan questions shall be permitted at any of its meetings, nor shall any nominations for political office be made.'

" The encampment also established *three grades* in the order called the ' Recruit,' 'Soldier ' and ' Veteran,' the latter only, being admitted into full membership; and also adopted the following articles of Rules and Regulations which are in full force at the present time:]

" OBJECTS

"' The objects to be accomplished by this organization are as follows:

"' First: To preserve and strengthen those kind and fraternal feelings which bind together the soldiers, sailors and mariners who united to suppress the late rebellion and to perpetuate the memory and history of the dead.

"' Second: To assist such former comrades in arms as need help and protection; and to extend needful aid to the widows and orphans of those who have fallen.

"' Third: To maintain true allegiance to the United States of America, based upon a paramount respect for, and fidelity to, the National Constitution and laws; to discountenance whatsoever tends to weaken loyalty, incites to insurrection, treason or rebellion, or in any manner impairs the efficiency and permanency of our free institutions; and to encourage the spread of universal liberty, equal rights and justice to all men.

"' ELIGIBILITY TO MEMBERSHIP.

"' Soldiers and Sailors of the United States Army, Navy or Marine Corps, who served between April 12, 1861, and August 20, 1866, in the war for the suppression of the Rebellion, and those having been honorably discharged therefrom after such service, and of such State regiments as were called into active service and subject to the orders of U. S. General Officers, between the dates mentioned, shall be eligible to membership in the Grand Army of the Republic. No person shall be eligible to membership who has at any time borne arms against the United States.'

" From that time to the present the growth of the Order has been steady and prosperous. The ' boys,' finding that they were not to be used as ' somebody's tool ' for political purposes, gradually came forward and joined the various Posts, manifesting a willingness to be identified with an organization whose aims and purposes were purely and unequivocally: FRATERNITY, CHARITY and LOYALTY.

"The *fourth* National Encampment was held at Washington, D. C., May 11 and 12, 1870. John A. Logan was re-elected commander-in-chief for a third term.

"This encampment adopted resolutions calling upon Congress to make Memorial Day (May 30) a legal holiday. A 'Badge' for the order was also adopted, the same as now worn by the members of the G. A. R., and may be described thus:

"A five-pointed bronze star made from cannon captured in decisive battles of the civil war, and donated by Congress for the purpose. The design upon one side presents the Goddess of Liberty to represent *Loyalty*, and on either side of her is a soldier and sailor clasping hands to represent *Fraternity*, while two little children, receiving benediction and assurance of protection from the comrades, represent *Charity*. On each side of the group is the national flag and eagle, representing *Freedom*, while the axe and bundle of rods or *fasces*, represent *Union*. In each point of the star is the insignia of the various arms of the service, that is the bugle for Infantry, crossed cannon for Artillery, crossed muskets for the Marines, crossed swords for the Cavalry, and the anchor for the Sailors. Over the central group are the words 'Grand Army of the Republic ;' under the group, '1861. Veteran. 1866,' commemorating the beginning and close of the civil war; also the date of the organization of the G. A. R.

"The *other* side of the star presents a branch of laurel— the crown and reward of the brave—on each point of the star. The National shield in the center, surrounded by the twenty-four recognized corps badges in the order of their number, each on a keystone, and all linked together, are arranged to show that they are united, and will guard and protect the shield of the Nation. Around the center is a circle of stars representing the States of the Union, also the Departments' composing the Grand Army of the Republic.

"The clasp of the badge is a bronze eagle with outstretched wings, holding a naked sword over crossed cannon and piled ammunition, representing *Defense*—always ready to defend the flag of the United States, which, as the emblem and ribbon of the order, is suspended from the *clasp*, and sustains the *star*.

"The *fifth* National Encampment was held at Boston, Mass., May 10 and 11, 1871.

"A. E. Burnside, of Rhode Island, was elected commander-in-chief. The 'grade system' was abolished, and only one degree for full membership established.

"The *sixth* National Encampment was held at Cleveland, Ohio, May 8 and 9, 1872. A. E. Burnside was re-elected commander-in-chief.

"The *seventh* National Encampment was held at New Haven, Connecticut, May 14 and 15, 1873. Charles A. Devens, of Massachusetts, was elected commander-in-chief.

"The *eighth* National Encampment was held at Harrisburg, Penn., May 13, 1874, Charles A. Devens being reelected commander-in-chief.

"The *ninth* National Encampment was held at Chicago, Ill., May 12 and 13, 1875. John F. Hartranft, of Pennsylvania, was elected commander-in-chief.

"The *tenth* National Encampment was held at Philadelphia, Penn., June 30, 1876. John F. Hartranft was re-elected commander-in-chief.

"The *eleventh* National Encampment was held at Providence, R. I., June 26 and 27, 1877. John C. Robinson, of New York, was elected commander-in-chief.

"The *twelfth* National Encampment was held at Springfield, Mass., June 4, 1878. John C. Robinson was reelected commander-in-chief.

"The *thirteenth* National Encampment was held at Albany, New York, June 17 and 18, 1879. William Earnshaw, of Ohio, was elected commander-in-chief.

G. A. R. BADGE.

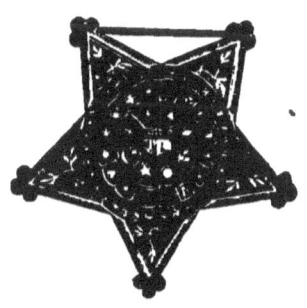

REVERSE OF STAR.

"The Adjutant General reported a gain for the past year of 4,048 members, and a total membership of 31,415.

"The *fourteenth* Annual Encampment was held at Dayton, Ohio. Commander Earnshaw positively declined to be a candidate for re-election, saying that he wished to establish the precedent that no man should hold the office of commander-in-chief for more than one term.

"Louis Wagner, of Pennsylvania, was elected commander-in-chief.

"The Report of the Adjt.-Gen. showed a membership of 44,802 on December 31, 1879, being a gain during the year of 13,387.

"The *fifteenth* National Encampment was held at Indianapolis, Indiana, June 15 and 16, 1881. George S. Merrill of Massachusetts, was elected commander-in-chief. The gain in membership during the previous year was 15,876, and a total membership of 60,678.

"The *sixteenth* National Encampment was held at Baltimore, Maryland, June 21, 22 and 23, 1882.

"Paul Vandervoort of Nebraska, was elected commander-in-chief. The gain in membership during the previous year was reported at 25,178, and the total membership at 85,865.

"The *seventeenth* National Encampment was held at Denver, Colorado, July 25 and 26, 1883. Robert B. Beath of Pennsylvania was elected commander-in-chief. The Adjutant General reported that on Dec. 31, 1882, there were 131,890 members in good standing—showing a gain of 46,034 during the year. He also reported that on March 31, 1883, there were 145,932 members and 971 Posts in good standing, or a gain in three months of 174 Posts and 14,042 members. All over the country the order is reported as in a flourishing condition. New Posts are springing up in every direction. Even away out on the frontiers, in the Territories, strong working Posts may be found. Each year, wherever the National Encampment has been held, the citizens have received the veterans with open arms, and have done their very best to make their stay agreeable. Nothing was too good for the men who had hazarded their lives to save the Nation as *one* country and under *one* flag.

"It is now well understood that the Grand Army of the Republic is *not* a huge political machine, that it favors no political party, and indorses no man for office. As an organization it inculcates a spirit of patriotism in the rising generation. As an organization the members do not forget 'that fraternity of feeling which binds them together as *comrades*, that charity which prompts them to the noblest sacrifices for the needy and destitute wards of the Grand Army, and that *Loyalty* which binds them together as citizens, and to an undying vigilance which is the price of liberty.'

"In an address to the encampment, Commander Devens said: 'The objects of our Association are such as should commend themselves not only to those who have fought under the flag of the Union, but to all good citizens also. Against our organization it has been especially charged that it was secret in its character, and that all secret societies were dangerous in a republican government. Plausible as this remark sounds, it is obvious that it can have no proper application to those societies whose purposes are well known, and whose secrecy is limited entirely to the Ritual by which their proceedings are conducted, and to their modes of recognizing their fellow members. *The Grand Army has no purpose that it is unwilling to reveal to the world;* it has no obligation that any citizen soldier, who is the same man to-day in thought and feeling that he was in the hour of trial, cannot take without hesitation or reservation; it has no political bearing or significance; any effort to turn it to any such object is to be resisted with our utmost resolution. As the old army was always broad enough to include all (no matter what might be their differences of opinion as to men or measures) of loyal and true devotion, so this Association is broad enough to welcome to its ranks every veteran whose heart still beats responsively to the music of the Union. In this connection I deem it proper to say that sometimes *attempts* have been made to secure the influence of our organization in matters merely political, such as aiding in elections of, or securing appointments for, particular individuals. Such attempts have *never* received, and *will not at any time* receive, any encouragement at the National Headquarters. They are not only in violation of the whole *spirit* of our order, but of its *letter*, as expressed by its Rules and Regulations. Let it be understood that our organization has no system of politics except that great and grand system in which all true men are agreed, whether citizens or soldiers—those principles of devotion to the death, if need be, for Liberty and the Laws, for the Constitution and the Union, which we once preached with our rifles in our hands and our country's flag above our heads, amidst the smoke and fire of an hundred battlefields. Let it be known that by these principles alone we are united, that this society does not exist for any personal ends or selfish purposes, and that it is not to be used by any man, or any set of men. If those who have enjoyed life together as schoolmates or classmates, delight to renew the scenes of their former life, and to live over again in each other's company the days that are passed, surely the tie of affection which binds together men who have not only enjoyed much but suffered together, must be one of no ordinary character.

"'Unless hearts were flint, no man could be insensible or cold to him by whose side he had stood shoulder to shoulder in the ranks of war, upon whose fidelity and courage he had known that his own life depended, and felt reassured as he looked upon his resolute brow and kindling eye, and to whom he had been all that is expressed by the simple but dear word—*comrade.*

"'Agreeable and delightful as are the social characteristics of our association, it has higher aims than these, to guard and cherish the memory of those of our comrades who have passed away; to teach the inestimable value of the services of those who—unused to the trade of arms—did not hesitate, when the hour of trial came, to leave the plow in the furrow and the hammer on the anvil, and commit themselves to the shock of battle, appealing to the God of battles for the justice of their cause, is with us a most sacred duty. And this not alone that the *dead* may be *honored,* but that the *living* may be *encouraged* to imitate their example, and that the strong spirit of nationality and loyalty to the Government which bore us up so bravely through four years of unexampled trial may be fostered and strengthened, and that we ourselves may be consecrated anew to the cause for which so many have suffered. But, although it is our object to do justice to the memory of our dead, it is our aim to do justice to the living also; to secure a fair and just recognition of their claims, and to protect their rights by all suitable means within our control. Above all, as true homage must consist not in words but in deeds, we have always held that no higher honor could be paid to the just fame of the brave men who have defended the Republic than to assist by kind words and material aid all good and true soldiers who by wounds, disease, old age or misfortune, have become dependent, and tenderly to care for the widows and orphans of the fallen. The motto which our order bears—'Fraternity, Charity and Loyalty,'—is the brief summary of its principles.'

"In his address to the National Encampment, said Chaplain-in-chief, Lovering: 'So far as the faith and morals of the G. A. R. are concerned, I have this to say: Its faith has its religion, and its religion has the devout obedience of every worthy member of our order. I do not refer to *any* religion, sectarian or universal, liberal or conservative, Christian or Pagan, as such. Whatever disputes there may be outside of our organization concerning them, do not affect us. Religion means *bond*. The highest religion casts out all spirit of fear and makes its 'bond' that of love. Our religion, within the terms of our organization, claims that highest bond. It is permeated, it is saturated with the spirit of that love. That love is *love of country*. That religion is the religion of patriotism.

"'Its altars are the graves of the unforgotten and heroic. Its symbol is the flag of our Union. Its priests are all those, within its organization, who confess this soldierly creed: I believe in a fraternity which joins in indissoluble union, justice and right.

"'I believe in a charity that, while merciful to a conquered foe, does not stultify itself by surrendering the fruits of victory; that never forgets the brightness of that cause which has been made illustrious by the heroic sacrifices of those whose graves should be the shrines of the Nation's reverence.

"'I believe in loyalty that acknowledges *"one country and one flag*;" that makes American citizenship honorable everywhere; that calls rebellion a crime, and the penalty of treason—*death*.

"'I believe that, in fraternity and charity, we should stand shoulder to shoulder, willing at all hazard of favor or fame to defend the G. A. R. as the standard bearer of the nation's loyalty.

"'There is one word I wish to emphasize. It is the rallying word of our whole body. It gives the pulse beat to every heart in every "Post." It is written upon every altar of patriotism we call a soldier's grave. It speaks to us in the honorable scars which wounds or disease, or the wasting hand of time has made on those who in the fullness of manhood stood forth to battle for the Union and the right. It is woven into every thread, red, white, or blue, of our glorious banner. It shines in every ray of light that gleams from the stars we have plucked with full hands from the skies to brighten and glorify our flag. It is the *one* word that is above the taint of political partisanship, and which seals our allegiance to one country and one flag. Cicero, the Roman orator, when he denounced the traitor and conspirator, Cataline, said, " Let it be written upon the forehead of every citizen what are his views concerning the republic." *Our* views have been written upon the pages of our Nation's history in ineffaceable characters. The ink was *blood;* the pens were *bayonets* and *sabers.* One word focalizes these views. It is written upon the forehead of every soldier. The spirit of it beats in the heart of every soldier. The temper of it toughens every muscle and thrills along every nerve of every soldier. That word is "*Loyalty.*" '

" Commander-in-chief George S. Merrill in his address said : ' The Grand Army is to-day the representative organization of the soldiers and sailors of America, the *one* great association which includes the veterans of every army and all ranks ; the men who followed the flag upon the land, and who fought beneath its folds upon the sea ; men of every nationality, color and creed ; the officer who wore the well worn stars of a general, and the private whose only badge of distinction was in patriotic and faithful service in the ranks— all upon the common level of *Comrades* of the flag with "*Fraternity*" which would bind in closer ties the veterans who offered *all* that they possessed upon the altar of country; with "*Charity*" which would protect and care for the needy ones among all the Nation's defenders, their wives and little ones, and "*Loyalty*" which would keep ever brightly burning that spirit of patriotism leading a free people to rise, in the majesty and might of 1861, to defend the unity of the republic, and secure to generations yet unborn a government from, by and for all the people; let the success of the past be but an inspiration to greater efforts in behalf of our organization in the future, and rest and sleep come not within our tents until every honorably discharged soldier and sailor who merits our confidence is enrolled in the Grand Army of the Republic.'

"Said Commander-in-chief Vandervoort in his address : 'We stand in line to-day as we did when we marched to the front burning with loyalty, breaking asunder the ties of party and meeting on one common platform, waving aloft a torn and honorable discharge, and exemplifying fraternity, charity and loyalty. I have heard the doctrine advocated that the sentence in our "installation service" "That we should stand by the soldier though the whole world assail him," means that we should do so if our comrade is a candidate for political office.

"'The Grand Army fetters the conscience of *no* member. It gives the largest liberty to all. It stands aloof from the strife and clash of parties. "It will stand by the comrade though the whole world assail him" in sickness, in distress, when the old wounds re-open, when the wife and children are destitute. It will take old veterans from the "almshouse." It will remove their bones from a pauper's grave, and bury them in holy ground. It will procure employment. It will lighten up the desolate home with the glowing illustration of Charity, but in all political and religious affairs we will hold our independence of thought, and our conscience as something we will not surrender to any order in the land.

"'To close I can not do better than to give an extract from a poem by Emily Hawthorne :

"'In years agone, a fearful strife was ended:
And hosts of valiant men who came together
At their country's call,—summoned to combat,

Whose name was legion when they started forth,
Were now dispersed; o'er this broad land
From East to Western shores were widely scattered,
And resumed their peaceful avocations
In field or shop, as ere they went to war.
The clanking swords and sabers in quiet
Graced the wall, with gleaming bayonets sheathed;
The muskets now in dusty corners stacked,
Rested, and rusty grew, while, bent to duty,
The patient shoulders where they had been borne,
Were placed to move the wheels of honest industry
Which once more sang, with an unceasing hum
The song of peaceful labor, honest toil.
As erst my muse declared was warfare ended,
And e'en a twelve month, too, had passed away,
Since "Grand Review" and final muster out;
When a strange germ in memory's garden grew;
For months this tender thought had lain, deep hid,
Like a spring flower that sleeps 'neath wintry snows,
Till balmy seasons call its tendrils forth;
Thus mem'ry touched the germ in many hearts
And woke Fraternal feeling in the breast
Of comrades who had shared the weary march;
From same canteen had quaffed the cooling drink,
Assuaging thirst intense, of famished men,
Who, shoulder to shoulder, had met the foe;
Where fiercest carnage raged had borne the brunt,
And had together faced its scenes of horror.
Then midst the loyal lads o'er all the "States"
In field and shop, and busy mart wide severed,
The feeling grew, a yearning unsuppressed,
To see and greet again those fellow soldiers.
This longing found expression and reply;
Some met, were thrilled with joy, and organized
This loyal, true, and mighty brotherhood,
" Grand Army of Republic." 'Thus was formed
The nucleus small of numbers few,
Round which now stand *two hundred thousand* comrades.
Loyalty was its test and basis firm,
And with *Fraternity* presided there;
These two were wed, and from this union true,

Came *Charity*, which greater is than all.
These soldiers' hearts are swayed by unseen motors;
They are united by a wondrous tie;
A mystic link inured by battles dared,
Strong joined, aye, welded too, by dangers shared.
By camp-fires lighted in a thousand towns,
Do comrades bring the wealth of memory's stores;
The symbols keep of war's vicissitudes;
Join hands in holy realm of sympathy,
And annually the "Grand Encampment" meets,
And year by year grows large with added numbers.
So shall this order prosper, lifted o'er
All party wrangle or dissension's strife,
And gather hosts of veteran recruits,
Till *ten years* pass—fast fall the soldiers old—
And then shall surely come the lessening ranks.
With no more volunteers from whom to choose;
Then one by one shall *all* be mustered out,
Yet, answer to a glorious reveille,
And join the comrades who have gone before.
In Heaven shall gather an army grand,
To form one universal brotherhood.' "

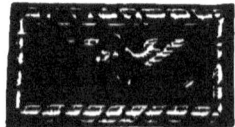

CAMP-FIRE XXII.

A ROMANCE OF THE WAR—A STORY STRANGE BUT TRUE—
WHAT AN INSANE FISHERMAN CAUGHT.

GATHERED together this evening—a very comfortable one—the veterans chatted miscellaneously for a time before commencing business. Finally the commander fired up the pipe of peace, and then called the assembly to order. But in his eagerness to proceed with the chats he somehow forgot to pass the pipe around, thereby totally disregarding the traditionary custom of his majesty, the redskin. Since it was the commander who abused the tradition, the comrades each concluded to light a pipe for himself, after which Captain M—k spoke:

" In the summer of 1862 our regiment was stationed along the line of railroad from Decatur to Courtland, Alabama. Small parties of us, from time to time, went out foraging on our own account, and on one of these expeditions I had an adventure which had never recurred to my mind until an event which happened a few years after the war recalled it forcibly.

" After the cessation of hostilities there was considerable talk throughout the North of forming colonies to settle in the West and South. Well, I got the 'colony fever' and conceived the idea of getting up a colony to settle in Northern Alabama, probably near our old stamping ground.

" With this project in view I went from Chicago to Decatur, Alabama, and from there by rail still further South toward the Black Warrior River. Reaching my journey's end

I concluded to return on horseback by a round-about way, and visit some of the back country; so I hired a horse and started out, first gathering information as to where I could find accommodations on the road, for houses and settlers are very scarce in that part of the world, so that it behooves a traveler to get his 'points' before setting out on a journey. My calculation was to reach the house of a certain settler at about seven o'clock in the evening. Seven o'clock came, but no settler's house in sight;—eight o'clock—nine o'clock—*ten* o'clock, and still no house to be seen.

"By this time I was thoroughly convinced that I had lost my way. I was tired out, and my horse was completely jaded. I rode on about an hour, and at last to my supreme delight I spied a light which I made for at once. I found that it proceeded from the window of a log cabin to which I rode up, and dismounting and hitching my horse, I attempted to enter the yard, when three savage dogs with angry growls disputed my further advance. But I finally succeeded in safely reaching the porch. I gave a knock on the door which roused the proprietor of the place, whereupon the following dialogue ensued, through the closed door:

"'Who's there?'

"'A traveler who has lost his way.'

"'What do you want?'

"'I want accommodation for myself and horse till morning.'

"'Well, you can't stay here. I don't keep tavern.'

"'How far is it to the next house?'

"'Seven miles.'

"'It's not possible for me to go seven miles, for my horse is completely tired out.'

"'I can't help that; my wife is sick, and I can't have you around.'

"'Can't you give me some feed for my horse, and a blanket for myself? I'll sleep on the porch.'

"After considerable parleying and urging, this request was finally granted. Soon the door opened and a tall, powerful man emerged, carrying a lantern which he held squarely in my face for a moment in order to get a good look at me, after which he led the way to the stable, where he groomed and fed my horse, and then we returned to the house.

"At the porch I halted, expecting him to go in and get me a blanket; but as he entered the door he said:

"'Come in, stranger; I want to talk to you.'

"I entered the cabin and sat down. He threw a few pine knots upon the smoldering fire and soon a bright blaze illumined the room. Then placing himself squarely in front of me, and giving me a searching look, he demanded in an imperious manner:

"'Now, stranger, I want to know who you are, and what is your business in these parts?'

"'I have already told you that I am a traveler looking for a suitable location to establish a colony from the North.'

"'Looking for land, hey! Going to establish a colony? Now, stranger, that story is altogether *too thin!* Men don't go round at midnight hunting for land. Now tell me the truth—who *are* you, and *what are you after?*'

"'I have already told you who I am, and my business; and if you don't believe me it is not my fault.'

"Again he searchingly eyed me, and then with an earnest emphasis, said:

"'Stranger, you have been in these parts before!'

"'Yes.'

"'You were a Yankee soldier, then?'

"'Yes.'

"'In 1862, and stationed near Decatur?'

"'Yes.'

"'While out foragin' one day with another Yankee you stumbled into Roddy's confederate cavalry camp; but before you were discovered you turned back and escaped?'

"'Yes.'

"'Just as you left Roddy's camp you met one of Roddy's men with a neck-yoke over his shoulders, and carrying a couple of buckets of water in his hands?'

"'Yes.'

"'*You put your pistol to that man's head and forced him to go over a mile to the rear with you* to prevent his giving an alarm?'

"'Yes.'

"'Stranger, *I am that man!*'

"It seemed to me, about that time, that he meant business, and intended to settle the old affair there and then. But putting on a bold front, I remarked as unconcernedly as I could:

"'Well, you have a mighty good memory.'

"'Yes, I remember some things. You bet I knew you the minute I set eyes on you; and I'll remember you as long as I live.'

"Meanwhile his wife had made her appearance, and, lighting her corn-cob pipe, seated herself near the fireplace, prepared to enjoy the fun.

"I hardly knew what would come next; but, after a pause, the man changed his position and manner, and said:

"'Now that I've told you who *you* are I'll tell you more about myself. I staid with Roddy's Cavalry Company for about three months after I saw you, and then my brother and myself deserted and enlisted in the First Alabama Union cavalry regiment, where we staid till the close of the war. After the war we came home; we were obliged to sleep in caves and keep concealed for a long time, as our former companions sought to kill us, and hunted us like wolves. Our lives were in danger every minute—but lately they don't trouble us much.

"'But I say, stranger, how's things up North? Is there

going to be another war? We think there will be soon. If there is you may count on me in going in for *Union!*'

"He now brought me out a lunch to which I did ample justice, and then I asked for a blanket that I might go to sleep upon the porch, as agreed.

"'No sir,' said he; 'no blanket for you; I've as good a bed as there is in this part of the country, and you are welcome to it!'

"After sleeping till morning I found a fine breakfast awaiting me, and that my horse had been already taken care of; and when I started off again my landlord accompanied me for several miles to show me the way."

"That's a good story," said Colonel Van Buren, of the 192d New York; "but let me tell an incident that will remind many of you of a hundred similar schemes which the homesick invented to get discharged.

"You all know how the boys tried the insanity dodge. Well, there was one fellow in my regiment who played it most successfully. We were at Fort Grebel in February, 1862. Fort Grebel was on the branch of the Potomac, opposite Arlington Heights.

"One night there was a very heavy rain, and in the morning, before the other soldiers began to stir about the camp, this fellow—I have forgotten his name—tied a string to his bayonet, took a position on the parapet, began fishing in a shallow pool, and to all appearances became entirely unmindful of his surroundings.

"An hour passed. No one interrupted him, and still he could be seen quietly but regularly lifting his gun with the string from the pool, as though the gun were a fishing pole, and that he had a bite. By and by the sun came up, and while the other boys were going about camp preparing for breakfast, the fisherman still kept up his weary stroke, lifting his supposed fishing-tackle from the water almost as regularly as though it were done by a clock.

"The surroundings and occasion were such that it was only necessary for a sane man to look once in order to be convinced that something was lacking about the 'head-work' of the machine which was fishing in the pool.

"The boys all began to talk about the matter, many of them jesting in a manner wholly amusing. But no cessation in the regular stroke of the fisherman. Finally the matter came to the notice of the captain, who at once proceeded to the interesting scene of operations.

"'What are you doing there?' he demanded.

"No response. The gun and string were lifted with the same regularity as ever.

"'Halt!' commanded the captain.

"Not a single movement of the fisherman. Up went the pretended fishing-tackle again.

"'Shoulder arms!' again commanded the captain, thinking that hearing an accustomed order might bring the soldier to his senses.

"But the warrior's countenance was as rigid as ever, and the fixed stare seemed riveted on the string which hung from the point of his bayonet and dropped carelessly down into the small pool before him.

"The captain now concluded to report the matter to the colonel, and started off on the errand at once. He suddenly met the colonel who had also beheld the fisherman, and was coming to investigate. The captain then returned to the scene with the colonel, when the same experience was repeated.

"The colonel concluded to call the surgeon, who came and examined the fisherman,—as well as possible while the incessant raising and lowering of his gun was being carried on,—and recommended that the insane fisherman be given a discharge, which was accordingly written out and handed to the captain; but before it was given to the soldier, the colonel asked:

"'What are you fishing for?'"

"No reply.

"'Well, I guess you can give him the document,' continued the colonel, and the captain handed it over to the fisherman, saying loudly:

"'Here! take this!'

"'*That's what I was fishing for,*' replied the fisherman as he threw down his gun, pocketed the discharge, and immediately left camp, much to the amazement of the colonel, the captain and the surgeon, and *very* much to the *amusement* of all others who had heard the conversation."

CAMP-FIRE XXIII.

THE WRONG OX BY THE HORNS—THE TABLES TURNED ON AN OFFICER'S STRICT DISCIPLINE—A DECISION BY MANSFIELD, GENERAL—RIVALRY IN RELIGION.

"A FEW evenings since," said Mr. S. W. Rodgers, "a reminiscence of General Nelson was given, in which something was said about strict discipline. I remember a similar incident in which an officer was compelled to take a dose of his own medicine. It was in the fall of 1863, after the army had advanced beyond Chattanooga. Fortress Rosecrans, Murfreesboro, was garrisoned by disabled batteries—to man the guns and do guard-duty they kept a picket line around the fortress.

"Some of the officers in command of the post were not liked as well as they might have been, had they been more deserving. One of these, who was officer of the day at one time, and who had not been accustomed to holding office of any kind, much less to commanding soldiers, concluded that he would like to show his authority. So he gave strict official instruction to the pickets, each to halt at twenty paces, dismount, advance, and give the countersign.

"All this passed off well enough, the boys executing the order to the letter. But finally the tables were turned. The officer tried to catch some of the boys asleep at their posts, but of course failed, most ludicrously. On the bank of Stone River, where the line crossed, there happened to be a resolute young fellow who could not be intimidated nor imposed upon.

"The pickets saw that the officer in discussion was trying to impress upon the minds of the boys the fact that he had been promoted, and his vigilance, the picket, at once concluded to muster and control all his accustomed wariness. The officer approached from the opposite side of the river. The picket, however, had previously ascertained the fact that it was precisely twenty paces from where he was standing to the middle of the river. It may have occurred, however, nothing being found in the annals of history to the contrary, that the picket previously moved his post a few feet from its original location toward the river, in order to have the middle of the river exactly twenty paces from his post; but this has never been proven.

"Whichever way that may have been, these two things are certain: That the officer rode into the stream with considerable pomp, and that the picket stood at his post with just as much pomp, like the hero that he was, probably thinking of Casabianca and a certain incident in the navy when the deck was on fire.

"When the officer had reached the middle of the stream," continued Mr. Rodgers, who had been interrupted by the throwing of more twigs on the camp-fire, " the picket immediately commanded:

"'Halt! Who goes there?'

"'I'm the *officer* of the *guard*,' replied the officer.

"'Dismount, advance and give the countersign!' was the further order from the picket.

"'Why, don't you know me, sir?—I'm the officer of the guard, sir,—*officer* of the *guard!*' repeating the emphasized words with much importance.

"'I'm not supposed to know any one. I abide by the code, sir,—*abide* by the *code;* I must *obey orders*, sir,—*o-b-e-y orders!*' responded the picket, with the same kind of emphasis that had come from the man in the river, and the picket raised his gun to fire.

"'Hold on!' cried the officer, "*I'll dismount!*' and down he went into the river, the water of which had been a month or two before considerably warmer than it was then. Any one who was listening might have heard an unusual amount of swearing by the '*officer* of the *guard*;' but this had no effect on the picket, who waited patiently for the officer to dismount, advance, and give the countersign. Next day the picket was put under arrest at the instance of the enraged officer, and was tried by court-martial, but of course cleared."

Then General I. N. Stiles remembered a decision by Mansfield, the general, which the legal fraternity may compare with one by Mansfield. the justice.

"When the rebel ram, Merrimac," said he, "first appeared at Hampton Roads—March 8, 1862,—General Mansfield was in command of the land forces. The ram had sunk the Union war vessel 'Cumberland' and had disabled the 'Congress,' which was run ashore to prevent her being captured by the 'rebs.'

"Seeing this, General Mansfield ordered the 20th Indiana Infantry to deploy along the beach, behind a sand ridge, to prevent the 'Congress' from being hauled off by the enemy. This vessel, now helpless and at the mercy of the Merrimac's guns, had run up a white flag in token of surrender. Captain R., of the 20th Indiana, who had been as good a lawyer at home as he was now soldier in the field, suggested that it would be a violation of the laws of war to prevent the enemy from taking possession of the vessel, since 'she had already surrendered.'

"I know the d—d *ship* has surrendered,' replied General Mansfield, ' but I want you to understand that *we* haven't.' The decision was final."

After the foregoing incident a veteran who, through modesty, declined to give his name, told a religious (?) anecdote. His name being unknown, the S. P. U. H. chroniclers might have attempted to describe him, but he stood behind the smoke which was then rolling in clouds from the fire, so that he could not be seen. His story is this :

" After we had settled down to some reliable routine of spending our time in the army, and had established what may be termed army society, our brigade and the one which was usually next to us became the most earnest rivals in almost everything.

" The colonels of the brigades seemed to catch the inspiration, and the friendly contests which we had, generally centered in them.

" Well, one season there was a religious revival in our brigade, which furnished an interesting programme for some time. The boys had been given a season of rest, and having much time to reflect upon their active wickedness, they became passive, and concluded to be at least entertained by the exercises.

" The other brigade saw that we were excelling them in this respect, and they determined upon a revival. Then an excitement arose, and the interest increased until finally twelve of our boys 'got religion,' and desired to be baptized. The baptism was administered, and soon a report of the occurrence came to the ears of the colonel of the other brigade, who called up the chaplain at once, and said:

"' Here! Chaplain, you have let that brigade over there get ahead of us! Go and detail at least thirty able-bodied men for baptism immediately. We'll not be outdone by them.' "

CAMP-FIRE XXIV.

THE WRONG KIND OF A CAT—"MORE ABOUT THE BROKEN WINDOW," OR CRAWFORD AGAIN.

JUST before Sherman started to Vicksburg," said a comrade from the 76th Ohio, " the river became so low that it was exceedingly difficult to make any speed with the boats. The nights were *very* dark, on account of the thick fogs, and we therefore gave up trying to run at night. As soon as it began to grow dark, the boats dropped anchor, and then came the time for rest and recreation, especially the latter, the opportunity for which was generally improved by hunting something fresh to eat.

" Two of us left the boat as soon as we could get ashore, and started off for a neighboring wilderness. We hurried along and were soon lost from the sight of the river and the dim outlines of the boats as they were 'tooting' and puffing to and fro over the sand-bars.

" We passed an old deserted log-cabin that well represented to my mind the birthplace of some illustrious statesman, as indicated by some imaginative pictures. On our first approach to the place, my heart bounded in the hope that we would soon have our stomach filled with something a little more palatable than hard-tack and bacon, but the nearer we approached the place the nearer our hearts approached our boots. No inhabitants, human or otherwise, could be found. It was the first domicil I had ever seen about which there was absolutely no living thing,—that is, nothing large enough to eat. The situation was very apparent—as much so as the growing darkness would allow. Curiosity, however, led us to explore. Old memories began to haunt us. I remembered the 'poet's lines,' in the 'Return of the Dead:'

> "'The bolt flew back with sudden clang;
> I entered; wall and rafter rang.'

"But the application of this was not practical, for two reasons: First, there was no bolt, and probably there never had been any; and second, there was no door, and with equal probability, there may never have been any. I thought of the two lines of poetry again, and at once concluded that they would be appropriate if I should change the punctuation. Hence, not thinking what I was about, I repeated the couplet aloud:

> "'The bolt flew back with sudden clang;
> I entered the wall; and the rafter rang!'

"No sooner had I repeated the lines than I adopted the conclusion, and thought to try the experiment. I called to my comrade:

"'Come on; let's go in, and see what's here, any way.'

"'All right,' he replied, and soon was around on my side of the concern. We stepped nearer to the old hull. I put my hand against a log to try its firmness. That whole part of the building fell in! Sure enough, I did then enter the wall, my comrade following. We were now inside of the building. For my own part, I felt a little strange. Everything was quiet, of course. I looked around carefully without moving. There were many dark corners, and many openings to the habitation, the principal one of which was overhead; in fact, the entire roof was made of sky. We looked and listened for a moment longer. There was a slight dull sound that startled us. Then there was an unpleasant odor—perhaps from the rotten wood. We immediately left the premises, but the scent did not leave us, and the only unmistakable and unsatisfactory conclusion that we could adopt was, that a certain kind of a cat lived there.

"Undaunted by this," continued the narrator, "we became only the more determined to have something to eat before returning, so we started on down the road. Before we went very far, however, we saw a light, and soon found this proceeded from the present abode of the people who had once lived in the dilapidated hulk which we had just left. We were now very tired, and concluded to purchase something to eat instead of looking farther. We bought six chickens and a few other things for five dollars, and, to the relief of the householders, made a short stay, returning hurriedly to the boat to change our clothing. As we approached the boat,"—

"Wait!" said the commander of the camp-fire. "Don't tell the rest of it."

"No! your story is too long now," added the reporter, and the comrade sat down amidst applause.

Mr. Crawley then supplemented his reminiscence of Crawford with the following:

"On the march and in camp Crawford always improved every opportunity to make fun for the boys; but it was in 'winter-quarters' where his propensity for fun found its full vent. With the aid of powder he invented all sorts of explosives, keeping the camp in a continual uproar; and that, too, without getting into trouble. He was always able to conceal the origin of his mischief, for, while many of the officers and men suspected who was the real author of all the fuss, but few of them could have testified to it, and they could not have been induced to betray him.

"One evening, I remember, as the men were falling in for roll-call, there occurred a terrific explosion which created the wildest commotion. Horses broke loose from the picket-line; men rushed for their arms, and the excitement at once

BATTLE OF LOOKOUT MOUNTAIN, TENN.—NOV. 24, 1863.

spread over the camp. The enemy was thought to be right down on us, and immediate preparations began to be made to resist an attack. The adjutant was sent to investigate, while the regiment sent up a yell which ended in a general laugh, with cries, ' Crawford again! Crawford again!'

"A little later I met Crawford with the same sad expression on his face, and taking me aside, he showed me what, before it had exploded, had been a *lead cannon.*

"'How did it come to explode?' I asked; for after bursting it had bulged out in the middle and had more the appearance of a steel rat-trap, when set, than anything else. He was now seized with another fit of laughter, during which he caught me by the arm and executed the 'Highland Fling' schottische around me, occasionally striking me in the back to give zest to the performance.

"When the fit was over he said that he took half a canteen and put the edge of it on a split stick. This contrivance served as a ladle in which he melted bullets. These he poured into a miniature well, in the center of which he had placed a small round stick perpendicularly, and around the stick wrapped a piece of wet paper. The molten lead was then poured into the well until it stood above the end of the stick. After allowing the lead time to cool he dug it out, pulled out the stick, filled the lead cast thus obtained with powder, closed the muzzle by hammering it together, bored a hole about midway between the breech and muzzle, and then the concern was ready for business.

"'Why did you use lead?' I asked, after he had finished describing the process of manufacturing the bogus cannon.

"'Because,' he replied, 'it is safe. Lead will tear apart but not break into pieces; and being soft, I could close the muzzle and get a much louder report. See? And then if anybody should happen to find it, they wouldn't know what to do with it;' and he laughed again.

"I shall never forget the night Crawford persuaded Jim Haliday into his tent to play 'seven-up.' Jim was a 'recruit,' and had just begun to be fascinated by the game of cards. Crawford had always felt morally obligated to teach the recruits all the methods of army life, and generally had a new mode of initiation for each one. Jim, of course, could not be allowed to remain long in camp uninitiated.

"On this particular night, Haliday played with the usual peculiar luck which attends beginners, and frequently made 'high, low, jack and the game,' and probably could have had the 'gift,' by asking for it; but he did not know that the piece of candle which burned within a foot of his head was *loaded*, nor that above him was suspended a bucket of water neatly on a pivot from which a small cord hung innocently by the side of Crawford; nor was he aware that beneath him, and beside the box on which he sat, lay at least a quarter of a pound of *loose powder*. Haliday held wonderful hands; he had just scored the inevitable 'high, low, jack and the game,' and the eager, flushed face, and sparkling eye, bespoke the excitement and pleasure born of victory, when the candle explodes and a piece of the burning wick sets Haliday's hair in a blaze, the powder is ignited beneath him, and while he and Crawford are both fighting the fire in Haliday's fore-top, Haliday is treated to a cold shower bath from above. Haliday was so badly frightened that he never got angry until next day, when he proposed to 'lick' Crawford; but Crawford convinced him that the true policy was to claim, that while writing a letter home to his mother in his tent, he thoughtlessly got his head too near the candle. Crawford told me a few days after this episode, while convulsed with laughter, that he regarded it as an outrage that so few of the boys called on him at his tent. He also stated (and I believe truly) that the setting fire to Haliday's head, by the piece of burning wick, was wholly unforeseen and unintended. It may have been only imaginative, but it never seemed to me that Haliday held as good hands, or played the game with the same eager, unreserved, child-like confidence, that he did before he encountered Crawford.

"For 'winter-quarters,' near Brownsville, Arkansas, some of the men built regular log-houses with chimneys and fire-places; others put up frame structures, six feet by ten, using a tent for a roof, but even these structures had small chimneys with fire-places; two bunks were constructed, one above the other, at right angles to the fire-place, and in front of the lower bunk a board or box was placed in front of the fire for a seat. One dark rainy night while walking down the 'tent-line,' old man Seward and Bierman jumped out of the top of one of these structures, carrying the tent roof with them, followed by a cloud of smoke and ashes. I had heard a noise before I left my quarters, but noises were so frequent that I paid no particular attention to this one. Seward and Bierman, who 'bunked' and 'messed' together, were members of the church, and were trying to lead a consistent life; and they succeeded as well as their surroundings would permit, but it was a terribly uphill-business. On the evening in question it seems they had 'read a chapter,' and were engaged in singing the familiar and comforting hymn:

> 'It may not be my way,
> It may not be thy way,
> And yet, in His own way,
> The Lord will provide,'

whên the 'back-log' exploded, and threw consternation, ashes, live coals, and burning brands, all over the interior of the 'domicile of the faithful,' and Seward and Bierman, in the excitement and hurry of the moment, and doubtless as a matter of convenience, escaped through the roof.

"I hunted up Crawford, finding him in his bunk; he reached for me, and clutching me tightly by the arm with one hand, with the other he would stuff the corner of the blanket in his mouth, and shake and kick. He finally became composed enough to tell me that it had been raining all day, and supposing that somebody would need a 'back-log,' he had prepared one, and had been careful not to cut it *too long;* that with a half-inch auger he had bored a half dozen holes in it and charged them with powder, and placed it where everybody must pass over it, in walking up and down the 'tent-line;' 'and do you know,' said he, 'I watched it for four mortal hours, before anybody took up with it, and yet every man in the company has stepped over it, from one to three times, and I know that fully two-thirds of them were out of wood, and too lazy to cut any; but at last Bierman carried it in, and he and Seward made a good fire and sat down and began to sing hymns. Everything was so quiet that I began to grow restless and uneasy, and concluded to drop in on them and inquire how they were getting on; they were very friendly, but somehow I couldn't make myself at home, and presently when a piece of the bark of the 'back-log' threw the 'fore-stick' into my lap, I told them I guessed I would go, that it was getting late, that I had been 'on duty' the night before, and was tired and sleepy; they mentioned that the wood was green and popped badly, and I told them that I had noticed the same thing myself; as I was leaving they were re-adjusting the 'fore-stick' and sweeping up the litter, but before I got to my tent I heard her go off, and saw them climbing out through the top; then I got in my bunk with my boots on, and began to snore. I am glad I called on them, for I would hate to have them suspect *me*,' and again he clutched me by the arm and stuffed the blanket in his mouth, and shook and kicked. I always thought that Seward suspicioned Crawford as in some way connected with his being blown up, and Crawford thought so too, for he told me that he noticed a change in his manner. But in the fight at Mulberry Creek Seward had his horse shot under him, and while fooling around trying to save his saddle, a retreat was ordered, and the old man was left behind, nearly 'tuckered out,' and the surroundings generally were unpleasant. Crawford went back and took him on behind him and got away with him, fraternally, as well as physically. When the news reached us that Lee and Johnston had surrendered to Grant and Sherman, that the Southern Confederacy had collapsed, and the war was over, we were inhaling the perfume of the magnolia, and a grateful sense of peace took the place of the hideous nightmare of civil war that had oppressed us for four long terrible years, and all eyes, except Crawford's, turned gladly homeward. He alone seemed gloomy and despondent, and went about with the air and expression of one who had been deeply wronged and injured. I ventured to inquire the cause, and he told me that he had prepared a series of entertainments for the boys that would consume at least a year, and yet the war had been abruptly brought to a close, that he had no notice of it, and had not even been consulted in the matter, and that he knew the boys would be disappointed. I do not know whether he is still alive or not, but if he is living, and his eye should rest upon this brief, hasty narrative, I am sure he would not be offended, for two reasons: First, because it is literally true, and secondly, because there never was and never will be, two more devoted friends than we."

CAMP-FIRE XXV.

A RAW RECRUIT'S ANXIETY—ANOTHER STORY ABOUT ANOTHER MULE—ON THE ST. FRANCIS RIVER—A GENERAL INCOG. REFUSED A CUP OF COFFEE—A CONFEDERATE'S IDEA OF WHAT THE GOSPEL IS.

S the tones of the previous speaker died away with the soft noise of the wind through the branches of the trees that overhung the glowing embers of the fire, R. C. Coyner, of the 38th Indiana, Vol. Inf., remarked: "I had just enlisted from the school-room at Hanover College, near Madison, Ind., when we were ordered by General Sherman to head off Buckner, who was raiding the northern part of Kentucky. We were in company with the Louisville Legion, the 6th Indiana, the 1st Ohio, and the 15th Indiana regulars. We were all raw recruits except the 15th Indiana, and knew about as much concerning discipline and drill as so many school-boys; nevertheless, we thought ourselves the flower of the army. After leaving New Albany, Ind., we marched to Louisville, then took the cars to Lebanon Junction, and then marched to Elizabethtown, Ky. After we reached this point we went into camp.

"One day Captain Pointdexter, our captain, detailed me for detached service, and I was ordered to report at General Sherman's headquarters. Upon my arrival I was put in command of a squad whose duty was to guard the general's quarters. I relieved the guard on duty, and posted my men to the best of my ability. The day grew apace, and toward night General Sherman emerged from his tent and began to pace a beat in front, with his hands behind him, and his head bent forward, seemingly in a brown study. My inexperience and unfamiliarity with the scenes and customs of military service rendered me all the more alive to my ideas of a soldier's duty, and as I beheld our commander pacing to and fro, the idea occurred to me that the responsibility of guarding our general was one of no mean importance. We had no idea of the proximity of the rebel forces, but the night was coming on and I began to fear that, in case of a surprise, the guard was ill fitted to protect the person of our chieftain. The more I thought of it, the more solicitous I felt.

"At length I concluded that I would ask the general if it would not be the proper thing to double the guard about the headquarters.

"Accordingly I stepped up, and after saluting the general, asked:

"'General, don't you think it would be a good thing to double the guard for the night?'

"The general looked at me in a surprised sort of way, and said, after a moment's reflection·

"'What did you say?'

"'Don't you think the guard should be doubled for the night?' I repeated.

'Sir, you are drunk!' was the reply that fell upon my astonished ears.

"'General, I mean what I say—you can make inquiry of my colonel and captain as to my habits if you have any doubts as to my sobriety,' I ventured to remark.

"The general laughed in an amused kind of way, and raising his long arm and waving me a curious salute, said:

"'Ah, I have been accustomed to having regulars for my guard. I do not think there is any use of doubling the guard to-night, sir.'

"The full force of his remark did not dawn upon my

peaceful mind until I had seen more service, but I can assure you, boys, that I know now just what he meant."

Comrade Coyner's anecdote brought a smile to the face of every veteran present, and each recalled the first time he shouldered his musket and went with a squad of "greenies," of whom which was the greenest it was hard to tell, to learn the drill.

The smiles were still lingering upon the fire-lit faces, when comrade Coyner supplemented his story with the following:

"At the battle of Perryville, and, by the way, boys, that was one of the hottest fights I saw during my three years of service, I noticed a mule out in front of our line, and directly in the line of fire, quietly grazing. He continued to nibble the grass as unconcernedly as though he were a thousand miles away from a battlefield. I was wondering at the splendid nonchalance of the long-eared beast, when a small cannon ball struck him in the upper part of the neck and tore a huge hole. The animal staggered a little, and, as if unmindful of his hurt, began to graze again,"—

"How big was the ball that hit him?" asked an ex-army teamster.

"Well, I should judge it was a twelve-pound shot, judging from the size of the hole it made," replied comrade Coyner.

The audible smiles of those present made the air quiver with fun, and the good-natured elves who have always been in attendance upon the scribe of the S. P. U. H. during his stay at these camp-fires, indulged in a fantastic minuet in order to allay their propensity to get into mischief.

A broad smile irradiated the visage of J. O. Henderson of the 80th Ohio, who related the following:

"We were lying at the mouth of the St. Francis River, a small, swiftly-flowing stream which empties into the Mississippi above Helena, and one afternoon we were detailed to board a small stern-wheeled steamer, and go up the river to capture some Confederate commissary stores. We got off finally, yet we made but little progress, as the river was very swift, and our boat ill adapted to stem such a swift current.

"We puffed and wheezed along at a snail-like pace, hugging the shore, and the night came on. The weather was misty, and the night pitch dark. We ran out of wood and went ashore to get a supply. Having loaded up, we cast and swung into the current. After some hours' steaming we ran out of wood the second time, and seeing a light on shore, hailed it, and asked if we could get wood there. The reply being in the affirmative, we landed and again renewed our stock of fuel. Again we cast off, and went on our way.

"Toward morning we were also in need of fuel, and hailing another light, arranged to obtain more wood, the owner saying as we touched the shore:

"'I guess that you can have it at $3.00, bein' as you fellers have got wood here twice before to-night!'

"The fact was we had not been over half a mile from that wood yard all night long, and when it was light enough to see, it was apparent that our vessel could not make any progress. We therefore turned around and went back."

The amanuensis of the S. P. U. H. having made his notes of the foregoing, was sharpening his pencil for further work, when a comrade of Smith Hancock of Co. D, 80th Ohio, narrated this incident:

"While we were encamped near Farmington, down in Mississippi, Smith Hancock had built a fire one morning and was cooking his breakfast, when General Hamilton came along with a small coffee-pot in his hand, and asked if he might make some coffee.

"'Naw, ye can't!' said Hancock.

"'Well,' said the general, 'I'm half sick, and I want to make a cup of coffee. I won't disturb your cooking at all.'

"'Oh, go to h—l and make your coffee,' retorted Hancock.

"Notwithstanding the protest, the general placed his coffee-pot on the fire, when Hancock stepped up and kicked it away some twenty feet, and said:

"'Lookee here, if you try that again, I'll lick h—l out of you!'

"'All right,' said the new comer, who began to pull off his coat.

"As his coat came off, Hancock saw the general's stars, and he uttered an expression of surprise and bolted into the bushes, as if the Old Nick was after him. We could hear him crashing through the bushes for three hundred yards.

"It wasn't ten minutes until the story spread among the boys, and, as it went along, the yell went up, and the progress of the yarn could be plainly distinguished along the line.

"Hancock did not come in for a week, and when he did put in an appearance the boys tormented the life nearly out of him."

"Another funny thing occurred down in Vicksburg," said a gray-haired man who had listened attentively to all that had been said. "Chaplain Howard, of the 42d Illinois, approached a knot of Confederate prisoners and accosted a long, lean, lank specimen, with:

"'My friend, have you the Gospel among you?'

"'Waal, I can't tell ye, stranger; I dunno nuthin' about it here—don't think we've got it, but I hearn that it has broke out awful bad down in Camp Douglas!'

"The Confederate thought the chaplain was talking about some disease.

"As soon as the chaplain recovered from his surprise he retreated in good order, and before night-fall the story was all over camp."

THE LATEST NEWS.

CAMP-FIRE XXVI.

THE SEQUEL TO THE FARMER AND THE WATERMELONS—
THE UN-WISDOM OF A RAW RECRUIT—A JOKE ON
THE GENERAL—THE TEMPERANCE MAJOR—THE CAP-
TAIN WHO DIDN'T WATER HIS WHISKEY.

IN August, 1864," said Mr. A. M. Peck, "our regiment was stationed at Paducah, Ky., and a little incident occurred there which is similar to one told at the first camp-fire. Realizing that the soldiers were often without fresh vegetables for weeks at a time, and sometimes without any, the citizens frequently brought garden truck, fruit, melons, etc., into camp, where such things usually found a ready market, especially when the prices were anywhere near reasonable. But occasionally there would a fellow come along, who had most wonderful ideas of the value of his goods, vividly reminding us of the sutler. To pay for the privilege of selling to the boys the traders usually took a liberal measure to headquarters.

"One pleasant day the cry of 'Here's yer mule!' rang through the camp. All the boys were on the alert for some fun, if it was to be had. The mule was a small one, hitched to a dilapidated old wagon, with an old skeleton of a horse which one would think would need weather-boarding to keep the hay that he ate from blowing away.

"In the wagon were a few bushels of apples, but from their appearance one could never guess what they really were; knotty things about the size of green walnuts, black and muddy from having lain on the ground so long before gathering, and were really unfit for first-class hog-feed. In all probability the apples had once been thrown to the swine, which had turned away from them, the apple merchant then collecting and offering them to the soldiers. He had heard that anything eatable could be sold to soldiers at a big price, and now expected to make a small fortune.

"But his hopes soon vanished. The boys gathered around, and of course sampled the apples as fast as they could. Only a few, however, were fit to be sampled. The driver thus saw the choicest (if this adjective is applicable) pieces of his fruit rapidly vanishing without any pecuniary return, or even promise of such. He at once concluded to make a desperate effort to save what was left, and whipped away at his sad-faced donkey and his almost fleshless horse, until first the horse and then the donkey began to approach something like a trot, as near as could be judged by soldiers who had had considerable experience in equestrianism before the war. But before the celerity of the team attained the before-mentioned desired gait, the top of a hill was reached, which achievement, however, was made after a certain other event took place, namely: The boys kept even pace with the wagon, and also kept abstracting apples therefrom until the vehicle had been dragged nearly to the top of the hill, when, by some sleight-of-hand, one of the boys slipped out the hind gate of the wagon box, and, sad to tell, the countryman's apples, severally and collectively, suddenly retreated and were captured by a large number of soldiers, who were in the reserve, while the driver, now finding it easy to persuade the mule and the horse to proceed faster on account of the down grade,—looked not back, but accepted the result, sadly concluding that there was great falsehood in the rumor he had heard about such high prices being obtained from soldiers for such a low grade of fruit."

Mr. W. B. Cowan then said that he remembered an

incident about raw recruits, "while on the march to Atlanta, that created fun for us soldiers.

"As was our custom, we had halted along the road for a few minutes' rest, and as soon as the 'Halt' was sounded every fellow immediately tumbled down into a fence corner, or where the fence corner should have been, in order to get all the rest possible before the 'Forward' was sounded. All the old regiments at that time had received a good many new recruits, and they had not become acustomed to old soldiers' ways. When we would halt for a rest, new recruits would be passing frequently, to catch up with their regiments. You could always recognize one of them by the load he carried— a big knapsack with a change of clothes, a blanket or two, and almost always with the bayonet on his gun. We halted one warm day away down in Georgia, and one of those recruits, with an unusual big load on his back, and a new, bright bayonet on his gun, came dragging himself along, when one of the old boys in our regiment, a droll wag of a fellow, raised up on his elbow, took a good long look at the recruit, and said: 'Hello, soldier!' The fellow stopped. 'Where did you git that gun sharpened?' The fellow could make no answer. It raised a yell that did not die out until the *recruit* had gone out of sight."

The drum major of the 72d Illinois Infantry, Mr. Edward B. Potter, then said, that "immediately after the fight at Franklin, Tenn., (I have forgotten the date), the supplies were, for some unknown reason, slow in coming—so much so, that our regiment was fed on roasted corn for about five days. Of course some of the boys objected, and cursed the government for not having better food ready for them at the proper time; but they composed a very small per cent. The great majority laughed and chatted, taking it all in good fun, and watched their opportunity to play a joke on the general. After a few days of corn rations, and immediately after breakfast one morning, an orderly sergeant of one of the companies took a rope and tying six or eight of the comrades in a string, started down the road. Wondering what on earth the sergeant meant, the astonished general rode up and inquired:

"'What in (Hades) is the matter here? What have these men done, sir, that they should be treated in this manner?'

"'Well, general, said the sergeant, with a very guilty look, as if he had really assumed the authority to punish the boys for some supposed wrong,—'well, general, I have just fed my mules their corn, and am now taking them down to water.'

"'Ha! ha! ha!' burst from all who could hear the remark, which, indeed, was loud enough.

"'Sold again!' said the general, who kindly saluted them and rode off."

"As short stories seem to be in order, here is one," remarked a comrade from the East, a guest at the camp-fire.

"In the fall of '64 the artillery brigade to which I was attached, was under the command of a major from Maine, who had unfortunately departed from the temperance principles for which that State has for so many years been noted. It was my misfortune for a time to have charge of the whiskey at the headquarters, to which the major's brigade was attached, and many laughable incidents occurred, one of which comes back fresh to my mind on the present occasion.

"In anticipation of his birthday, and a celebration with friends, as I surmised, the major, the day previous to that anniversary, rode up to headquarters and accosting me by name, inquired how much whiskey I had on hand.

"Not thinking our supply of stimulant needed in the direction mentioned, the major already being far too much under its influence, I evaded a true statement, and replied:

"'Only a small quantity, major.'

"Not satisfied, he again put the question in the same thick, unsteady voice before used. This time, still wishing to convey the idea of a very limited quantity, I answered:

"'I may have about two gallons.'

"The major straightened himself up as best he could and, with a most disappointed and disdainful look, exclaimed:

"'What is, hic, two gallons of whiskey among one man!' and slowly rode away.

"And let me tell you in this connection about the captain, having charge of the commissary department at the headquarters of the corps lying next to ours, who did not water *his* whiskey.

"Riding upon one occasion with several fellow officers to our headquarters, they all dismounted and came in, as they said, to sample our whiskey. I immediately set before them the best we had, which was considered a fair article for army use.

"But the captain, after imbibing, declared it to be very thin and badly watered (a statement containing more truth than poetry), and invited us to ride over to his corps where we should be furnished with the 'simon pure' article, which we could water to suit ourselves.

"The invitation was at once accepted, as good whiskey was very scarce at that time, and no opportunity was allowed to pass unaccepted by those accustomed to the beverage.

"On arriving at his quarters a fresh barrel was tapped, a measure drawn off, and the glasses filled. I noticed something peculiar in my glass, and while the captain was calling attention to the fact that his whiskey was not watered, I extracted from the contents of the glass given me a little dead fish about an inch in length, which had doubtless come from the brook that flowed at the rear of the captain's commissary tent, and holding it up to the gaze of all just as he concluded his remarks, I asked·

"'Do you suppose such a specimen as this to be contained in all pure Bourbon from Kentucky, captain?'

"The look of consternation that overspread his face can better be imagined than described, and he never after boasted the superior purity and strength of his whiskey over that of others."

CAMP-FIRE XXVII.

HOME ON A FURLOUGH—A PREMONITION OF DEATH—
HOURS OF PERIL.

"FURLOUGHS," said one present, who had taken a very active part in the home end of the war, " reminds me of an experience of John Curry, who came home in the spring of 1864, I think, for a short rest. He had been gone three years, in which time he became inured to the customs of army life, and was indeed a splendid example of how a man may change nearly his entire life, especially his every-day habits and his health, simply by change of surroundings,— provided these are at all favorable, and he adapts himself to them.

" Mr. Curry had been home only a few days when I called to congratulate him on his safe return. His description of camp-life and recollection of incidents then fresh in his memory, seemed almost endless, but were none the less interesting. I sat with my mouth and eyes open for two and a half hours, or longer, and listened with all possible attention.

"I accepted a second invitation to come around again in the afternoon, and was there promptly.

"The happy face of Mrs. Curry welcomed me at the door. Her voice, I noticed, still had the accent of the Fatherland, as she invited me in and told me that she did not like to arouse her husband, who was then asleep and needed all the rest he could get. She then entertained me by telling how different her husband seemed 'since he vas in dzhe war,' particularly as regarded his food. Pork and beans were very relishable to him now, but three years previous he could eat nothing but the best of beefsteak; she said corn-meal cakes were better than pastry, and coffee with cream and sugar in it was not fit to drink, he thought. She hardly knew how to prepare anything for his taste. He had undergone another radical change; he would not sleep in a bed, but when the sunshine was warm enough would take two rails, place them about a foot apart, with one end of each resting on the yard fence and the other ends on the ground, then lie down on the slant thus formed, and sleep for two or three hours. He was now sleeping on the floor in the adjoining room, and she asked me to step in and see how comfortable he looked. I did so, and indeed, he was the personification of comfort.

"It recurred to my mind that if some of the chronic growlers from general debility would shoulder a musket for a few months, or engage in some similar occupation as trying to the body, thereby creating the demand upon the stomach for food, there would be less dyspepsia and grumbling, and more health and happiness.

"'Schon! Schon!!' called Mrs. Curry, with her usual accent, now concluding that her husband had slept long enough. But John did not awaken. The same deep, contented breathings were still regularly drawn.

"'Schon! *Schon!*' she called again, but could not arouse him.

"'Let me show you how to wake him,' I suggested, at the same time telling her that as he had not heard his first name called for three years he had probably failed to recognize the sound, especially when he was asleep.

"'All right,' she replied.

"'To arms!' I said sharply, and John bounded to his feet so suddenly, with a motion of shouldering arms, that both of us were startled. After comprehending the situation he rubbed his nose and eyes, then, after a little explanation on my part, we were again talking over old time experiences."

Mr. Bailey then gave this reminiscence of a death presentiment to a comrade at the battle of Fredericksburg:

"It was the night before the battle that six of us, all of Company H, stretched our weary limbs under the warm cover of an A tent to get rest and strength for the struggle on the morrow. The evening before had witnessed the close of the bombardment of Fredericksburg, and the day had been occupied by the crossing of the Union Army over the Rappahannock, and the usual marches and counter marches requisite to getting into position. Our army lay in the open plain which intervened between the south bank of the river and the range of mountains back of the city, both flanks resting on the river, with the center pushed forward about a mile and a half, forming an oval line three or four miles long. Our position in the line was the right center of the left grand division, commanded by Major-General Franklin. In the wooded hills in front, blue with the smoke of camp-fires, lay the rebel army in ominous silence watching our every movement, and quietly waiting for the battle sure to come with the dawn of another day. In our immediate front lay the corps of Stonewall Jackson, with whom we had measured strength on several previous occasions, and with whom we were again to dispute for the possession of the natural fortifications of which they had taken advantage. The cavalry, artillery and infantry had been placed in position, and our patriotic commander, General Burnside, had ridden along the whole line at the close of the day to personally inspect the entire position. Already the darkening shades of the clear, cool, December night, was hushing into silence the two great armies, and the twinkling stars were looking down upon the fatal plains so soon to be filled with dead and mangled men.

"Our suppers had been finished, pipes smoked, tents pitched, and we prepared for our last sleep before the battle. Our gallant Captain Carle, a regular army soldier, had been wounded at second Bull Run; was not yet fit for duty, though he had accompanied us for the purpose of seeing the battle; Lieutenant Pratt, recently married to a young and lovely girl, had returned from a furlough home only a few weeks before, and was temporarily in command of the company; Jack Gibney, he whose skillful hands prepared the salt horse and coffee for all hands; Jimmy Moore and Hobart Ripley, noble, generous hearted boys as ever carried a musket, and the writer, lay down that night together under the only A tent of which our company could boast, and were soon wrapped in peaceful slumber. And yet all did not sleep that night. About midnight I felt a pull at my elbow, and rousing up saw Lieutenant Pratt bending over me, motioning for me to come out of the tent without disturbing our sleeping comrades. We had been warm friends and next door neighbors for years before entering the army, and I thought I had for some days detected a shade of sadness in his countenance, and more than once had found him engrossed in melancholy thought, but I had attributed it to the fact that his mind was on the wife and friends he had so recently left behind him. We walked out to the dying embers of the fire and sat down for some moments without speaking; he probably thinking whether or not it would be better to tell what was on his mind, and I waiting to hear.

" At last, with deep feeling, he said:

" 'F—, I have had a premonition of death. Six weeks ago, while on my way from home, I stopped in Washington over Sunday, and on Sunday evening attended church. When I crossed the threshold of the church the gas lights dimmed, and then recovered their usual brightness. The presentiment came to me in a moment, that I should be killed in the next battle, and I have not been able to overcome it since. I feel as certain, as that you and I are here, that I shall be killed tomorrow.'

"I tried with the best argument I could to dissuade him from the idea, and to show him the fallacy of tracing any connection between a thing which he had so often seen and was of such common occurrence in his own life. But argument was useless, and he seemed as sure of his death as though it were a positive certainty. I knew that he was morally and physically a brave man, and his deeply religious soul would have rebelled against anything like superstition, so that his feelings could not be attributed to cowardice, or a desire to shirk the dangers before us; besides, he had been tried on hard-fought fields, and proved true as steel. With him the idea was a wrought conviction admitting no doubt, and I pitied him from the bottom of my heart; though not a believer in presentiments, I could not feel with him that his death was a foregone conclusion. After an hour's conversation on the subject we again retired; he to a sleepless preparation for the death of which he felt so sure, I to indulge in selfish slumber.

"With the first breath of dawn we were aroused to eat a hearty breakfast and fall into line. A dense fog covered the whole plain, and we moved cautiously forward, unable to see more than a few yards. Soon a skirmish line encountered the rebel pickets, who promptly fell back after a few shots. A halt was called, and our division, the old Pennsylvania Reserves, received orders to unsling knapsacks, and we knew we had been selected to make the charge on the left. Moving forward we were placed in close column by brigades, in support of a battery, and ordered to lie down. The rising sun soon cleared away the fog and revealed our line of battle face to face with the enemy who were concealed in the woods about 600 yards distant. Then the dogs of war were let loose, and the several batteries along our line began to pay their respects to the enemy, who answered the compliment with vigor. The solid shot from the enemy's right raked our lines from left to right, while spherical case, screeching through the clear morning air from the front, exploded over our heads. Our regiment, which lay in the front line, suffered very little, but the regiment of new troops in our rear lost severely, in one instance a solid shot sweeping seven men out of a single company. The position was one of constant suspense to men compelled to lie idle, waiting to see where the next shot would strike. Activity, even in much greater peril, would have been infinitely preferable. Through all this trying ordeal Pratt kept his self-possession and strove only to do his duty, though no one but myself knew the deep and silent agony he was struggling to conceal.

"At last, to our relief, we were ordered to fix bayonets and charge. Never did the gallant 6th keep a straighter line on a dress parade than it did while charging across the 600 yards of open field which lay between us and the enemy. The railroad which ran along the skirt of the woods was the point at which we were to stop, but finding the position untenable by reason of a battery which swept the track, we entered the woods and kept after the enemy, whose first line was broken and now in full retreat, mowing a track the width of the division through the rebel lines. A lull occurring in the firing, Pratt again approached me, and leading the way a few paces to the rear, said, with a voice choking with emotion:

"'I shall never leave these woods alive. I am going to meet death here this afternoon. If you get out alive, I want you to tell Jennie I was prepared for death, and that my last thoughts were of duty to her, my country, and my God.'

"I was deeply impressed with his earnestness, and begged him to go to the rear out of danger, but of no avail. He felt he was going to die, and he would meet a soldier's death as a soldier should.

"'Forward,' came the order along the line, and with a hasty 'Good-bye' and 'God bless you,' we sprang to our places to encounter the rapidly forming lines of our enemy's fresh reinforcements.

"That was the last time I ever saw Pratt. The straggling shots deepened into that loud, monotonous roll, and the stray whiz of the minie ball changed into that storm of leaden hail when sounds lose their individuality, denoting the desperate nature of battle. A sharp twinge in my shoulder gave me a ticket to the rear, and I left the boys still pressing forward. For five mortal hours the old Pennsylvania Reserves kept their faces to the foe, unrelieved and unsupported, while thousands of fresh troops were lying in the rear behind stacked arms. But it is useless to dilate upon the errors and jealousies among generals, which lost that battle to the North at the expense of 13,000 brave men, for the results at all points of the line were alike disastrous. Night mercifully put an end to the slaughter, and the lines were reformed near where we started in the morning.

"With great anxiety I sought out our company, with several others who had been wounded, to learn how it had fared with the rest of the boys. Out of the six who had slept together the night before, five went into the battle, two of whom were killed, and two wounded. Almost the last man killed was poor Pratt, struck in the forehead with a minie ball. He never spoke afterward, and the boys being hard pressed, were reluctantly compelled to leave his body where he fell. His presentiment was no idle tale. His prediction proved as true as he felt it to be, and was carried out in all its terrible reality. With the flickering gas in the church at Washington the light of his life went out in the fullness of the undying fame due to the dead heroes of the war for the Union. Among the serried hosts of immortal spirits which are gathering in silent array on the battlements of heaven, he rests with the coveted crown inscribed 'Faithful unto death.'"

Immediately as the last speaker finished, George W. Scott

of the —— Illinois, narrated the following, which brought so vividly to the minds of his listeners the desperate ordeals of the long ago that more than one present drew a long breath and felt for the moment a sudden rush of the old feeling when death stared every one in the face.

" It was at the battle of —— that we were ordered to charge a line of the enemy's works. We were the third line of battle. Just beyond a small stream lined with willows the enemy were strongly entrenched, and heavily supported by artillery. From where we lay, the ground, which was clear and open, sloped gently to the stream, and the guns of the enemy could be distinctly seen a few hundred yards on the other side of the willows.

" The order was given, and the boys ahead of us gallantly charged over the open ground and endeavored to pass the obstructions at the creek, formed by stakes and interlaced willows. Immediately a sharp fire was poured into them from the works beyond.

" The first line staggered and almost recoiled, when they were hurried on by the second line which came up just behind them. The fire from the enemy became hotter and hotter, and men dropped on every side, but the impetus of the second line carried them down into the creek, where partial shelter was afforded by the low bank.

" At this juncture the order was given to follow and charge the works, and we started down the slope at double quick.

" The musketry and guns poured an avalanche of death among us, and before we had gone over half the space the ground was strewn with the wounded and the dead. It was a terrible moment. The shells howled through our ranks, and bursting overhead and upon the ground, filled the air with flying fragments, which, with the bullets, made fearful havoc.

" In less time than it takes to tell it, we had traversed the open ground and had reached the willows. We found these a serious obstruction, and, in face of the terrible fire, they were almost impassable. Our line was in confusion and nearly demoralized, and as we were about to fall back, the order was shouted, to lie down, and take shelter in the creek.

"As we lay there with but half of our bodies protected, the enemy increased their efforts to dislodge us by sending a veritable hail of missiles.

"The minie balls and buckshot fell upon the ground in an incessant shower. Cannon balls plowed up the ground and begrimed us with earth, while above the air quivered with the uninterrupted passage of lead and iron. From various parts of our line where sufficient shelter was afforded, our boys kept up as rapid a fire as possible, but from where I lay the bank was so low that to raise an arm or head meant a wound or certain death. The man who lay next to me ventured to look at the enemy's works, when he was struck by a shot that completely severed his head from his body.

"In our struggle to capture the position our colors were shot down three times. The last man who carried the flag gained a position behind a tall stump, and three different times the stump was struck by cannon balls and cut partly away. It became too dangerous a place, and the brave fellow held up the colors while he lay flat upon the ground.

"This situation of things remained the same until night came on, when we were enabled to crawl down the bed of the creek under cover of darkness. In the morning a flank movement drove the enemy out of their works, and we occupied the position."

CAMP-FIRE XXVIII.

DINNIS M'GINLEY AS THE "SECRETARY OF WAR"—MART M'COY AND THE GENERAL—HOW THE 15TH CORPS CAME BY ITS BADGE—THE ROMANCE THAT A SPENT BALL BROUGHT ABOUT—HOW WHEELER'S CAVALRY GOT SOME CORN MEAL — SENSATIONS UPON SEEING A COMRADE KILLED BY A BULLET.

IT is a well-known fact that the imaginative faculty is more active after night-fall than during the day, and that fire-light has the peculiar influence of stimulating memory. The association of glowing embers and burning brands with the unwritten history of "the late unpleasantness" is the cause of these pages. The well-remembered appearance of the hastily-made fire with the old familiar camp-kettle slung over the blaze, instantly recalls a score of events which have almost staggered out of sight down the aisle of the past.

It seemed to be so as the old-time soldiers gathered about the crackling sticks this evening, for, with every snap of some withering twig as it was consumed and slowly changed into smoke and heat, some one present recollected a story. A feeling of *bonhomie* lent its cheer, and a spirit of jovial companionship reigned in the circle.

An uproar of laughter in a group across from the meditative scribe of the S. P. U. H. arrested the attention of all, and it was immediately decreed that the cause of the hilarity should be exposed for the edification of every one. It was discovered that Capt. Fred. Maxwell, of the 3d N. Y.

Cavalry, had "spun a yarn," and accordingly he was invited to repeat it.

"Well, boys, if I must, I must, I suppose, and I will narrate one of the funniest incidents that I ever observed. The long years that separate to-night from the days when we followed the Stars and Stripes to 'the front' have not dimmed its humor for me, in the least. It occurred when we were near Poolesville, Md.

"At 'retreat roll-call,' one day, Captain McNamara, a son of the Emerald Isle, was the 'officer of the day.' Accordingly he went to the 'guard house' to inspect the guard. A member of Company F was one of their number, and Captain McNamara knew him almost as well as he did himself. One by one the boys were inspected, and the member from Company F came in turn. The captain found his cartridge box minus ammunition, and in its stead numerous letters. There were not forty rounds of powder and ball in it, but dozens of letters. Instantly the captain's face assumed the grim expression of outraged discipline.

"'Shtep three paces in fhront!' commanded the captain, and the order was obeyed.

"The captain looked at him in a curious, questioning way, and then went to the guilty soldier and scrutinized his cartridge box with great care. Walking slowly around him, he inspected every accoutrement zealously. Then, in a severe tone, he asked:

"'An' phat moight be yer name?'

"'Dinnis McGinley, sur!'

"Again the captain went around the man and looked into the misused cartridge box, and turning to its owner, he repeated:

"'An' phat did ye say was yer name?'

"'Dinnis McGinley, sur!'

"Pointing at the letters, the captain ejaculated upon the

heels of the reply to his question, with an astonishing look of surprise:

"'By me sowl, oi thought ye was the Secretary of War!'"

As the merriment subsided somewhat, Lieut. S. M. Witt, of the 10th Indiana, followed with these remarks:

"We had a droll kind of a character in our regiment by the name of Mart McCoy, who had formed the habit of saying, on all occasions, both appropriate and inappropriate, 'Halt! d—n you, halt!'

"We had just been mustered in at Camp Morton, Indianapolis, Ind., and were about as green a set of recruits as any *rendezvous* had the fortune, or misfortune, to see during the war. Our captain had been an old Mexican soldier, and we thought that he was the only one in camp who knew anything about tactics, and it was currently believed that we were not obliged to obey any officer but our leader, Captain Kice.

"We were sent to Rich Mountain, and soon were marched to where we had work to perform, and were treated to our first experience under fire.

"We had been ordered to lie down, and in order to escape the bullets, we had taken shelter behind the brow of a hill.

"While lying upon the ground, General R—— happened to pass along the line, and ordered firing to cease. Mart McCoy was lying upon his back holding his gun in a perpendicular position, muzzle upward, and was inadvertently playing with the lock of the weapon. Just as the general was passing by, McCoy's piece was accidentally discharged, and so near the general that the report startled him.

"As soon as the general recovered himself, he clutched McCoy by the collar, administered a forcible reproof for the apparent violation of orders, in the way of shaking him and asking, in a severe manner, if he meant to obey the commands of his officers. As the shaking process was going on, McCoy was ever and anon the recipient of several not very gentle applications of boot leather. Yet, notwithstanding the rough handling he was receiving, McCoy managed to gasp out:

"'Halt! d— you, halt!'

"The general loosened his hold and looked at McCoy in astonishment. McCoy, realizing that, for his manner of addressing a superior officer, he was liable to punishment, immediately vanished down the hill, followed by the guffaws of his comrades."

It will be remembered that certain army corps were designated by different badges, such as stars, acorns, etc., etc., and Capt. H. B. Reed, of the 129th Illinois, said the way that the 15th Corps of Sherman's army came by its badge occurred in this wise:

"One night some of the boys had built a log fire, and were enjoying its genial warmth, when they were joined by an Irish soldier. He was hailed by:

"'Hello! Where are ye from? What corps do ye belong to, Paddy, and what's yer badge?'

"'Me badge?'

"'Yes—what's yer badge?'

"'Me badge, did ye say?'

"'Yes, d— you; what kind of a badge does yer corps wear?'

"'Arrah, ye insultin' blackgarruds, oi belong to the 15th Corps,' and turning around and showing his cartridge box, 'an' this, wid 100 rounds, is me badge!'

"The incident was reported to headquarters, and as the 15th Corps had not received its badge, General Logan declared that a cartridge box with the number '100' upon it should designate them, and the order was carried into effect."

Among the myriad of incidents which happened daily

along the lines, many of which are stranger than the marvelous events traced upon pages of fiction, one told by Oscar F. Avery, corporal in the 11th Michigan, seems like a portion of a play upon the stage wherein the finale is made to come out just right for the hero.

Corporal Avery said: "It was at the battle of Stone River, early in the morning, that our regiment was lined up at right angles with the main line, and while standing in this position a comrade at my side, by the name of Robert Thomas, was struck just above the eye by a spent ball. He sank to the ground, and several of us placed him in as comfortable a position as possible, and were ministering to him the best we could under the circumstances, when we were ordered to form a part of the main line. This took us away from the prostrate form of Thomas, who lay beside a tree, apparently breathing his last breath.

"After the second day's battle I was detailed to look after our wounded. I searched for my comrade, Thomas, but could find no trace of him. We supposed that he had died, and been buried by the rebels.

"Nearly a year afterward, in 1863, while we were marching across to Bridgeport, with our line of battle extending a distance of thirty-two miles, who should rush out of the bushes and into the arms of the boys of his own company, but Robert Thomas!

"He told us his history from the day of the battle of Stone River, and we learned that he was taken prisoner while lying under the tree where we had left him. He laid in a hospital for nine months, and after recovering sufficiently so as to be able to move about, he took an opportunity to board a train with one of two regiments who were being transferred, and by saying that he belonged to the regiment just ahead, he arrived at the front, and, taking French leave of his train, he slipped through the pickets, stumbled upon us, and fell in with his old company, after being gone almost a year, and not having seen during that time a Union soldier, nor the Stars and Stripes."

Captain Reed asked if we had heard how he ground corn all night for some of Wheeler's rebel cavalry.

We responded in the negative, and when about to insist upon having the particulars of the incident related, a member of the captain's company, who helped do the grinding, said:

"Captain, tell the boys about our grinding that corn for Wheeler's cavalry!"

"Well," said the captain, "I was in command of a foraging party during our 'March to the Sea,' and one afternoon it happened that we came across an old corn mill. We concluded to gather some corn from the surrounding barns and grind it. We collected a large quantity, and in a little while had the old mill doing its best. Having no sacks, we took dresses and skirts that we found in a deserted dwelling, and by tying up the ends of them, soon had a goodly number of serviceable sacks.

"We kept the old mill going till toward morning, and had about finished our job. We had slung some of our improvised sacks across the backs of our mules, and were engaged in filling others and preparing for departure, when our pickets rushed in and reported rebel cavalry coming down the road.

"We rushed to our guns, but before we could use them, a volley from the enemy's carbines rattled through the mill, and a chorus of yells stampeded our mules.

"In less time than it can be told, our little party had scattered, and our mules were flying in all directions. Some of them strewed meal over the fields for miles, and the way feminine apparel was distributed was ludicrous to behold.

"The early morning air was filled with meal, shots, curses, brays, flying petticoats and yells. Confusion reigned supreme, and bedlam was outrivaled.

"It is needless to say that we made ourselves scarce, and with the exception of two or three who were captured, we gained our camp in safety. We had lost our corn meal, but we thought ourselves lucky to have escaped being taken prisoners and sent to Andersonville."

Probably thousands of readers will remember their feelings upon seeing, for the first time, a comrade struck lifeless. Such sensations are always remembered, and the impressions then received are invariably carried to the grave. Powerful as such events were in causing emotion, their rapid and familiar occurrence dulled their horror, and lessened their repulsiveness. The dread and sickening loathing created by many a corpse on a battlefield, is by familiarity and constant view transformed into a stoical indifference. Were this not so, the awful carnage of some battles would have made deserters of thousands of soldiers.

Sergt. J. H. Goff, of the 129th Illinois, told the effect of seeing a soldier shot dead, and said:

"It was at the battle of Resaca, Ga., that I beheld, for the first time, the death of a soldier by a gun-shot. He was standing about twenty feet in front of me in the next line of battle, and just as I happened to glance at him he was struck in the neck by a musket ball. He let fall his gun and dropped, turning toward me as he fell, and as he did so, by a convulsive movement of the muscles of his throat his tongue was forced out of his mouth to its utmost extent.

"A sickening shudder involuntarily passed over me at the fearful sight. A feeling of great sympathy and pity welled up in my heart for the poor fellow, and I longed to go to him and take him in my arms, minister to his wants, and seek to ease his pain. My attention was then attracted to the enemy by their rapid fire and by the humming of their bullets above us, and as I realized that it was by one of their bullets that the poor boy in front of me had met his death, a savage desire for revenge and retaliation drowned out the finer emotions which had just filled my breast, and I was eager to put my desire into execution. I clutched my gun with firm fingers, and with every muscle steady, and every nerve calm, my whole mind was concentrated in my determination to avenge the death of the man who lay upon the ground cold in death. In a few minutes I found myself loading and firing as rapidly as possible, and during the subsequent movements of the regiment I forgot, for the time, the death of the soldier."

The recital of Sergeant Goff caused the faces of all to assume lines of gravity and sadness, and it was plainly apparent that this incident had awakened in the minds of each memory of war's most horrible phases, and an oppressive silence pervaded the camp.

It was some time before the usual flow of good-natured spirits resumed its course, and after several more stories the motion to adjourn was decided to be in order, and ere long the camp-fire was a smoldering heap of ashes.

CAMP-FIRE XXIX.

THE TRUTH ABOUT THE CAPTURE OF THE GUERILLA CHIEFTAIN, JOHN MORGAN—AUDACIOUS AUDACITY— THE LAST PLANK OF THE SHIP OF STATE.

G. BIRCHFIELD, of the 13th Tennessee cavalry, said: " There have been several letters published claiming to describe Morgan's death, but I have never yet seen one which came anywhere near the truth of the affair. I was one of those who, when the shadow of war darkened the entire land, lived in the Sunny South; but having been raised by one of those truly loyal men, one who loved his whole country, and whose father had fought at King's Mountain, and, moreover, being in that truly patriotic section of Southeast Tennessee, whose loyal sons fought on every battle-field, I could not be otherwise than true to my country in that sad hour. So I have had my share of the hardships and fun, and the incident to which I refer was one of the perilous ones.

" It was in Greenville, Penn., Sept. 4, 1864. We had been encamped at Bull's Gap, sixteen or eighteen miles west of there, for four or five days, and about midnight on the third we were aroused and ordered to saddle up. It was pitch dark, and the lightning played around the clouds as we marched out east of the gap and across the country southeast, until we struck the old Newport road. Then we turned east toward Greenville, when the rain began to fall in torrents. When within two miles of Greenville, just before daybreak, we learned that the Confederate pickets were posted in an old house one mile ahead.

"Colonel Ingerton ordered two companies to the right through the woods and fields. They got between the reserve pickets and town, and the rest of the regiments closed in on them. We took them without a shot, and then marched to within about three-fourths of a mile of Greenville, when Colonel Ingerton ordered Company G to take the road toward town. Captain Wilcox commanded the company. The rest of the regiment were formed in line across Blue Spring road, facing the west.

"Captain Wilcox marched up the top of a hill to the west of town, and into the main street, and halted; then rode forward to where he could see from end to end of the main street, and it seemed to me, in the gray of the morning, that the street was alive with men. The Johnnies getting in late the night before, had camped in the street, and on the rising ground to the east. Captain Wilcox ordered the company to 'Forward march! Trot! Charge!' and in an instant we were among the Johnnies, some of whom were still wrapped in the embrace of Morpheus on the sidewalk. When they were roused by the yells and firing, they left hats, guns, blankets, horses and all, and jumped over fences, darted through doorways, and into stores, and around buildings; and in fact, there was general confusion, forty-four boys in blue being mixed up with one or two thousand Johnnies who were running in every direction. We did not even stop to take prisoners of those who would throw up their hands, but dashed through the main street to within one or two hundred yards of their battery, which we could see was making ready to give us a welcome. Lieut. John M. Wilcox, John Turner and Sol. Turner, John Humphrey and eight or ten others made a dash for the battery, which fired one shot. This from bad range or some other cause, struck a church; but the boys went for those guns and drove the rebels away, and captured them; but since they could not remove them, they left the guns and joined the company in town, where we were employed in picking up Johnnies.

"I rode up to the hotel, where I was acquainted with Mrs. Col. David Fry, the noted bridge-burner and Union scout. She was standing on the porch. I said, 'Good-morning, Aunt Catherine.' She was very much excited and replied, 'General Morgan is in that brick house at the rear, and you must take him.' I galloped to where Captain Wilcox was standing near the church east of the hotel, and told him of the vicinity of General Morgan. There were fifteen or twenty men with Wilcox. He ordered them to surround the block, which they did. In a very short time Andrew Campbell went to the west side of the block, near a stable that stood north of the hotel that Mrs. Fry occupied. Captain Wilcox ordered John M. Wilcox and myself to go into the grounds in the rear, and east of the old church on Main street, passing north toward the brick house that Mrs. Fry designated to us. When we had gone about half-way, we passed by an outhouse, which stood on the southeast corner of the lot on which the house of Mrs. Williams was situated. John H. Morgan had made his quarters there the night before. As we passed this, two officers, Johnson and Clay, I think, were their names, came to the door, threw up their hands, and said they would surrender; but just then we saw a man start from behind the building in his shirt sleeves and bareheaded, and run toward the brick house on the north side of the block; so we did not stop to take the two, but hurried up to catch the other fellow, as we saw that some of our boys were just behind us.

"We passed by the side of a grape arbor twenty-five or thirty feet, and through it to the east side, where we could still see Morgan pushing toward the house. We got between him and the house, and ordered him to surrender, which he refused to do, and fired. The ball passed very near Lieutenant Wilcox and myself. We were about twenty or thirty feet from where he stood. He then turned and passed through a bunch of grapevines, and snapped his revolvers at us again.

"Just at this time I saw Andrew Campbell ride out from behind the stable and fire. Lieutenant Wilcox and myself both yelled at Campbell not to shoot, for Morgan was right in line between us and Campbell. Morgan turned and went five or six paces toward Campbell, when Campbell dismounted, and was taking deliberate aim, when Morgan wheeled and faced Wilcox and myself with his pistol raised. Campbell fired his second shot, which took effect just below the left shoulder-blade, and passed through his body, and out below his left nipple. Morgan threw up his hand and exclaimed, 'Oh God!' and fell dead without a groan. We then placed his body on Campbell's horse, and he carried it about one mile west of Greenville, where we met General Gillam. Campbell said, 'General, here is the old Kentucky horse-thief, I guess he won't get away this time.'"

A witness of the following audacity then told this:

"About the boldest thing I ever saw done was an achievement by Dan Ellis, a famous pilot and scout, who before the close of the war succeeded in piloting over 12,000 men in squads of from one to three hundred in one direction or another, through the mountains of East Tennessee. He had been trained in the vocation from his boyhood, learning his wit by hard knocks and from the rough teachings of experience rather than from book larnin', yet a little, or even a great deal of the said 'larnin'' would not have injured him materially, since he could neither read nor write, though he was as eloquent and as fluent a talker as could have been found in that part of the country. His reputation as a successful guide was well-known throughout the whole State, and when the Johnnies heard that Dan was leading a column, extra effort was made to head him off, though, in the nature of things, they rarely heard of him, for, figuratively, he stepped lightly and filled up his tracks.

"But even with him everything did not always slip smoothly. He was captured at least once to my certain knowledge. It was in October, 1861, just after the burning of the Union bridge, near Holstein. The operations in that vicinity for a few days previous attracted some attention from the Johnnies, and before we knew it, the Confederate Colonel Leadbetter, with one thousand infantry, escorted by a battalion of two hundred cavalry, were down upon forty of us with Dan Ellis at the head. They caught us in a tight place, almost unawares, and we simply and quietly surrendered. It was a part of Dan's policy, he said, to surrender like a fellow confessing his guilt on the gallows, when we were caught in a trap, since that would tend to make the enemy more merciful toward us, and continued gentle submission would throw them off their guard. So we went on with our captors almost as well as if we had been a part of them, until we arrived at Taylor's Ford.

"Leadbetter turned us over to Major McClelland to take to Elizabethton and put into jail until further orders; but when we arrived at the Ford, Dan concluded that he had gone far enough with his Confederate escort, so he at once began to carry out a plan for escape which he had by that time matured in his own mind. Riding up to a house near the road, his guard following close by his side, he leaned over the picket fence and called out for a cup of water. The lady within was not long in coming to the fence with it, and then the fun commenced.

"The woman held up the cup of water to him, and Dan held out his hand to receive it, at the same time calling out loudly to the guard who was with him, as though he were startled:

"'Look! look! See that Yank and Johnnie back there,' pointing to the rear.

"'Where?' asked the guard.

"'Way back—half a mile,' continued Dan.

"The guard looked long and steady, but saw nothing. Meantime, instead of taking the cup of water from the lady, Dan placed his hand on the fence, leaped over, and was several rods across the field before the guard discovered him. The guard was so fully absorbed in looking for the Johnny and Yank to whom Dan had so kindly called his attention, that he did not hear Dan say:

"'Drat my buttons, if that wa'n't a pretty narrer jump, an' it hurt my hand,' as he jumped the fence; and, indeed, the first thing that called the guard's attention to the fact that Dan was leaving the country, was the shooting from the other guards, which soon numbered a hundred or more shots. But the bullets were too slow, and Dan was soon out of their range. He was at this time on the crest of a low hill, and turned and saluted the Johnnies, who fired another volley at him, which closed the adventure. It was of no use to pursue since he had the advantage on any footman of at least sixty rods, and the fences and hedges were such that a horse could not be used, so that Dan Ellis escaped after all.

"In this connection, with almost these same circumstances, there occurred another incident which shows what mother wit can do for a fellow sometimes, and which I will relate with the permission of the camp-fire."

"We will refer that to the S. P. U. H.," said the commander. It was accordingly referred, and the society replied that they had always disliked the principle of usurpation in history, but asked that the comrade be allowed to tell his story on this occasion, so he continued:

"Just previous to the capture of Ellis and the rest of us, while we were preparing ourselves for business at the front, an incident occurred, the sequel to which was unique. Elizabethton, Tennessee, if I remember correctly, was the home of Congressman N. G. Taylor. At any rate, he made a ringing speech there while an enrolling officer for the Union army at that place, and grew eloquent in the cause which had sent him to Congress twice. He said that the Union was still strong, but needed to be still stronger; that the flag still waved over hearts that would remain loyal to the end; that all who considered themselves men would remain under the folds of the national ensign, and permit no strange banner to appear in our skies; that he, for one, would hang to the ship of state until the last plank, sundered from the others, would float out upon the ocean of anarchy, and *then he would still be on that plank!*

" This brought the cheers from the audience, and the enrolling proceeded rapidly, so that it was only about two weeks after, when a company of a hundred or more of us encamped at Doe River Cove.

" We had been there about a week, and some of the boys began to be impatient because there was no fighting or anything else to do. Soldiering seemed to be rather dry business, and gradually homesickness, thus early, and even a desire to repudiate their oaths, began to possess the boys.

" Taylor staid among them, and all the while cheered and exhorted them to remain loyal. But finally the climax was reached. It now appeared that the practical part of war had never dawned upon the minds of the boys, and when it was rumored through the camp that the long-looked-for enemy were actually coming, and that there would in all probability be a battle, there was a general dropping of countenances. Captain Gourley, with a small force, was sent out to reconnoiter, and before long he sent back a messenger, who announced that the advance of Colonel Leadbetter's Confederate brigade had been met and vanquished with due promptness; the messenger also bringing a request for moie men to assist Captain Gourley. The whole camp was accordingly ordered into line of battle at once. Every volunteer toed the mark, but just as they did so, a screech was heard off to the left, and soon there came through the bushes a man on horseback, with his face bloody, swinging a sword in one hand and a butcher's knife in the other, crying at the top of his voice:

"'Run, (hic) boys! Run! They're comin'!' the crier being one of those mis-made men whose idea of chivalry or knighthood, and especially modern soldiery, was that the first act is to get 'gloriously drunk.' The first act having been completed, it did not take long for the drunken man to imagine that the whole Confederate army was *upon him*, and, having fallen from his horse several times, the knocks and bruises therefrom bled freely, and soon gave him the appearance of having been just where he reported himself to have been. The young soldiers who beheld him in this condition were at that time just in the proper state of mind to take fright at anything like war, so that they did not need a second warning for each to betake himself to some hiding-place near. Within five minutes from the first warning sounded by the drunken soldier (?), the original line of battle could not be distinguished from a light gust of wind, so shadowy and absent were the previously brave soldiers.

"No one could be seen except Congressman Taylor and Captain Boyd. They saw the last of their following secrete himself, and then saw the drunken man fall from the horse with that certain thud which gave strong evidence that he would lie there some time before regaining his consciousness. Then Congressman Taylor said to Captain Boyd:

"'Well, captain, there may be something in it, after all,' referring to the sudden disappearance of the soldiers from the supposed enemy. 'We had better be on the safe side, at any rate, and I think the safe side is the side of this embankment right here.' So saying, the congressman and the captain stepped down the bank, and when they were well hid, Congressman Taylor sadly reflected aloud:

"'Ah, captain, the last plank of the ship of state *is* now out upon the anarchical billows of rebellion, but I am still on it.'

"Sure enough, before many hours, the Confederates under Colonel Leadbetter came, and they picked up most of those who had formed the line of battle earlier, the Confederates having captured the reconnoitering party under Captain Gourley, who could not stay their advance under such great odds.

"After hunting out the line of battle from the various nooks and corners, and capturing its members, the Johnnies finally found Congressman Taylor and Captain Boyd, who surrendered without much hesitation. All the captives were taken to Elizabethton and jailed. The last plank of the ship of state now appeared to be getting the worst of it—to be sinking, and dragging the congressman down with it. He was in a sorry fit. The enemy would have no mercy for him who had incited so many to take up arms against them only a short month before. He sought the advice of his brother-in-law. I believe it was he who told him that the best thing he could now do would be to confess his guilt, and make a speech in behalf of the Confederacy. This he concluded to do, and when he was brought up to take the oath of allegiance to the Confederacy, he seized the opportunity and made a rousing speech, closing with the following ambiguous words:

"'Yes, dear friends, the ship of state has gone to pieces, and the last plank *has* floated out into the Confederacy, and I here solemnly declare that I am upon that plank.' The assertion received applause, and was accepted as an oath of allegiance, but the congressman still stuck to the plank, soon slipping away from the Confederate ranks, and the plank in turn still staid under him, for after the war he was elected to a third term as a reward of merit."

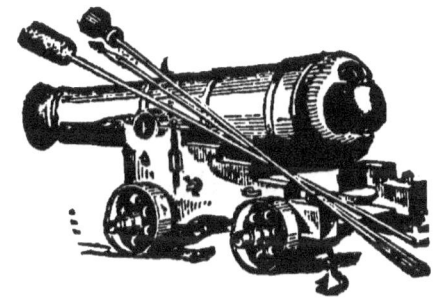

CAVALRY CHARGE.

CAMP-FIRE XXX.

A MULE DRIVER'S PECULIARITIES — FORAGERS — MAJOR COLLINS' NEGRO BOY, FRACTION—THE SAD STORY OF AN UNKNOWN MICHIGAN SOLDIER.

COMRADES, listen, while I tell you about a mule-driver of the Twenty-sixth Illinois," spoke up one of the boys.

"Frequently private soldiers became widely known in the army for some peculiar characteristic, but perhaps few were more so than the one I am about to describe. He was about six and a half feet high, long, lank and angular, with an ungainly, swaggering kind of gait, though when astride a mule he was at home. He was generally known as 'Stackpole,' the mule driver of the 26th Illinois. He always had a good team, and if he lost a mule he could soon pick up another, since he did not concern himself as to where the mules belonged, if he wanted them. In the fall of 1864 he took a span from General Schofield's headquarters team, and shaved, cropped and painted them, till the driver passed them on the road a few hours afterward, hunting his stolen mules, but never dreaming they were before him.

"This same driver had an undying thirst for good commissary whiskey, and when the roads were in the most fearful condition, and teams balked and floundered in the mud till it almost seemed nothing would ever again induce the mules to pull a pound, if only the quartermaster would send for 'Stackpole' and promise him a pint of good whiskey, the balkiest team would soon be pulling for dear life. He would vault into the saddle, straighten up the leaders, touch up every mule in the team, and when all were alert and ready, it really seemed he could make his whip play round like a streak of lightning, hitting all at once; then he would halloo till you could hear him for miles, not omitting of course the traditionary 'cuss words,' and things would go, however deep the mud might be.

"Starting loads recalls the 'March to the Sea' with Sherman, and through the Carolinas in the winter of 1865, which developed many expert foragers, and the enormous loads that some soldiers could carry into camp would astonish people in civil life. But the improvised carts and conveyances would also make them open their eyes. It was a common thing to see mules and horses led in loaded down with provender, but to see a nice family carriage driven in, with the elegantly cushioned and costly upholstered seats piled full of bacon or pickled side meat, was not at all unusual.

"At Lynch's Creek in South Carolina, owing to high water, crossing was delayed several days, and the sparsely settled country was soon stripped of almost everything eatable, until finally nothing remained to live upon but a scant supply of ear corn, which was rendered palatable by being parched. Officers had to watch their horses while they were eating, to prevent the famishing men from stealing all their corn. After crossing, the foragers struck out to collect food, and when they returned about 2 o'clock in the morning, the men got up, cooked, ate, and sat round the camp-fires, singing and making merry, apparently as happy and contented as if in the midst of plenty."

James Houghton, of Plymouth, Indiana, a member of the 29th Indiana, then took the floor.

"At Stone River, on the afternoon of December 30, 1862, the regiment was ordered to move up and take a position for the fight on the morrow.

"Major Collins, of that regiment, had a negro servant whom the boys, for some unaccountable reason, had nicknamed 'Fraction.' While being placed in position, Fraction espied a mulatto boy passing to the rear with an old fashioned 'horse pistol' in his possession. A sudden idea seemed to strike the servant, and he yelled, 'Wha' yer gwine wid dat shootin' iron?' The boy answered, 'Gwine to de reah, to take car' the 'Cunnel's hoss.' 'Fraction' then said, 'Jess han' dat shootin' iron ober to me,' and the boy, like a true soldier, quickly obeyed the order of his 'superior'(?). 'Fraction' then followed along till the regiment was placed in position, borrowing ammunition from several of the soldiers. When the fight commenced the following morning, he disappeared very suddenly, and not turning up at nightfall, nor the next day, the regiment came to the conclusion that he had been killed or taken prisoner.

"On the third day, while a bevy of regimental and company officers were seated under a tree, cracking and eating nuts that had been shaken off during the previous day's engagement, one of the officers descried 'Fraction' coming toward them. He was immediately assailed by a volley of questions as to his late whereabouts, and after much taunting and more coaxing, seated himself, and assuming a very important manner, gave the following account with the utmost gravity:

"'Well, gemmen, when dat fightin' commenced, and de boys 'gan to drap like dey was hurt, an' de rebs 'gin runnin tow'd us purty fas', I jess 'cluded dat I could run faster dan dem. I jess got dat hoss pistol all ready, and away I went. Purty soon I he'rd somebody ridin' arter me, and when I looked 'roun', I tell you dat my legs trimbled, for I seed one ob dem rebel hoss offica'hs comin' like de berry debil. I didn't stop to take aim, but jess histed dat gun over my left shouldah, and pinted it in the d'rection of dat man, and pulled de' triggah, an' I'll bet a possum' dat I killed dat fellah, but I didn't stop, no sah! I jess kep' on runnin', and when de bullets 'gan to go whiz-z-z-z, and de big shot sing whir-r-r-r, I jess dodged to one side, an' lay down in de fiel' wha' I bin eber since! You don' catch dis chile foolin' wid dem rebs any mo',—no sah,—de bullets cum too clus, an' 'sturb my appytite!'"

"As a contrast to the anecdote just given, I offer a tribute to the memory of a brave Michigan boy who gave his life to his country," said Isaac N. Phillips, corporal of Company A, 47th Illinois Infantry, 16th Army Corps:

"We had been for ten or twelve days lying in the trenches in front of the frowning batteries of old Spanish Fort, one of the defences of the city of Mobile. About the fort proper were breastworks inclosing a large extent of land, with several smaller forts having mounted batteries. The 13th Army Corps lay upon the left of the 16th to which I belonged. I, with a large number from our brigade, was doing detail duty as a sharp-shooter up in the saps near the rebel works. The main line of the corps lay several hundred yards in our rear. The fighting had been done principally with artillery, and, day by day, as the siege progressed, and the tremendous siege-guns were put in place back on the main line, the cannonade upon the Union side grew more terrible and deadly. The leaden rain poured into the port-holes of the forts by the vigilant sharp-shooters (whose well-directed bullets made it almost impossible to man the rebel guns), with the still more terrible fire from the batteries, and the ponderous shells from the mortars far back of the main line in the woods, made the situation of the 'Johnnies' precarious in the extreme.

"Those great mortar shells! Who that has ever heard the sound of their journey through the sky can ever forget it! When night settled down, and the cannonade would cease, the stillness semed unearthly, because of the contrast, no doubt, between that and the great turmoil and noise of the day; and this stillness was only broken by an occasional musket shot, or by the firing from the immense mortars in the rear. A dull, heavy report, followed by silence, was all that indicated the starting out of a thousand-pounder on its mission. Looking intently in the direction of the battery, some comrade would exclaim: 'There it goes!' and where his finger pointed would be seen slowly climbing the sky what appeared to be a little waving torch. Listening intently we could hear the hissing sound of the burning fuse as the immense shell turned over and over in its progress. ' Wsh-wsh-wsh-wsh '—nearer and nearer it came, making a slow, majestic progress up and over the blue dome of the sky, until, with almost miraculous precision, it dropped into the fort just in our front; and the fuse, which had entertained us with its little harmless pyrotechnics, during the long aerial voyage, never forgot to do its fatal work just as the shell came down. It would seem almost two minutes from the firing of the mortar to the explosion of the shell—minutes of dreadful suspense to those inside the doomed fort. It was a rare accident for one of the shells to miss its mark, or fail to explode at the proper second of time to make its mission effective.

"But it is not of bomb-shells alone that I am to tell you. One night the news came along the line of sharp-shooters that the rebels were thought to be evacuating the fort. It was between midnight and morning. We were not positive of the correctness of our information; but we were not long in verifying it. Pell-mell we ran, in the wildest disorder, over the trunks of fallen pines and among the rifle-pits skirting the rebel breastworks, scampering recklessly over ground, which, wild rumors of buried torpedoes and infernal machines had, only a few hours before, made us view with profound reverence and awe.

"Sure enough, the rebels had left the works. We picked up a good many stragglers in the timber of the inclosure skirting the bay; and a few of us crept down in the dawning morning light to the water's edge where, under cover of the trees, we could see the last boat-load of rebels embarking from a little island some three or four hundred yards off the main land, which island was connected with the shore by a plank bridge wide enough for two men to walk upon it abreast. The water was shallow. The rebels had passed over this plank bridge, and as we lay near the shoreward end, two men dressed in butternut clothes came running back over the bridge toward us. We supposed them to be rebels, but as they carried no guns did not fire upon them. When they came near we called to them to halt, which they failed to do. One of them raised his hand, in which was a short stick and said, 'You are the men we want to see.' One of our party, noted for rashness and haste, mistaking the stick in the hand of the supposed rebel for a pistol, fired and instantly killed one of the two. The survivor called out that he was a Union prisoner making his escape, and begged us not to fire again; and then he told us a story that touched my heart with a feeling I never experienced in war before.

"He and his companion had been long in rebel prisons. They had been taken to Spanish Fort to work on breastworks, preferring hard labor to the festering *ennui* and filth of a prison pen. They had first met at the fort, only a few days before. The survivor did not know more than the given name of his dead comrade, and that I have now forgotten. He belonged to a Michigan regiment,—had been several months a prisoner; all else was unknown. The two had taken advantage of the confusion in embarking, to steal away and make their escape. Just at the moment when his heart was beating high—when he supposed himself to be emerging from the jaws of death and the mouth of hell, as it were, the poor Michigan boy had been shot by his friends.

"He was tall and handsome, and not exceeding twenty years of age. His fine features and cleanly person and habit spoke him one of a good family, and probably city bred. We searched his clothes, hoping to find his name or some address to which we could write and tell the sad story of his death, but none could be found. We made him a grave 'by the sounding sea,' under the shade of the cypress trees, and there he sleeps unknown to the multitude; but not, I trust, 'unhonored and unsung.'

"Lee and Johnston had already surrendered, but we did not know it. Doubtless his people—perhaps his mother—knew he was a prisoner, and at that moment her heart was beating with high hope at the great news of Union success which was soon to bring her boy to her arms. How she must have watched and waited and listened for the footsteps that never came! How she must have scanned the news of the returning prisoners whom peace had released from bondage; and who knows but she may still be searching for the name of her lost boy upon the headstones of the many populous prison graveyards! But no power less than that which shall reassemble all the dead, can ever bring to that Michigan mother the sad news of her lost boy; and then let us hope its great sadness may be turned into a still greater joy, for he gave his life for his country as much as though he had fallen while scaling rebel ramparts, bearing his country's flag."

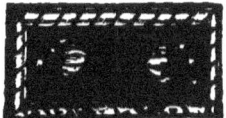

CAMP-FIRE XXXI.

"DESECRATED" VEGETABLES—WHAT THEY WERE, AND HOW THEY COOKED 'EM — SHAMING THE "BIGGEST LIAR."

"HERE is something that we used to eat during the war," said a veteran, and he held up a piece of something that appeared precisely like a plug of "navy tobacco" an inch or more thick, and about fourteen inches square.

"It looks (as has just been observed) like a huge piece of tobacco, and oftentimes the boys would have readily traded pieces of it for *half* its weight in that luxury. The designation donated to it by the War Department was 'dessicated vegetables;' but the boys changed it to 'desecrated,' which we thought more appropriate, for soldiers delight to call things by their right names. The statement may seem strange, but we actually made soup of the stuff of which I hold a sample in my hand, even though people not acquainted with the substance be unable to guess its use from appearance. Yes, my dear comrades, you all remember how many a mess we've had from this material. I remember one incident connected with its introduction among us."

The speaker here tossed the piece of pressed vegetables to the S. P. U. H., and after a casual scrutiny it was placed under close scientific analysis, and was found to contain the following ingredients:

1. Onions, with husks on.
2. Potatoes, prepared to be cooked in three styles.
3. Corn, with no particular pains taken to omit the cobs.

4. Beans, strung, unstrung, Boston, shelled, unshelled, and otherwise.

5. Cabbages, leaves, head, stalk and roots.

6. Tomatoes, dried, with an occasional vine hung on; though the latter was not necessary, and hence not always appended. This last observation will also apply to the roots of cabbages and husks of onions.

7. Sweet potatoes, occasionally a small piece, being very scarce and expensive. The vines were unattached to this ingredient.

8. Parsnips, the previous year's growth, which were strictly fibrous, and unable to be masticated.

9. Pumpkins, the cow variety.

10. Lettuce, radishes, parsley, celery, garlic, squash, horseradish, carrots, asparagus, mustard, and all other vegetables and semi-vegetables not included in the foregoing list. If anything in the vegetable line was not represented in each piece, it was not the fault of the manufacturers. It is said to be recorded that at one time a purse was made up among the boys, to be given to one who could name something which could not be found in these pieces of " desecrated vegetables." After numerous guesses the task was given up, and the purse had to be distributed among the original donors.

The ingredients were first dried separately, then pressed and dried together, then compressed and redried, until they occupied the smallest space possible. In their primary condition, fresh from the vines, three or four of these chunks of vegetables, 14x14x1¼ inches, would make nearly a wagon load of produce. After compressing and drying they could almost be put into a peck measure. They were mixed together without much regard for quality or proportion, then cut into pieces of regular size, as before stated.

But after all the hard things that were said about " dessicated vegetables," they proved a boon to the army, though they did not appear as a part of the regular rations until 1864. When they were issued, they supplied a real meal, since fresh vegetables could not be obtained under any circumstances during the winter months. By compressing the vegetables they could be shipped and handled with more facility, but a single incident will illustrate how some of the cooks were forgetful of the swelling principle in such vegetables as beans, rice, etc.

"When 'dessicated vegetables' were first issued to us, I remember," continued the speaker, "one cake was dealt out to each company as vegetable rations for three days. This preparation at first sight did not look very palatable, and when it was passed to the respective messes (numbering six to eight in each mess) the boys respectively and respectfully refused to eat any of this universal succotash, even if the cooks were willing to serve it.

"On the other hand, the cooks for each mess refused to use it, and so the whole cake went the rounds without being broken, until it came at last, to our mess, which numbered six of as venturesome fellows as any company in the regiment could boast. Our cook, a fellow by the name of Leander Turner, also refused to have anything to do with the new style of vegetable, since all the boys had come to the conclusion that, if they would give it a positive letting alone, the quartermaster would not issue it any more.

"But we told our cook to fix it up, whatever the results; we wanted to see what it would look like. Accordingly he gratified us. He took the regular ten-gallon camp kettle, nearly filled it with water, saying as he did so:

"'Well, let's try some soup from the fodder,' and he put the whole cake into the kettle of boiling water. Ere long the beans began to swell, the rice grains to grow larger, the dried corn extended its dimensions, and the other vegetables began to resume something of their original proportions; it is to be held in mind that this was only the *beginning*, though the 196 cubic inches of dried and pressed vegetables even at this time had absorbed most of the water, and were creeping over the sides of the kettle, having already pushed out into the fire a huge piece of meat, which had been put into the kettle before the vegetables had been put in.

"'What in thunder 'll I do with all this darn truck?' asked the cook, as the vegetables kept on coming out of the top of the ten-gallon kettle, and gave unmistakable evidence that they were burning in the bottom.

"'Jim, bring another kittle,' he said, speaking to the waiter boy.

"The boy brought another kettle, which was partly filled with water, and enough vegetables were taken from the first kettle and placed in it until the second kettle, too, was full. Then more water was put into the first kettle. But the cook had again miscalculated, for all of the water poured in the first time had been absorbed by less than half of the dried vegetables, so that there was almost as much cause for swelling the second time as the first. Add to this the fact that the kettle was already dry and almost red-hot in the bottom, so that as soon as possible water was poured in again, and when it had time to penetrate to the bottom, sufficient steam was immediately generated to bring about only one result—a terrific explosion, sufficiently loud to scare the cook near unto death, and cause most of those who heard it to start for their arms, while the manner in which it fared with the vegetables in the kettle can be summed up in a few words: The cook had drawn, in that one small piece of 'desecrated vegetables,' sufficient rations for one hundred men, three days for dinner, or in other words, three hundred meals; and when it came to putting the entire cake though small, into a ten-gallon kettle, with sufficient water to swell the ingredients into eatable shape, this was one of the physical impossibilities; so that at the time the explosion occurred, the vegetables had again risen to the top of the kettle, and consequently were scattered in the air, most of them, however, falling back into the kettle, and like a slumbering volcano, were soon ready for another explosion.

"But the cook rallied his courage, made for the kettle, and in his strength of madness, kicked the thing several feet from the fire, with the angry expression:

'Darn that Yankee stuff, anyhow; drat my gizzard if you'll get me to cook any more of it. I've cooked lots o' vegetables in my time, but I'll be dad burned if I ever saw anything that would swell twic't and then bust,' which ended the scene.

"We did not eat any from that cooking, but when the boys became accustomed to 'dessicated vegetables' we often had a fine pan of soup from a small piece of the preparation, which, no doubt, helped to keep away scurvy."

F. E. Huddle, of Company M, 10th Illinois Infantry Volunteers, who is also known as "Shorty," "The Clodhopper," "Grumbler-in chief," etc., now arose, and with a gesture indicating that he desired to be heard, began the following story, for the truth of which he vouches:

"Do any o' you boys recollect the first day o' the siege o' Vicksburg? No? Well I do. Several things happened about that time that I won't forget for two or three years yet. We were lyin' on our arms one night, spinnin' yarns, when some shootin' commenced on our left, an' cap'n says to me, says he, 'Shorty, I wish you'd go over thar an' find out what that 'ar racket's all about.' I wan't much anxious to go out an' get the top o' my head blowed off, but I couldn't go back on orders, so I made a break, an' met the picket comin' in as fast as his feet could carry him. I stopped and got behind a live oak, an' when the picket went by, I peeped out, an' blame my eyes if there wan't ten Johnnies comin' after him single file, as hard as they could run. They was strung out one behind the other, an' I stepped out, an' when they was all in a straight row, I let drive, an' what do you think? Why I killed every blamed gray in that squad, an' the bullet was found stickin' to the knapsack o' the last man. They war comin' up hill, an' of course they war leanin' for'ard, an' every mother's son o' the crowd fell with his face atwixt the feet o' the man ahead on 'im."

"Whose feet did the leader's head fall between?" asked comrade Brown.

"Why his head laid atwixt my feet. You see, they wan't more'n six feet off when I let fly, an' of course they all slid for'ard a little as they fell."

"What did you do then?"

"Well, sir, I went back to headquarters an' reported to the cap'n."

"What did he say to you?"

"He said: 'Well, Shorty, I reckon you're doin' a leetle lively lyin', but we'll go down thar an' see about the thing.' The hull comp'ny war formed an' marched out, an' when the boys seed them rebs lyin' thar, all on 'em cried out, 'Cap'n, Shorty's a tellin' the truth. It's the rebs as is lyin'.'"

"What did you do with the bodies?"

"Oh! We merely dug a hole in the side o' the hill, an' gin the first man a push, an' they all slid right down into it, an' we shoveled the dirt in an' left 'em as a monument to the cause. If I'd 'a been a rebel, an' been shootin' at Union soldiers, I don't believe I'd 'a been able to kill so many."

"I don't either," said comrade Black.

"Nor I," assented comrade White.

"The Lord was with you," broke in another.

"You're right," said comrade Huddle, "but the strangest thing about the whole business was the names o' them men."

"Their names?" asked the S. P. U. H., full of wonder, and with ready pencil to tablet wedded.

"*Their names!*" slowly and solemnly spoke the relentless story-teller.

"And what were they?" asked a chorus of voices.

"Ignatzky Volubkluskidinka, Roderigueza-de Bombulaskiloskidumpi, Sophoclesaskidasa Ratinetkswlinkatswelka, Bordeska Elakanatza Estenowskilownkiloskinowargatz, Pedroza Ednatkskilvoratk Linowndiskilotstovlsirodeutzanzaboluska, and—"

The members of the division began to feel the weight of years growing upon them at this point, and two or three, who had been listening, and who were young men when the story began, turned gray, and the S. P. U. H. adjourned on account of a message announcing the death of a prominent member, leaving the speaker alone, struggling with the last nine feet of the sixth name, which began, Titusolotskyblowskyadjuskkorilzaondaloskadeefrowskybombastitzajokowsky, Manadnaskyletotkskyowatkaletonkipedraskadulitzipoedozaintinzalototskedelankszawrtnolzullvyslknotzylkvwrzooskin———."

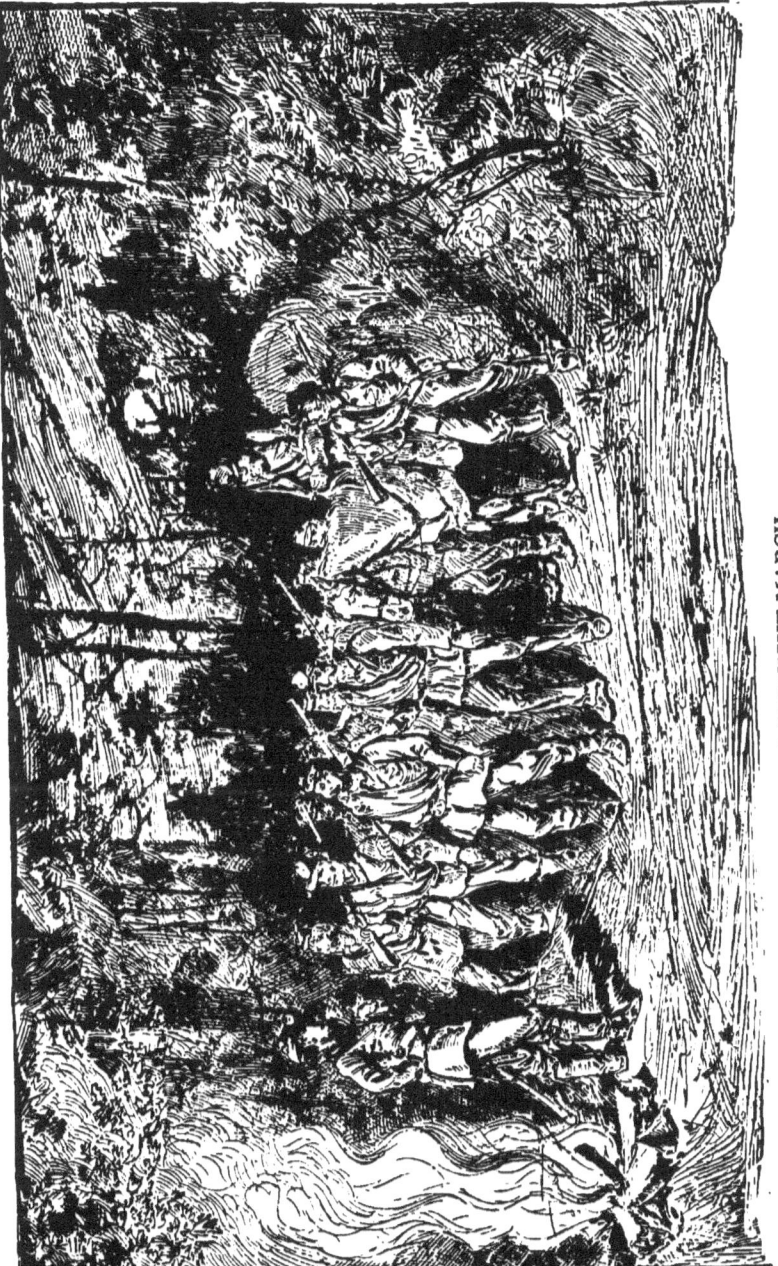

A MIDNIGHT MARCH

CAMP-FIRE XXXII.

TWO OF MOSBY'S MEN PERSONATE UNION OFFICERS—A SUCCESSFUL MILITARY MANEUVER—CHARACTER MAINTAINED NOTWITHSTANDING THE DEMORALIZING INFLUENCES OF ARMY LIFE.

MEMBER of Mosby's band in the East appeared before this camp-fire and desired to relate an adventure which occurred within the Federal lines. He was permitted, and spoke:

" After the winter's campaign in the mountains our band settled down for a time in the beginning of March, and during the latter part of that month the boys spent their time in individual and private enterprises.

" Mosby could trust his men. They were all devotedly attached to him, and were therefore allowed all the liberty they wished. They would organize private excursions into the enemy's country. By private excursions are meant those in which two or three of the boys would, without advice or attention from any officer, put their heads together, and lay plans for adventures within the territory of the enemy.

" One of these escapades is too good to be longer unrecorded. Sam Underwood was known among the boys as a mischievous, prank-playing, quick-witted, dare-devil-sort-of-a-fellow, not without a high sense of honor. He had been educated at the University of Virginia, and had both the culture and the powers of mind to have made a high mark in the world, but alas ! like thousands of others he had no tenacity of purpose, and when the war broke out the life of a partisan was too enchanting for him. After that he could not hold himself to any one thing long enough to achieve substantial results. But he was a fountain of humor, and his place under Mosby was just suited to his tastes—a freedom from responsibility, with all the liberty he wanted.

" He disclosed one of his plans to Bowie, and together they started to work it out.

" They found themselves after a day's and night's travel so far inside the Union picket lines that their identity was never suspected. They were loud-mouthed Union soldiers. They had clothed themselves in the captured garments of the officers who had been taken at the Dranesville fight. Mosby had possessed himself of certain papers which had thoroughly posted him in the names and numbers of the regiments of the enemy. These papers were captured with the Dranesville officers, and after Mosby had used all he wanted from them they fell into the hands of Underwood.

" The two daring guerillas were at least forty miles inside the Union lines, and stopping in one of the strongest neighborhoods of Shenandoah Valley, shook themselves in humorous gratification at having avoided suspicion. They gave out that they were quietly engaged in procuring information for the government at Washington as to how the soldiers of its armies were behaving themselves in Virginia. Their familiarity with all the operations of the Federal forces, the names of well-known officers, their commands and subordinates, begot confidence at once. They were secret agents, and this they gave out as the reason they did not stop in the towns—they could get more reliable information at a little distance, where their mission would not be suspected by the army.

" They had been in the neighborhood but three days when they received an invitation to a party to be held at the house of Daniel Maxwell, a celebrated Unionist of that country. The Maxwells held first place in the social ranks, and were really a cultured family. It consisted of Mr. Maxwell and wife, one son sixteen years of age, and two daughters, respectively eighteen and twenty years. They were indeed young ladies of intelligence and refinement, and finished education, having graduated at the head of their class in one of the most distinguished colleges of the North. And they were as beautiful as they were cultured. Indeed, they were renowned for their beauty, and for the exquisite grace of their demeanor.

"Into this family Underwood and Bowie had right of *entrée.* To confess the exact truth, as they afterward said when giving an account of the party, an 'eerie' sensation crept through their hearts as the evening of the party approached. They had rather stand in the face of a whole Yankee battalion than before the flashing batteries of those two beautiful girls. But there was no help for it. Underwood was every way qualified to move in any circle, but Bowie was a novice in the affairs of the drawing room and parlor. Underwood, however, after giving him a few lessons in etiquette, instructed him to be sure and not talk, or try to do so, on subjects he did not understand. 'I'll do most of the talking,' said Underwood. 'They'll expect us naturally to be quiet about our business, and if we let things run their own way they'll come out all right; and then we'll tell the boys, when we get back to camp, how we played it on 'em;' and he chuckled again.

"About 9 o'clock they mounted and rode up to the Maxwell mansion. The parlors and drawing rooms, cloak and hat room, were all brilliantly lighted. Most of the guests had already arrived. A couple of colored servants in livery stood at the gate to show them in, and they were at once ushered into the cloak room, where they divested themselves of their superfluous wraps, gave a few touches to their hair, a few whisks of the brush to their clothes, and were conducted down the broad stairway to the entrance of the drawing-room. They handed their cards to the servant who, with an overwhelming bow handed them to one of the Misses Maxwell who stood at the door to receive.

"Underwood gave no description of the lady's dress, but in answer to a question concerning it, replied: 'No one would ever think of her dress, who looked at her eyes. She welcomed us with a cordiality that made one forget he was a stranger. She took my arm first, led me to her mother and introduced me. She left me in care of her mother, who immediately introduced me to her husband. Then poor Bowie had to go forward, but he sustained the ordeal well—he couldn't do otherwise with so charming a companion. As soon as it was proper we were presented to the several members of the party, ladies and gentlemen.

"'But,' said Underwood, 'I surrendered. The only Yank" to whom I would ever yield was that charming Evelyn Maxwell. Bowie and I were made heroes. Every attention was paid us. Bowie was looked upon as a dignified, quiet gentleman of distinguished ability, and I had to pass as a sort of chatterer. But so goes the world. Bowie's silence, with an unruffled manner to maintain it, gave him much character.

"'The hours passed away as swift as merry chimes of Christmas. Supper was announced. And such a supper as it was! Think of it!—roast turkey with cranberry sauce and celery of home raising, moist and tender; roast beef and mutton, with vegetables to suit. Then the cake, wine, pastry, and relishes of a dozen varieties—Oh! oh! But didn't Bowie wade in! I was afraid his appetite would make him lose his brains. Never dignified man ate as he did. I was afraid that in satisfying the keen demands of his stomach he would lay himself open to the suspicion of being a "hungry rebel."

"'But to our consternation what should occur at this happy hour but the entrance of a Union officer who seemed to be at home in the house. The supper was ended, and the gentlemen were lingering over their cigars and wine. We were at once presented to him. He questioned us politely as to our command, inquiring into details a little too closely for comfort. Bowie shot a glance at me which the officer caught. I could see that suspicion was created. I tried with abandon and story-telling to efface it. I found afterward that we had made one fatal omission in our plans. We had given ourselves the character of two officers of Maine regiments located in the very line of the Confederacy, and we had forgotten that Maine men do not use the Southern "twang" in their pronunciation of words.

"'Here we were—Yanks talking in Southern dialect! This was what struck the Union officer. I felt certain that we should not be interfered with rashly, nor until after the party was broken up for the night. I gave Bowie a signal, communicated to him my suspicions, and we arranged to leave a little before the accustomed hour of departure. We effected our purpose quietly. Under the pressure of sudden news we aroused our host and hostess and expressed our regrets that we must cut short our pleasant hours. We bade them good-evening.

"'Our horses were pawing at the gate, and the darkeys were patiently holding them. We were accompanied to the door by Miss Evelyn Maxwell, and,' said Underwood, 'as we were passing along the hall I determined to kiss those beautiful lips if I died for it.

"'Bowie had passed out of the door, hat in hand, awaiting the close of the few words of good-bye. Miss Evelyn followed me out on the portico with warm invitations to return at any time.

"'Suddenly I put my arm around her drew her to me,

kissed her lips, and bounded away. Her sudden scream alarmed the house. In an instant I was mounted and with a dash of the spur our horses leaped off at a fearful pace. I did not say a word, only led the way.

"'"What the d—l is the matter?"' shouted Bowie. '"What did you do to the girl? Hold up, man!"

"'On I went. I had done a dastardly thing, but I'll swear by all the virtues of Diana I didn't mean to.

"'Soon we heard the sharp clatter of hoofs behind, and knew we were pursued. But we gave them the slip. We rode out into the brush till they passed. We recognized the Union officer with a following of eight or ten men.

"'We rode all that night and lay in the shadows all next day, and finally came into camp after an absence of ten days.

"'I have never been within one hundred miles of that neighborhood since,' continued Underwood, 'and I live in mortal fear lest I might at some unexpected moment run across that woman. But I'll swear to the last I couldn't help it. And if she could know that it was not meant for rudeness, but was the impulse of a romantic feeling as a tribute to her beauty, I do not believe—sensible girl that she is—it would be very difficult to make atonement.'"

One of General Sherman's admirers then asked to be heard for a brief time, and related the following:

"In that desperate battle on the 22d of July, 1864, when General McPherson fell, the Army of the Tennessee was on the east side of Atlanta, but in a day or two they withdrew from that position, and, marching in rear of the Army of the Cumberland, formed on the extreme right of the army, and there on the 28th of July fought the bloody battle known as Ezra Church, where the rebel troops repeatedly assaulted them before they had time to entrench themselves, but were in every instance repulsed with great slaughter. For nearly a month after this contest was one of outposts rather than great battles. The Union lines were steadily advanced, while in many places, as we afterward learned by actual measurement, there were less than sixty feet between the fortified picket posts, and a continual firing both night and day was kept up. The soldiers went to their posts under cover of the night, and had to remain close on the trenches all day, for if a head was shown but a moment, it was sure to draw a shot from the enemy.

"On August 26, General Sherman, in pursuance of a previously conceived plan, withdrew his whole army in order to make the flank movement below Atlanta and strike the railroad at Jonesboro and other places, for the purpose of cutting off their supplies.

"To prevent the rebels discovering this movement in time to attack, it was necessary to maintain the picket line for several hours after the army had left, and this duty was assigned to Col. Ira J. Bloomfield, of the 26th Illinois, with about 400 picked men from the 15th and 17th Corps. The troops began moving shortly after dark, and by 10 o'clock they were all in motion. The noise caused by the artillery and heavy ammunition wagons aroused the enemy, and several times they made a heavy assault upon the picket lines; but the men held their places with great bravery. About 1 o'clock some of the men, conscious that all hope of succor was miles away, and oppressed by the intense darkness of the night, and the ominous silence of the deserted camp where a few hours before all was bustle and confusion, and knowing full well that if a determined attack should be made, they must all be killed or captured, became alarmed, and it required the utmost exertion of the officers to hold them steady. But, after holding the lines until nearly 3 o'clock, they withdrew so quietly that the rebels continued firing at our picket posts, and did not discover our absence until daylight next morning.

"Before closing," said the last speaker, "I wish to call your attention to some effects of army life on character, and how these effects were overcome by the counter influences of peace and civilization.

"In glowing periods Lord Macaulay describes the facility with which Cromwell's soldiers gave up the profession of arms and devoted themselves to avocations of civil life, so that they were noted for their diligence, sobriety and prosperity; but never in the history of the world has such a mighty army been suddenly disbanded as in the spring of 1865 at the close of the rebellion; yet men accustomed for years to live by foraging, or taking by force whatever they needed or desired, quietly sank back into the ranks of civil life, and soon became distinguished for their energy, integrity and success in business, and no less so for their fidelity and zeal in support of the civil government of the country.

"Among thousands of instances that might be cited I will refer to a boy who enlisted as a private when between seventeen and eighteen years of age, from Tazewell county, Illinois. He was a mere stripling, slight of build, but rather tall. The hardships and exposure incident to the winter campaign under General Pope, around New Madrid and Island No. 10, in March, 1862, gave him the camp diarrhœa. His appetite failed, and his captain, thinking he would die if kept in the ranks, gave him permission to remain with the company wagon for two or three months, by which means he recovered his health, rejoined his company, and proved a faithful soldier, though he became an inveterate gambler. Whenever off duty he could be found playing poker or some other game for money, and such was his nerve and self-control that, though he lost or won hundreds of dollars, nothing more could be told of his feelings by looking at his face than at a board. His winnings, in time, became large, and he sent home several thousand dollars; and on the march from

Atlanta to the sea he won until his bundle of bank bills became so large he had to carry it in a rubber blanket. He, of course, at other times, had great losses; but when the army started north through the Carolinas, Jan. 31, 1865, he was left at Port Royal Inlet (because his time was out), nine miles from any Union troops, with over three thousand dollars about his person. He bade his comrades good-bye because refused permission to go along with them, went back to the coast, was mustered out of service, and came home by the way of New York. He invested all his money in land, and began farming and dealing in grain and cattle in his native county. He sold out all his property in Illinois a few years ago, went to Nebraska, entered some land and bought other tracts adjoining, located at the county seat, and is to-day worth a large amount of money; but above all, is a respected and exemplary citizen. This, however, should be said of him, that when he left the army he entirely abandoned gambling, and he most faithfully kept his resolution then formed, to do so. He is everywhere noted for his integrity, and his word once given is to him a bond."

CAMP-FIRE XXXIII.

REMINISCENCES OF THE BATTLE OF CORINTH—A BRAVE BOY IN GRAY—THE OLD CANTEEN.

"I can tell some facts," said Mr. J. W. Evarts, "of a detachment from the 15th Illinois Cavalry, "which I have never yet seen in print. They came under my direct observation, and will be recognized as true by many a comrade.

"I was with Stanley and Rosecrans at the battle of Corinth, which lasted three days, the heaviest fighting being done on the 4th of October, 1862. On the evening of the 3d, near sunset, Rosecrans left me to watch a road two miles west of the town, on which the rebels were expected to approach in force, and invest the place that night. Price had sent Rosecrans word that 'he would take dinner the next day at the Tishemingo hotel, or in h—l!' I rode a fleet horse, and planted myself behind a large tree on the north and south road, at the junction of the road leading eastward into Corinth. Our entire army had gone into camp behind the forts and earthworks. I was probably the only Union soldier outside of our lines. A half hour's watching, and I saw a dust rising up the road to the north. A moment later, and a long column of rebels were in full view; in the scattering timber for some distance the rebel skirmishers were deployed, and approaching in line. I waited motionless till I could identify the personages riding in front, the descriptions answering for Generals Van Dorn and Lyttle. On reaching within fifty yards, realizing my safety had reached its limitation, I put spurs to my horse and darted toward Corinth under a shower of bullets. Reaching the tent of General Rosecrans, I made my report, and the battle of the next day verified the identity of those rebel commanders.

"The most tragic scene of the battle of Corinth was the charge on Fort Williams by the 'Rebel Forlorn Hope,' in which four hundred volunteered under Colonel Rodgers to capture the fort or die in the undertaking. The fight commenced at daybreak, and had raged hot till about noon, with terrible slaughter on both sides. Our troops numbered 27,000, and an area of five or six square miles around Corinth was thoroughly fortified, and long-range guns were so planted as to rake the rebel columns lengthwise wherever they formed. A deep ravine, stretching along the west of town, was covered with fallen trees, making a tangled abattis so great that it was difficult to cross; but the rebel legions climbed from limb to limb over tree-tops, and jumped from log to log across a dangerous bayou, all under a raking fire of musketry and artillery, many dropping dead or wounded among the brush; and to the number of several thousand they charged through line after line of our bristling bayonets and the slashing sabers of three thousand of our cavalry, reaching their goal, the Tishemingo hotel. Our cavalry rallied in force, and charged them back; but their onslaught grew more desperate, and they repeated the charge the second time, and were a second time routed, retreating over a thousand acres strewn with the dead and wounded of both armies. This weakened the spirit of the rebel commanders, and they called for the fated four hundred to capture our greatest stronghold, Fort Williams, whose guns were pouring a steady stream of destruction into their decimated ranks. It was but a moment after Colonel Rodgers responded to lead, that the four hundred daring men were in line, and at a little after noon they rushed like mad demons upon the fort, crossing the ditch and scaling the walls, as if by superhuman dexterity. Many were killed at the first charge by the hundreds of rifles that were blazing at them from every direction. The charge was repeated with more dauntless heroism, if possible, than before, and the rebel flag was no sooner raised than its brave bearer fell, a corpse. One by one this heroic band fell dead in the ditch or in the parapet, when, last of all, Colonel Rodgers himself grasped the broken and shivered standard, waved it above his head, shouted victory, and the next moment he, too, fell, pierced through the heart. Perhaps there was never a more exciting scene in the annals of modern warfare. Those who witnessed that terrible charge, could not feel any but the deepest admiration for such unparalleled bravery.

"Colonel Rodgers was probably the largest man engaged in the war on either side, standing six feet and seven inches, grandly proportioned, and weighing about three hundred pounds. He was a lawyer by profession, and resided at Holly Springs, where he was highly esteemed for his nobility of character, and was regarded as one of the ablest and most scholarly attorneys in Mississippi; and though a confederate soldier, we can do no less than reverence his wonderful bravery."

"We are all ready to pay our devotion to true courage wherever we find it," said the presiding officer, and now 1 will offer a tribute to ' The Old Canteen,' that staunch friend of true courage and all other virtues, by inviting Lieutenant Page to recite some beautiful lines on the subject, from an author who, though unknown, makes us feel that he has tested its friendship.

In response, the following was rendered in the most appreciative manner:

THE OLD CANTEEN.

Send it up to the garret? Well, no; what's the harm
If it hangs like a horseshoe to serve as a charm?
Had its day, to be sure; matches ill with things here;

Shall I sack the old friend just because it is queer?
Thing of beauty 'tis not, but a joy none the less,
As my hot lips remember its old time caress,
And I think on the solace once gurgling between
My lips from that old battered tin canteen.

It has hung by my side in the long, weary tramp,
Been my friend in the bivouac, barrack, and camp,
In the triumph, capture, advance, and retreat,
More than light to my path, more than guide to my feet.
Sweeter nectar ne'er flowed, however sparkling and cold,
From out chalice of silver or goblet of gold,
For a king or an emperor, princess or queen,
Than to me from the mouth of that old canteen.

It has cheered the desponding on many a night,
'Till their laughing eyes gleamed in the camp-fire light,
Whether guns stood in silence, or boomed at short range,
It was always on duty; though 'twould not be strange
If in somnolent periods just after "taps"
Some Colonel or Captain, disturbed at his naps,
May have felt a suspicion that "spirits" unseen
Had somehow bedeviled that old canteen.

But I think on the time when in lulls of the strife,
It has called the far look in dim eyes back to life;
Helped to staunch the quick blood just beginning to pour,
Softened broad, gaping wounds that were stiffened and sore,
Moistened thin, livid lips, so despairing of breath
They could only speak thanks in the quiver of death;
If an angel of mercy e'er hovered between
This world and the next, 'twas the old canteen.

Then banish it not as a profitless thing,
Were it hung in a palace it well might swing
To tell in its mute, allegorical way
How the citizen volunteer won the day;
How he bravely, unflinchingly, grandly won,
And how, when the death-dealing work was done,
'Twas as easy his passion from war to wean
As his mouth from the lips of that old canteen.

By and by, when all hate for the rag with the bars
Is forgotten in love for the "Stripes and the Stars;"
When Columbia rules everything solid and sole,
From her own ship canal to the ice at the Pole;
When we Grand Army men have obeyed the last call,
And the May flowers and violets bloom for us all;
Then away in some garret the cobweb may screen
My battered, old, cloth-covered, tin canteen.

CAMP-FIRE XXXIV.

THE LAST CAMP-FIRE—END OF THE SEASON—THE S. P.
U. H. VALEDICTORY—A HYMN OF PEACE.

IT WAS spring; not one of the springs which poets dream about, but just simply spring—the annual return of that season which, in the latitude where the chats had been held, consisted of a muddy March, a rainy April and a flowery May. It was the same as any other spring. The morning had been just as frosty, and the edges of the small streams and mill ponds just as icy (and no more so) as any other spring; so the noon-days grew just as warm and pleasant; so the evenings were just as comfortable and chilly alternately; so the birds sang just as sweetly; so, later, when the thick, rich mud had changed to yellow clods, the grass grew just as fresh and green. All in all, no one could have any cause for special self-congratulation; but all alike were happy.

The man of brainwork and the man of business each again could brush back the ruffled locks from his forehead, and, drawing a long breath, plainly see his blessed vacation in the distance of a short month or so; while the rested, burly plowman could husk himself from his winter haunts, circulate in the fresh, free air of an American field, and bend to his labor in the full hope of a beautiful and abundant harvest.

In thorough and strict keeping with the spirit of the occasion, and desiring to be in harmony with nature, the veterans, therefore, in camp-fire assembled, passed a resolution which gave positive instructions to the janitor to abstain from igniting the fagots until further orders; the resolution to take effect when this fire had burned itself out.

The evening was devoted, not to the regular order of business; but to general leave-taking, dreamy remembrances of the enjoyment which had been offered, and to a sort of review of the former camp-fires. Now it was time to say "Good-bye." The fire began to wane, and would soon be out, according to resolution. Business must be hurried if any were to be done.

At this time an idea struck a veteran. He would call on the S. P. U. H. for a speech to close.

"Moved and seconded," said the commander, "that the Society for the Preservation of Unpublished History be, and the same are hereby requested to furnish a speaker for this, our last camp-fire." Carried.

The society refused to comply, of course; they would not be human if they complied on being asked the first time. To their amazement and chagrin, however, the veterans did not make a second request for awhile. But finally, another invitation was extended, which the society, having selected one of their number for the occasion, was very careful to accept, simply for the reason that the comrades might take offence, since they had originally assembled at the instance of a similar request from the society.

Everything thus arranged and agreed, the unfortunate member of the S. P. U. H. who must speak, suggested that if the commissary would serve coffee and hard-tack, it would allow him a little time for reflection. Granted. The veterans then drank coffee; the society man drank coffee, and reflected. What would he speak about? The war had been the subject at every camp-fire all winter. Reconstruction was threadbare. No topic of sufficient interest presented itself. The time for the speech was now at hand. The speaker arose.

"WORTHY COMMANDER," said he, with great dignity, "I recall to memory everything which is of no interest. The comrades, I know, are weary. We have just had supper. Supper, dear veterans, is the only meal I really enjoy, except breakfast and dinner."

"That's enough of that harangue, said the commander. Spring is the season for fresh things."

"Well, there's nothing to talk about," said the speaker. "It is not proper to exhort your patriotism to fight another war; that only one flag shall rule us, has long been settled; and, indeed, there seems no demand for but a very small army. What shall I speak about? The plowshares of the regenerated people are warm with energy; honest manhood among them is flush in the hope of great fruitage, nor is this hope misplaced; while the smoke from factories, new and old, rises from a thousand hillsides. Only a few unruly ones tamper with what has 'ceased to be even remains.' Ever thus it has been. When a child burns his finger in the fire, he naturally becomes mad at the fire; but it is only necessary for him to thrust in his hand once more to find that the fire will still burn. The garment of charity soon covers the wound, which may be healed by proper doctoring; and when the child pushes his finger through the garment, it needs the hand of not only a stern, but modest, mild, and loving father to administer gentle but firm reproof, which makes the family complete, congenial and co-operative, when they can gather around a camp-fire and swell the chorus in

A HYMN OF PEACE.

The echoes of war now have traveled
The valleys the last time for aye;
And the hills and the forests are silent,
As the Angel of Peace wanders by;—

While the unknown now sleep where they suffered—
    In the land where brave charges they led;
Where the moss droops her tendrils in mourning,
    And the mocking bird sings to the dead.

Unmarked are the mounds where they slumber,
    Their names are unsung and unwept;
But their deeds are not lost nor forgotten,
    For they're in eternity kept.

And while nature's monuments freshen,
    In merry spring over each grave
Of the loyal sons of the nation,
    May her emblem in gratitude wave.

And, too, while the bosom of ocean
    Bears the harvests away on her tide,
May the olive branch bend in the sunshine,
    And brotherhood ever abide.

Then let all the hearts that are heavy
    Be cheered by the smile of the glad,
And every one who may be happy,
    Make happy all those who are sad.

THE END.

www.ingramcontent.com/pod-product-compliance
Lightning Source LLC
Chambersburg PA
CBHW032048220426
43664CB00008B/914